T0247901

LOUIS B. MAYER AND IRVING THALBERG

Louis B. Mayer

and

Irving Thalberg

The Whole Equation

◆◈◆

KENNETH TURAN

Yale

UNIVERSITY

PRESS

New Haven and London

Yale University Press books may be purchased in quantity for educational,
business, or promotional use. For information, please e-mail sales.press@yale.edu
(U.S. office) or sales@yaleup.co.uk (U.K. office).

Frontispiece: Mayer (*left*) and Thalberg choosing sides for a 1930s studio
softball game. (Marc Wanamaker/Bison Archives)

Set in Janson Oldstyle type by Integrated Publishing Solutions.
Printed in the United States of America.

Library of Congress Control Number: 2024938762
ISBN 978-0-300-25449-5 (hardcover : alk. paper)

A catalogue record for this book is available from the British Library.

This paper meets the requirements of ANSI/NISO Z39.48-1992
(Permanence of Paper).

10 9 8 7 6 5 4 3 2 1

Jewish Lives® is a registered trademark of the Leon D. Black Foundation.

To Ross Thomas and Andy Dowdy,
    may their memory be a blessing.

To B, always.

CONTENTS

CONTENTS

LOUIS B. MAYER AND IRVING THALBERG

Introduction

On September 15, 1936, the Spanish Civil War ("German Planes Turn Tide to Rebels in Madrid Drive") was the main news on the front page of the *New York Times*. Elsewhere in the sixty-page broadsheet was a story on former president Herbert Hoover catching a "good-sized" bluefish in the waters off Montauk Point, while obituaries clustered on page 29. Centrally placed was one that detailed a death the previous day that was simultaneously shocking and not completely unexpected. "I. G. Thalberg Dies; Film Producer, 37," read the headline, while the cluster of subheads laid out the highlights of a life both celebrated and cut harshly short:

"Boy Wonder" of Hollywood
Was Called Most Brilliant
    Figure In His Field.
Regarded as Pacemaker
Made Succession of Hits and Had

Developed Many Stars—
Husband of Norma Shearer.

Taking up two full columns, including a photo, the Irving Thalberg obituary was the biggest on the page, and nearly half its length was taken up by tributes from clearly unsettled movie notables to the most successful producer at Hollywood's most successful studio, Metro-Goldwyn-Mayer, a man who, despite battling serious health issues since childhood, had always acted as if he were invulnerable.

First among equals was Nicholas Schenck, as president of both MGM and Loew's, Inc., the man who was Thalberg's boss. Schenck called him "the most important man in the production end of the motion picture industry. He was important personally even more than officially. We all loved him. It is difficult to bear such a blow."

Over the next few days, tributes to and stories about Thalberg filled newspapers on both coasts, an outpouring of public grief for a Hollywood executive, not a beloved star, unequaled before or since. Director Frank Capra, whose MGM experience was mixed at best, noted that Thalberg "was one man whom everybody trusted," Howard Hawks called him "the great genius of the picture business," Charles Laughton "the most brilliant producer in the world," and W. R. Wilkinson, who owned the *Hollywood Reporter*, wrote dramatically, "IRVING is dead! The King is gone and there is no other king."

Most impressive, if more subdued, the august *Times* in a rare editorial tribute to an entertainment figure said that Thalberg "helped, perhaps more than any other man in Hollywood, to make the motion picture a medium of adult entertainment, and by many thousands of theatregoers his talent and vitality will be missed."

A little more than twenty years later, when Louis B. Mayer died at the reported age of seventy-two in 1957, he also merited a major *Times* obituary, though the October 30 story was not quite as long or as shell-shocked as Thalberg's. For unlike his erstwhile colleague, Mayer had not died young or at the height of his power but half a dozen years past his unceremonious ouster (officially he had resigned) as MGM's production chief after twenty-seven years in the job. If Thalberg died too young, with prime years still ahead of him, Mayer had lasted too long, out-living his perceived value and usefulness.

Mayer's obit certainly did not lack for deserved praise, call-ing him "the czar of Hollywood movie producers," mentioning condolences sent to the family by Vice President Richard M. Nixon (Mayer was a fervent Republican), and noting that for seven consecutive years he had been the highest paid executive in the United States.

If Mayer did not get a *Times* editorial marking his passing, he did get a *Time* magazine obituary that said for three decades "L. B. Mayer was the most important man in Hollywood," and his erstwhile son-in-law David O. Selznick looked back even further and called him "the greatest single figure in the history of motion picture production." Never to be outdone in fulsome praise, the *Reporter*'s W. R. Wilkinson started his Mayer tribute with a call-back to his Thalberg piece: "MR. MOTION PICTURE is gone."

Thalberg gets no more than a brief name-check in Mayer's obituary, and Mayer had barely done better in the younger man's. But during the years they worked together at MGM, the ne plus ultra of movie studios, the place that had the most of everything, including profits, their collaboration was arguably the most con-sequential in Hollywood history.

In little more than a decade, their Mr. Inside/Mr. Outside partnership created a model for movie production which, though currently somewhat down at the heels, has lasted for close to a century.

Jointly and separately, they supervised hundreds of pictures and ran an enterprise the size of which is almost unimaginable for a movie studio today. At MGM's Culver City location as many as six thousand employees toiled on some thirty stages, 177 other buildings, and numerous multipurpose backlots spread over approximately 175 acres. Rival studios either embraced this system, tried to improve on it, or defined themselves in opposition, but no matter what, MGM was the standard by which others were judged.

Though there were exceptions, Mayer was in general the business-minded public face of the studio and Thalberg formed unequaled bonds with the creative corps, especially writers. Working the levers together they could do no wrong. Until, to borrow Ernest Hemingway's phrase, gradually then suddenly they fell apart, a rupture that was an open secret in Hollywood even before Thalberg's death.

If, speaking of the partnership's beginning, L.B.'s perceptive daughter Irene Mayer Selznick could poignantly say "my father never loved anyone the way he loved Irving," there were also reports that in the immediate aftermath of Thalberg's death, Mayer gloated to a confidant, "isn't God good to me." What began in bliss ended in something bordering on rancor.

Each man was significant in his own right, and a number of well-researched and impressive biographies have been written about each. Nor have they gone unnoticed in literature, F. Scott Fitzgerald's unfinished *The Last Tycoon* (whose studio executive protagonist Monroe Stahr is unapologetically based on Thalberg) being perhaps the most celebrated example of their grip on the creative imagination. What Fitzgerald famously wrote of Stahr, calling him one of the "not half a dozen men [who] have ever been able to keep the whole equation of pictures in their heads," could be said with even more justice about their joint activity.

But despite the turbulent drama inherent in their relationship, which seemed at times like the joining of potent but unstable nuclear particles, only one book has set out to treat both men jointly, Samuel Marx's engaging *Mayer and Thalberg: The Make-Believe Saints*, published in 1975. But because Marx, as MGM's longtime story editor, knew both men personally, his book serves as source material as much as analysis.

Though there was but fourteen years in age between them, Mayer and Thalberg had the tension of a father-son dynamic to contend with, but that is not all. The pioneer-protégé clash was in them as well, plus a rift in the nature of their Jewish experience. Mayer was a serial eastern European immigrant, first to the United States, then to Canada, and then back to the United States, while not only was Thalberg born in this country but his family was also German Jewish. In the complex hierarchy of American Judaism, the two men faced each other across a broad social divide.

But different though they were in some respects, Mayer and Thalberg managed to share the same goals even if they had divergent ideas of how to go about achieving them. They were unlikely participants in the high adventure of creating an art form that stormed the world, and though they tended to favor different kinds of films, they shared the messianic notion, unusual at the time, that the right movie stories could not only make a profit but change the culture as well as individual lives. One was a tough junkman's son, the other a cosseted mama's boy, but they dreamed the same mighty dream, and the movie business they jointly helped create has never been the same.

1

Mayer Before Thalberg

THE WORLD KNEW him as Louis B. Mayer, but that was not his name.

The initial B supposedly stood for Burton or Burt, but in truth no middle name existed. And his supposed birthday of July 4, 1885, was a fabrication.

There is perhaps no better way to understand the almost unimaginable psychological distance an impoverished infant traveled to become one of the most celebrated men in America than to contextualize exactly how great that distance was, how mired in the miasma of Pale of Settlement poverty his family of origin was and how unlikely it was that he of all people would become a key arbiter of cultural taste for the world.

It is a measure, then, of both the destitution he'd come from and how desperately both he and his parents and siblings wanted to escape it that almost nothing about his original name, date, and place of birth is known for certain.

Mayer's official MGM biography doesn't mention Europe at all, giving that July 4 birth date (apparently picked in celebration of the country that had been so good to him) and implying that he was born where he grew up, his parents' immigration terminus of St. John, New Brunswick, Canada.

The best guess of Mayer's birth is sometime in July 1884 in the village of Dumier in northern Ukraine, though Lithuania and the Belarusian capital of Minsk are also contenders. His family name at birth might have been Meyer, Meir, Meher, or Baer: "only God knows," said one of his daughters, "where the Mayer came from." The boy's first name was Lazar, which soon became Louis when the family immigrated first to the New York area and then, for reasons unknown but probably economic, to Canada.

Mayer was perhaps three when the family left Europe, seven or eight when they finally settled in the maritime town of St. John, so far off the beaten path that when actor Walter Pidgeon truthfully told Mayer he was from the same place, the studio head, suspecting chicanery, "became enraged . . . and offered to wrestle me to the ground." It was in St. John, where he was raised with two sisters and two younger brothers in a Yiddish-speaking family, that he learned a mean streets philosophy. Explained writer Budd Schulberg, son of one of Mayer's great Hollywood rivals, "Louie Mayer grew up in the street. The Jew-baiting that was one of the year-round sports of Saint John made him tough, and rag-picking made him resourceful and opportunistic." Filmmaker Mervyn LeRoy, in likely expurgated fashion, said Mayer advised him in a similar fashion: "Look out for yourself, or they'll pee on your grave."

Mayer always insisted that he'd never picked rags, and his studio biography, written by masterful MGM publicity chief Howard Strickling, offers a parallel anecdote that may well have something of the truth in it: "He was eight when, entirely of his own volition, he made his first 'business venture.' With his pocket money, he bought a red wagon of the toy variety and used it to collect the metal parts discarded by various shipbuilding plants in St. John. These parts he sold—and that was the start of what eventually became the marine salvage business of Jacob Mayer & Son."

Mayer's parents, father Jacob and mother Sarah, both had considerable influence on young Louis, but the nature of that impact was starkly different.

Perhaps the least complicated relationship in Mayer's entire life was the one with his mother. By all accounts, especially his own, she loved him deeply and unreservedly, and, Mayer's daughter Irene Mayer Selznick later wrote, when Sarah died unexpectedly when he was twenty-nine, "no kind of emotion in his life ever matched the grief he felt at her death. He was totally devastated and mourned her passing the rest of his days. From that time on until he died, a large portrait of her hung over his bed."

This veneration affected his relationship with talent—he reportedly got into fistfights over the nature of mothers with both John Gilbert and Erich von Stroheim—and even the kinds of roles that were featured in his films. As Mary Astor, who played many a matriarch at MGM complained, "Metro's mothers never did anything but mothering. They never had a thought in their heads except their children."

Perhaps Sarah Mayer's greatest service to her son was protecting him from father Jacob, by most accounts a stern, unbending, and possibly physically abusive man. "The harshness of St. John's climate," wrote Jacob's granddaughter, "was matched by this man's nature."

Initially, like many immigrants, a peddler, Jacob took advantage of St. John's bustling harbor to become a scrap metal dealer and then transitioned into a marine salvage business. Some say it was the son who started the business (hence the red wagon anecdote) but whatever the case, Irene Mayer Selznick relates a remarkable story of her father, who left school to work full-time at age twelve. "My father would be sent out to bid at auctions, and he would have the money sewn into the lining of his coat. It never occurred to anyone that this pale, undersized boy was a serious bidder. I think he did very well because the other bidders didn't take him seriously, and he learned about negotiating, when to speak up and when to make a move, and he learned to make judgements early." Making the same point, but with markedly less sympathy, was F. Scott Fitzgerald, who told his notebook "Mayer started as a junk dealer—now he is again."

A surviving photograph from later in this period shows Mayer with one of his salvage crews, a self-possessed man with evident self-belief. Among the group of eastern European Jewish emigrants who drifted in from a variety of occupations to create Hollywood, few if any came from a work environment that was as strenuously physical as his.

It was probably junk business that drew Mayer to Boston, the nearest American metropolis to St. John, but much about the city proved to be to his liking. He moved there in 1904, looking for the main chance. What he found first was a wife, and he didn't have far to look.

Right across the street from where Mayer rented rooms was a kosher butcher shop run by Hyman Shenberg, a religious man who also served as the cantor at a local synagogue. His daughter Margaret, a kind and pretty woman who had a high school diploma and experience as a bookkeeper, caught Mayer's eye and within months, in June 1904, they were married. The wedding certificate also marks the first appearance of that mysterious middle initial B in Mayer's name.

That mark of prominence, if that was what it was, did not stop Mayer from experiencing financial reversals, including a near bankruptcy. But in 1907 came one of those fortuitous, life-changing moments: Louis B. Mayer discovered the movies, and nothing was to be the same for the medium or for him.

The movies in 1907 were humble and inexpensive, hence the name nickelodeons. These establishments, as Mayer couldn't help but notice, were booming, and the audience was largely lower class and poor, a demographic whose tastes Mayer understood without need of translation.

But what Mayer and his cohort also recognized, as Samuel Marx put it, was that "a great new industry was up for grabs. Nobody was experienced, nobody's father had been in it; there were no rules or traditions." Temperamentally Mayer and his fellow moguls resembled Willy Loman's brother Ben in *Death of a Salesman*, trusting their instincts, walking into the jungle confident they would walk out in a few years being able to proclaim, as Ben does, "And by god I was rich."

Seeing the crowds these theaters drew, Mayer decided to buy one of his own, possibly with the help of money borrowed from his family. The location was Haverhill, an industrial town north of Boston, the theater a run-down former burlesque house named the Gem but inevitably referred to locally as the Germ.

The refurbished theater, grandly renamed the Orpheum, opened on November 28, 1907. Mayer, unapologetically personally moralistic and just starting to understand that even at this early stage, movies could be uplifting as well as profitable, scored his first success by screening Pathe's *Passion Play*. That and other successes led to a second theater and then a third, the sixteen-hundred-seat Colonial, which opened in 1911. A distinctive feature of this establishment was an oil painting of the owner himself, prominently displayed in the lobby. This new business, Mayer had discovered, was not one that demanded personal modesty.

Determined to find better product for his theaters, which soon grew to five, Mayer first branched out into the nascent business of film distribution, starting a firm called the Louis B. Mayer Film Company. By 1915 that move had led, after some twists and turns, to Mayer's becoming a key part of a distribution and production entity called Metro Pictures. It was here that he first encountered a New York lawyer named J. Robert Rubin, quiet, well spoken, and genteel in a way that prefigured Mayer's connection to Irving Thalberg. Rubin would remain a key associate for decades.

It was a deal Mayer made outside of his connection to Metro, however, that was a major milestone in his rise. In 1915 the ever-scrambling distributor formed a separate company, called Master Photoplays, and was able to get a piece (the New England rights specifically) of what was to be one of the most profitable, and inescapably racist, films ever made, D. W. Griffith's *The Birth of a Nation*.

Mayer later melodramatically claimed to star Lillian Gish, "I pawned everything I owned—my house, my insurance, even my wife's wedding ring—just to get those rights." However he raised the money ($50,000 against ten percent of the net profits) it paid off. *The Birth of a Nation* made between $665,000 and $1 million in New England alone, and Mayer earned a tidy sum, probably somewhere between $100,000 and $250,000, though he was always dogged by accusations that, in silent star Miriam Cooper's words, he engaged in "outrageous cheating on paying off the percentage." No matter what, the end result was financial security and when Mayer told Gish, "I want to thank you for starting me on the road to success," he meant it.

To watch Mayer and his fellow early moguls maneuver in this new world is to be fascinated at how, like free climbers on an unknown cliff face, they went from handhold to handhold, figuring out what they were doing as they went along.

So, starting from owning theaters and then moving to distributing films in order to have something to present there, Mayer went to the next step, which was actually producing films himself. If he was to truly control his financial destiny, that step was inevitable and essential, but it could happen only gradually, and it involved one of the things that was to become

Mayer had a long-standing interest in child stars. The young actor in this pre-MGM image is Richard Headrick. (Collection of the author)

one of Mayer's much-commented-on strengths at MGM, the signing of stars.

Building on his position with Metro, Mayer convinced the vainglorious Francis X. Bushman, who was one of the great stars of the age and knew it, to make a serial called *The Great Secret*, which promised "chapters of the greatest mystery, the most noble romance, the finest thrills in the world." In part because Bushman had a not-so-well-kept secret of his own, an adulterous affair with his costar, the serial flopped, but Mayer was just getting started with producing.

He next set his sights on Anita Stewart, a key player for powerhouse Vitagraph Studios and sometimes referred to as "America's daintiest star." What especially intrigued the actress was the offer of a production company of her own to be called Anita Stewart Pictures, Inc., but extricating Stewart from her Vitagraph contract proved to be difficult, involving complications up to and including lawsuits. Writer Schulberg, no Mayer fan, said Mayer "virtually shanghaied" her, and part of the fallout was Mayer leaving Metro and becoming a producer on his own.

Mayer's first film with Stewart, *Virtuous Wives*, which costarred future gossip columnist Hedda Hopper, arrived in theaters in 1918. Critics were uncertain but the public approved, and that success led to a move that seemed inevitable if Mayer was to remain in moviemaking—he took his wife and daughters Edith (known as Edie) and Irene to Los Angeles, even then the American filmmaking mecca.

Mayer did not show up unannounced in California; he had already, for instance, been in touch with top director Lois Weber, grandly telegraphing her, "My unchanging policy will be great star, great director, great play, great cast. You are authorized to get these without stint or limit. Spare nothing, neither expense, time, nor effort. Results only are what I am after."

The newly minted producer had also made plans for where he was going to work, but these were nowhere near as grandiose. He would be renting space at the Selig Polyscope studios, a place familiarly known around town as the Selig Zoo not because that's what it had been but because that's what it still was.

Located on Mission Road in East Los Angeles, the Selig Zoo in its prime housed numerous animals, including more than a dozen Bengal tigers and a comparable number of lions, leopards, and bears. "Louis B. chose the Selig Zoo because it was the cheapest place in town," recalled Hedda Hopper. "The zoo was the stronghold of wild animals trained for pictures. All day long, while the actors were silent on the movie stages, the animals roared their disapproval in their cages."

The Selig enterprise had been started by Col. William N. Selig, an entrepreneurial former vaudevillian rather than an ex-military man, who had been in films so long he'd started as a competitor of Thomas Edison. It was not long before Mayer outgrew his rented space and made arrangements with Selig to have a new studio built on an adjoining property, a four-stage affair optimistically designed, according to biographer Bosley Crowther, "to resemble the château of Chenonceaux."

One reason Mayer needed more space was that Anita Stewart was no longer his only star. In a move that can only be seen as nakedly opportunistic, he signed a young actress named Mildred Harris, a woman better known (because a very bitter, very public divorce was then taking place) the way Mayer advertised her: Mrs. Charlie Chaplin. On a night in April 1920, both the celebrated actor and Mayer chanced to turn up in the Alexandria Hotel, words and blows were exchanged, and Mayer knocked Chaplin out. Other confrontations with actors were to come, as Mayer's unvarnished emotionalism was destined to get the best of him as often as not.

Still, Mayer in his early years in Hollywood definitely wanted to learn, both to polish off the rough edges of his St. John youth and New England apprenticeship and to figure out exactly how movies were made, the better to make them himself.

Though, like the other immigrant moguls, Mayer had simply stumbled onto the movie business, he'd dealt with enough hardship to know a good thing when he saw it, and he was not about to go away. If, as writer Anzia Yezierska trenchantly observed, Hollywood was no more than "the fish market in evening clothes," Mayer had reason to believe he could and would succeed.

Yet there were obstacles, including brusque and uncertain manners that some said never left him. Early on, silent star Madge Bellamy, called for a meeting, relates disapprovingly that "as I entered his office, he did not rise, nor did he take his feet off his desk. 'I'm thinking of using you in a picture,' he said, slowly eyeing me as he took the cigar out of his mouth." Florence Browning, his Selig Zoo secretary, told an interviewer, "He seemed to have absolutely no reticence, no inhibitions, no sense of embarrassment at his evident manifestations of conceit."

The flip side of this, however, was a genuine concern for morality in pictures, a passion for "moral uplift" his daughter Irene says was with him from the start. Hedda Hopper told Frances Marion, destined to be one of MGM's top writers, that "Louis B. is more puritanical about sex than my Quaker relatives," and at their first meeting Mayer himself told Marion that "his wife and two little girls, Irene and Edith, must never be embarrassed by any of his pictures."

All in all, as actress Ann Rutherford told biographer Scott Eyman, "I had been to his hometown. I knew from whence he sprang. He taught himself grammar. He taught himself manners. If anybody on earth ever created himself, Louis B. Mayer did."

That claim notwithstanding, Mayer of course did not pull off this transformation seamlessly or without help. Selig-era secretary Browning reported that she frequently put his dictated rants into "an orderly, comprehensible form." Grandson Daniel Selznick remembers that even later in Mayer's life personal notes from him were often ungrammatical and after the executive died a Mayer attorney told Selznick the man's papers had been burned. "We did it to protect your grandfather's reputation. His grammar wasn't perfect, and we wouldn't want anybody to know."

Similarly, to hear Mayer's speech in newsreels of the period is to hear not a trace of an identifiable accent. Though some sources disagree, according to Samuel Marx, MGM's first publicity chief Pete Smith wrote and supervised Mayer's early speeches, and in terms of diction Mayer "also received counsel from actor Conrad Nagle."

When it came to discovering the ins and outs of movie-making, Mayer was similarly relentless in pursuit of knowledge and whatever else he needed. He tried to be on the sets of his movies as much as possible, asking unending and often irritating questions.

Hedda Hopper reports, in an anecdote dating back to that 1918 *Virtuous Wives* shoot in New York, "a round little man kept getting in our way, peeking out from behind some bush just when we were ready for a take." Yes, that was Mayer. And silent star Miriam Cooper reports that Mayer was similarly persistent in an attempt to get her husband, director Raoul Walsh, to work for him. "He's always over-anxious to make himself agreeable," Walsh had written to his wife, and when Mayer showed up at their house, he refused to take no for an answer. "The more I retreated," Cooper remembers, "the more he came on. He backed me all the way from the front door to the backyard."

One director who agreed to work with Mayer ended up similarly perturbed. Marshall "Mickey" Neilan, who directed one of Anita Stewart's first Los Angeles films, *In Old Kentucky*, was an early-days auteur who believed that producers were best neither seen nor heard. He and Mayer were fated to clash and did so for years.

"My difficulties with Mayer in the early stages," he wrote emphatically to biographer Crowther decades later, "was simply the man was going to the school of HOW ARE MOTION PICTURES MADE and this was a 24 hr. way of living with the man." With Neilan ostentatiously not cooperating, eventually Mayer "would wipe the sweat off his brow and wend his way back to the front office WHERE HE BELONGED." He also never forgot.

Even when it came to his fellow movie entrepreneurs, Mayer seemed to have a gift for feuds. He got on the bad side of Samuel Goldwyn by bad-mouthing him to his future in-laws. Producer B. P. Schulberg, who shared studio space with Mayer at the Selig Zoo, became infuriated with his erstwhile partner when he left him holding the bag by secretly moving across town to join what became MGM. According to the much-repeated story, before he died B.P. had a request of his son Budd: "Put my ashes in a box and tell the messenger to bring them to Louis B. Mayer's office with a farewell message from me. Then when the messenger gets to Louis' desk, I want him to open the box and blow the ashes in the bastard's face." As writer Lenore Coffee, who had a long relationship with MGM that began with writing intertitles for silent films, summarized, "everybody fought with Louis B. Mayer, sooner or later."

If there was a professional relationship in Mayer's life that seemed to be the exception to that rule, it began inauspiciously enough in 1922. Always on the lookout for the next handhold up the mountain, Mayer felt the limits of being a one-executive operation, and a young man named Irving Thalberg, only in his early twenties and already head of production at major player Universal studio, was also wanting a change. Hoping to help, director Cecil B. DeMille had told Paramount's Jesse Lasky, "The boy is a genius. I can see it. I know it." Lasky's short-sighted reply: "Geniuses we have all we need."

A possible deal with comedy impresario Hal Roach did not materialize either, and in November of that year Mayer and Thalberg met at the home of a mutual friend, attorney Edwin Loeb. The talk was of movies, the compatibility instantaneous. Thalberg told his parents he'd never met anyone like Mayer, and Mayer for his part told Loeb, in a remark that could cut more than one way, "If he comes to work for me, I'll look after him like he's my own son." On February 15, 1923, the match was officially made: Thalberg signed as vice president and production assistant at Louis B. Mayer Studios. Whatever complicated amalgam of personal and professional needs and aspirations created this match, the results were something to see.

2

Thalberg Before Mayer

WHEN ACCOMPLISHED WRITER Allene Talmey, later a three-decade columnist for *Vogue* and a film reviewer for *Time*, put together a 1927 book-length collection of Hollywood profiles illustrated with elegant woodcuts and called *Doug and Mary and Others*, in classic journalistic fashion she did her best to find the fascinating, unconventional aspect of each of her subjects. Irving Thalberg, however, defeated her.

"Out of the dullness of middle-class complacency," she wrote, almost in despair, "there has come an unnatural phenomenon known in Hollywood as 'Irving Thalberg, the boy producer.'"

"There are no pathetic passages to be written about him," Talmey goes on; his story is rather "a tale even whose background is bleached of vitality . . . so smooth and bumpless that no broken strands of bark are left on which legends may catch. There are no prongs on which may hang gay, strange and amusing anecdotes." Rather, if anything Thalberg's life "has been a cold monochrome stretching from Brooklyn to Hollywood. . . . None knows whence he drew his knowledge."

From the vantage of almost a century, some things still look the way Talmey saw them, but only up to a point. What was most dramatic about Thalberg's early life was not the up-from-poverty incidents of his fellow moguls but a terrifying illness that defined the boundaries of his days from childhood through his marriage and beyond. He did die young as predicted, at age thirty-seven in 1936, just a few years older than Mozart, though the disease that took him was not the one that had been feared for so long. But illness aside, almost everything about the entirety of his life had been charmed except its chilling brevity.

Unlike Louis B. Mayer, who was already a teenager deep into the junk/salvage business by the time Irving Grant Thalberg was born on May 30, 1899, quite a bit is known about the earliest days of his future collaborator. In fact if not in spirit a child of the nineteenth century, he was born at home, at 19 Woodbine Street in the Bushwick section of Brooklyn, to William and Henrietta Thalberg.

Though never more than comfortably middle class, the Thalbergs were German Jews like their wealthy compatriots the Warburgs, the Lehmans, and the Schiffs. German Jews did not speak Yiddish, had gotten to America earlier than eastern Europeans like the Mayers, had assimilated faster and become successful sooner, and in general looked down from the heights of supposed gentility on their ne'er do well coreligionists.

"The tensions between the established German Jews and the insecure east European Jews had become severe, even rather nasty," wrote Irving Howe in his landmark *World of Our Fathers*, quoting the *Jewish Messenger*, a German Jewish weekly, as calling the newcomers "slovenly in dress, loud in manners and vulgar in discourse." These kinds of nettlesome ethnic and class divisions were hard-wired into the DNA of Jews of the period, and though it is unlikely Thalberg and Mayer ever spoke about

Thalberg as a well-behaved young Brooklyn boy. The image is in a
picture frame used by wife Norma Shearer. (Collection of Darin Barnes)

them to each other, it is hard to imagine both were not aware
of the gap and that their ultimate conflicts weren't affected by
them.

William was an importer of lace, an immigrant from Germany whose position in the family pecking order was not significant. As Thalberg's wife Norma Shearer wrote in an unpublished memoir, "Henrietta treated William more like an uninvited
guest she had to tolerate than like the head of the family."

As for Henrietta, also German Jewish, she was a different order of business, able to keep her significant position in her son's life for decades, and, unlike Mayer's similarly placed mother, she did not have to die to do it. Her successful family owned a department store, and her drive and intensity were impossible to disguise, visible even in photographs taken on nominally happy occasions, like her son's wedding to movie star Shearer.

Under a cloud from almost his first breath, Irving Thalberg was diagnosed as what was then called a blue baby, a skin color symptom of a lack of oxygen called cyanosis and caused by a congenitally defective heart. Doctors predicted he would not live beyond thirty, if that.

Henrietta Thalberg was not interested in medical predictions. She both coddled her young son and refused to let him be defined by his childhood illnesses, which were many, eventually including bronchitis and diphtheria, even rheumatic fever. Thalberg spent many months in bed, which finally would place formal graduation from high school out of reach, but his mother would not allow him to be idle.

Henrietta Thalberg not only brought his homework home to her bedridden son, but she also convinced teachers to visit and explain the lessons. And she went to the library to get him books to read. He was drawn to the pragmatism of William James, coming up with self-help maxims like "the clearness with which I see my goal determines my speed in reaching it." And he devoured classic literature to such an extent that one biography rhapsodized that the young Thalberg had "fought alongside the Three Musketeers, mounted the steps to the guillotine with Sydney Carton . . . brooded with Hamlet and climbed balconies with Romeo."

Although Thalberg had once thought of becoming a lawyer, his health issues made him seek immediate work. He learned Spanish and stenography and took some unremarkable jobs. Then something happened so unlikely, so the stuff of Horatio Alger legend, that the details have mythologized into multiple accounts. Only the result is not in dispute: in 1918, when he was just nineteen years old, frail high school dropout Irving Thalberg out of nowhere became the personal secretary to Carl Laemmle, the head of Universal and one of the bedrock pioneers of the movie business. And the best was yet to come.

Carl Laemmle was the most eccentric of all the founding studio heads. He did things very much his own idiosyncratic way, sometimes with splendid results, sometimes not. Giving a teenage Irving Thalberg a leg up in the film business was definitely one of the former.

Born in Laupheim, Germany, in 1867, Laemmle was older than many of his fellow pioneers, eighteen years older than Mayer, for instance, and he jumped into the movie business rather late in life. Naturally avuncular and given to being called Uncle Carl, he was described by best-selling novelist Edna Ferber as a "gnomelike little Oshkosh storekeeper who, like a figure in a fairy tale, had become a millionaire overnight because he had seen the possibilities of a thing called the nickelodeon."

Facing stiff resistance to his filmmaking efforts from Thomas Edison and the monopoly-minded Patents Trust, Laemmle in 1909 founded a production entity he called Independent Motion Picture Company, playfully known as IMP for short with a mischievous, not to say diabolical logo to match. Eventually, he gathered IMP and other small independent companies into the much larger Universal, a name he apparently came up with when he looked out the window and saw a wagon with a Universal Pipe Fitting Company sign rolling by.

Because so much had happened to him in a random way, Laemmle saw no reason to run his new studio (on a former San Fernando Valley chicken farm the U.S. postal service grandly recognized as "Universal City") other than haphazardly. But though neither of them knew it, like movie lovers who have no idea they're fated to meet, Carl Laemmle needed Irving Thalberg and Irving Thalberg needed him.

The meeting happened, unexpectedly enough, at a vacation location on Long Island called Edgemere. Thalberg's grandmother had a cottage there that by a quirk of fate was located next door to one used by Carl Laemmle, who, not surprisingly, liked to show movies outdoors at night to friends and neighbors.

Biographers differ on what happened next. Did Thalberg, a summer visitor at the cottage, get hired as a favor to his mother's mother, or by demonstrating acumen via pithy postscreening analysis? Did his mother, by a different account a friend of Laemmle's wife, put in a good word for him or did he refuse any hint of favoritism, getting hired by Universal on his own merits and then getting noticed by Laemmle as a familiar face in the office.

Finally, how it happened is not critical; what is key is that Thalberg became Laemmle's personal secretary in Universal's New York office and as such began to demonstrate a trait that impressed not only his first boss but everyone who worked with him from those days to the end: a seemingly innate grasp of how films worked, of how to adroitly tailor them to optimize audience satisfaction. David Lewis, who began as a close Thalberg associate and ended up a Warner Bros executive (and whose *The Creative Producer* is an astute memoir of the period), wrote that of all the people he'd come across only Thalberg, Mayer, and Jack Warner "would have been important in any phase of endeavor they entered." But he also felt that Thalberg's cinematic basic instincts made him stand alone in the movie world.

Also working at Universal's New York offices, as it turned out, was Samuel Marx, destined to be MGM's story editor and an engaging memoirist. "He handled all of Laemmle's correspondence and corrected his broken English while also arranging his appointments," remembered Marx of his newly made friend, "detouring the time-wasters, and channeling away the cries and complaints flooding in to the boss." He also had time to dream of a career in a business that he said "changes so fast that it offers unlimited opportunities." More than that, Marx remembers him vowing that if he had the opportunity to take on those who settled for mediocre films, "I'd make them do it my way so they'd never know if their way was better."

That chance came soon enough. Finding Thalberg to be an invaluable organizer, Laemmle made a spur-of-the-moment decision in 1919 to take his young employee with him first to Chicago and then on to Los Angeles. This first-ever trip away from the East Coast was so last-minute that a teary mother Henrietta apparently had to meet him at Grand Central Terminal with a packed suitcase for him to leave on time.

Laemmle may have been happy with his vision of Universal as a kind of Woolworth's five and dime, awash in a variety of inexpensive merchandise, but someone was needed to regulate the flow. Marx reports that sixteen managers had taken a shot at running Universal from 1915 to Thalberg's arrival, and all had been sacked.

After some time spent on a kind of listening tour of the studio, he deftly navigated a bureaucratic thicket ("I took charge because there was no one left to take charge") and, backed by Laemmle, was named its general manager in 1920, in charge of day-to-day operations before he was old enough to sign the payroll checks.

Not only was Thalberg young, if anything he came off as younger than he was, looking, remembered his associate Albert Lewin, "like a high school boy, rather sensitive, quite handsome," and photographs from these early days bear this out. A New York meeting with Louella Parsons, which the gossip columnist wrote about some years later, was the first recorded instance of a blanket refusal to believe this youthful individual could be a respected executive. When Thalberg introduced himself at their restaurant meeting, Parsons suspected someone was pulling her leg.

"I replied briefly and I fear none too gently, 'Well, what's the joke? Where is the new general manager?' 'I am,' replied the boy modestly. To save my embarrassment, Irving started ordering luncheon. Five minutes talk with him and I knew he might be a boy in looks and age, but it was no child's mind that was being sent to cope with the intricate politics of Universal City."

Once Thalberg got to Los Angeles and took over Universal, this you-can't-be-him situation picked up steam. Edna Ferber recalled "a very, very young and very, very bright lad . . . a wisp of a boy, twenty-one, so slight as to appear actually frail." Screenwriter Lenore Coffee, called to a meeting at Universal, remembers, "Although I had seen photographs I was not prepared for the slender body, the delicately boned and striking Italianate face. I thought immediately of how he would look as a Renaissance prince, for he had a princely air." More than that, Coffee says that the young executive, "with his sound instinct, created his own image right from the start, and it never changed. When you were shown into his office he was invariably standing behind his desk, looking at a letter or fiddling with various objects with an abstracted air, as if he were quite unconscious of your presence. After a good moment he would look up as if startled to find you there. 'You wanted to see me?'"

Several memoirs of the period include anecdotes uniformly insisting that Thalberg looked so inexperienced he was literally mistaken for an office boy. The great Lillian Gish reports a Union Station encounter where "Mother, mistaking Irving Thalberg for an office boy, gave him our baggage checks"; silent film divas Nazimova and Mae Murray were incensed to find "an office boy" at one of their parties; and even future wife Norma Shearer, as will be seen, apparently made the identical mistake.

Given all this, it's no surprise that the sobriquet "Boy Wonder," which was to stay with him through his obituaries and beyond, apparently started during his Universal days. A *New York Times* headline as early as October 15, 1922, proclaims "Great

Executive Job Held By a Boy of 22." Though Thalberg apparently disdained the "Boy Wonder" title (Marx says he coldly told Upton Sinclair's wife that he "never heard it"), jibes at his youth were ever-present. Screenwriter and wit Herman Mankiewicz even wrote in a parody of Hearst newspaper style "Irving Thalberg celebrated twenty-sixth birthday with bigger celebration than last year's twenty-sixth birthday celebration. Plan bigger twenty-sixth birthday celebration next year."

Thalberg had more serious things to worry about at Universal, however, than his disconcerting youth. At the top of the list of difficulties was Erich von Stroheim, one of the great directors of the age as well as a world-class self-mythologizer who had barely concealed contempt for anyone who had the temerity to stand in his way. Thalberg inevitably did, and the conflict between them, extending across several films, two studios, and half a dozen years not only made Thalberg's reputation, both pro and con, it also marked a sea change in how Hollywood motion pictures were thought about and made.

Though he was to make a career as The Man You Love To Hate, playing strutting, heartless Teutonic officers, Stroheim was not an aristocrat and likely had little or no military experience. Born Jewish in Austria, he simply added the von to his name when he arrived at Ellis Island in 1909 and began to act the part.

But like many actors since, what von Stroheim really wanted to do was write and direct. He had a story, "The Pinnacle," that he volunteered to direct for free, asking only to be paid to star. Carl Laemmle, a man who liked to gamble as much as he liked a bargain, said yes.

Concerned that audiences would confuse pinnacle with pinochle, Laemmle changed the name of the story of a neglectful American husband, a lonely wife, and a conniving European womanizer in a spiffy uniform (played by the director himself) to *Blind Husbands*. The film proved to be one of 1919's major successes and soon enough a similar von Stroheim–starring tale of amoral Europeans and gullible Americans, set this time in the gambling mecca of Monte Carlo and boasting the nicely book-ended title of *Foolish Wives*, was in the works. And it is here that Irving Thalberg, Universal's newly minted general manager, entered the picture.

Thalberg had taken up his position about halfway through the *Foolish Wives* shooting, which ended up lasting almost a year, and though he like everyone else admired the director's gifts, von Stroheim's profligate ways were anathema to him, especially since cost cutting was one of Carl Laemmle's mandates. An enough-is-enough confrontation between Thalberg and von Stroheim was inevitable. One version has von Stroheim snapping, "If you were not my superior I would smash you in the face," with Thalberg replying, "Don't let that stop you"; another has Stroheim point-blank refusing Thalberg's order to stop shooting by announcing, "Remove me as the director and you have to remove me as the star and you won't have a picture," adding dismissively to his staff, "Since when does a child supervise a genius?"

With the acting card as trump, the result was clear. In Samuel Marx's words, "this was Thalberg's baptism of fire with von Stroheim," but it was not the last word. Near the end of the film, when Thalberg thought one sequence had prompted sufficient retakes, cinematographer William Daniels reports, "When I went to the location next night the cameras weren't there. I got a car and went after the cameras, but I couldn't get them back. Thalberg had removed them permanently. By the time I got back they had taken the lights away. Thalberg was terrified, and I sympathize; spending all that time, and a million dollars, on a picture in those days was incredible, unheard of."

Despite von Stroheim's profligacy, because he was gifted and because his very name was associated with a style of daring filmmaking audiences responded to, Thalberg and the studio were reluctant to pass on the director's next movie, one it was still contractually owed. This feature, set amid the inevitably decadent aristocrats of pre–World War I Vienna, was to be called *Merry Go Round*.

Von Stroheim wrote and directed as usual, but Thalberg, who had learned from his *Foolish Wives* experience, stipulated that the director could not also star (the role went to Norman Kerry) and von Stroheim, probably thinking he was close to invincible, did not contest the matter. That proved to be a mistake.

Despite having agreed to stay on budget and on schedule, von Stroheim did no such thing. After six weeks of shooting, overseen for the first time by a unit production manager installed by Thalberg, the director was well behind where he was supposed to be. On October 6, 1922, von Stroheim was called to Thalberg's office and given a two-page letter signed by the general manager but likely written by Universal counsel Edwin Loeb, also in the room and later to be key in connecting Thalberg to Mayer, saying he was fired and detailing the reasons why. Stroheim did not make a fuss but almost immediately took a train for New York, where he expected, incorrectly it turned out, that his young adversary would be overruled by Carl Laemmle. In the meantime, Thalberg immediately installed a journeyman director to finish the film (eventually advertised as "Rupert Julian's Stupendous Production"), and the replacement's work was competent enough to make *Merry Go Round* one of the year's financial successes for the studio.

Read today, the Thalberg letter sounds like the declaration of war it was. It shoehorned seventy-two single-spaced lines of closely reasoned argument into two tightly packed pages, as if to emphasize that the studio's determination to economize extended even to the use of its Universal Film Manufacturing Company stationery. The heart of the matter was calling Von Stroheim to task for "your totally inexcusable and repeated acts of insubordination, your extravagant ideas which you have been unwilling to sacrifice in the slightest particular, repeated and unnecessary delays occasioned by your attitude in arguing against practically every instruction that has been given to you in good faith and by your apparent idea that you are greater and more powerful than the organization that employs you." As a result of this and other offenses, no surprise, "you are notified you are discharged from our employ."

A firing in Hollywood may not sound earthshaking, but when von Stroheim was let go it was. In these still-early days of the movie business the director was an absolute monarch, and producers and/or money people were supposed to quake in their presence and stay well out of the way. Directors never got axed, and von Stroheim himself well knew that his dismissal by Thalberg meant the pendulum had begun to swing toward the studio domination of filmmaking that was to be the rule for half a century. Years later fellow director Orson Welles was still furious about it. "Thalberg was the biggest single villain in the history of Hollywood," he told his friend Henry Jaglom. "He destroyed von Stroheim as a man and as an artist. Literally destroyed him."

As implacable fate would have it, von Stroheim and Thalberg were not free of each other. Both men ended up at MGM, where they tussled, as will be seen, over a pair of more celebrated films, *The Merry Widow* and the ill-fated *Greed*, but *Merry Go Round* was the one where the die was cast. As producer David O. Selznick told historian Kevin Brownlow, the executive's action "took great guts and courage. Thalberg was only twenty-two. . . . I can well imagine that Thalberg reasoned with him, but finding von Stroheim adamant, he had the courage to do what had to be done."

This action reverberated for Thalberg in different ways. On the most basic level, it gave him credibility; as profile writer Allene Talmey put it, "the kid secretary had proved himself." But it would be simplistic to think of Thalberg as a bean-counting enemy of creative filmmaking. In truth, both ways was the only way he wanted it: a great favorite of the majority of the writers and other creative folk he worked with throughout his career, he believed films could be artistic and not bankrupt the studio. Individual obsessives like von Stroheim did not interest him, and he believed in his filmmaking ideals as deeply as his adversary believed in his. It was not until Thalberg got to MGM, however, and joined forces with Louis B. Mayer that he was able to put his vision of artistic possibilities into consistent practice.

Thalberg's brief time at Universal also connected him with another major talent who was not a business-as-usual type, the singular actor Lon Chaney, but this time the results were salutary for all concerned, leading at Universal to one of Chaney's most iconic roles and later at MGM to the most stable and productive period of the actor's career. There were some bumps, but there was also the kind of mutual respect that was not the case with von Stroheim.

Best known today as the original Phantom of the Opera, Lon Chaney was a man of a thousand paradoxes as well as faces, "the star who lived like a clerk," according to frequent director Tod Browning, the performer who was reclusive enough to insist, "between pictures there is no Lon Chaney." An actor who achieved stardom by taking roles that are almost too strange to characterize, Chaney specialized not in monsters with human faces but in humans with monstrous ones.

Though Thalberg was to make his reputation with unashamedly straight-ahead material, it's worth noting that he also had an unexpected taste for the frisson of strangeness that Chaney brought to the screen. It was at Universal with 1923's huge hit of *The Hunchback of Notre Dame* that the two first worked together, and Thalberg's particular gift for seeing and seizing opportunities came to the fore.

As with most movie success stories, the question of who had the original idea for a new version (there had been six previous ones) of the Victor Hugo novel about Quasimodo, the misshapen cathedral bellringer, and the beautiful Esmeralda, daughter of the King of the Gypsies, is open to dispute, with the likely truth being that Chaney and Thalberg had the same thought at different times.

It would have been natural for Thalberg, who read voraciously during his long periods of childhood illness, to have suggested *Hunchback* as a feature. But the actor expressed an interest in the role as early as 1920, according to Chaney authority Michael Blake, and even tried to secure the rights for himself. Thalberg went with the reliable Wallace Worsley as director, and the role of Esmeralda went to Patsy Ruth Miller, who remembers the actor with the forbidding exterior as the giver of shrewd advice: "You don't have to live the part, just act it," Chaney told her. "The point is not for you to cry; make your audience cry."

Hunchback was shot on the Universal lot, where some of the $1.25 million Thalberg had convinced Carl Laemmle to spend had gone toward a replica of the cathedral's façade. Sixty workmen transported cobblestones from a river miles distant to create the eleven-acre cathedral square, and Chaney himself daily spent three-plus hours in makeup, looking so fierce that future director Tay Garnett, on the set as a fan magazine boy reporter, remembered, "Even the jaded extras avoided looking at him."

As good as all this was, it came to Thalberg to add the finishing touches. Viewing the completed film, with theaters ever hungry for product clamoring for the chance to show it as soon as possible, the general manager, as he was to do often in the future at MGM, saw a chance for something more.

Feeling the film could use more spectacle, at the not inconsiderable cost of $150,000 he took the gamble of ordering director Worsley back to the set to shoot additional crowd scenes, some at night, when expensive arc lights would be required. Laemmle, who was always after Thalberg to keep expenses down, was in Europe at the time and could not stop the plan. *Hunchback* proved to be precisely the prestige item Thalberg intended, as well as the studio's highest-grossing film of 1923.

Despite these kinds of high-profile machinations, life in Hollywood was not all production difficulties and balance sheets for Thalberg. Though he worked long hours and lived near his parents, whom he'd moved out to Los Angeles in 1921, along with his sister Sylvia, Thalberg had as much of a romantic life as his mother Henrietta, unceasingly vigilant because of her fears about his health, would allow.

Perhaps the earliest and most appealing glimpse of this side of Thalberg comes from Bessie Love, an actress of beauty and presence whom the young executive was taken with, as she relates in an anecdote from her autobiography, *From Hollywood with Love*, that's charming enough to quote at length.

> Irving Thalberg had called to see me that evening and was there when word came about my father [who had been taken ill at his central California ranch]. Irving was a beau of mine: not serious, but a beau. He was a sweet boy with good manners, who blushed easily. So did I. . . .
>
> Irving was new to Hollywood. He knew nothing of California distances and drove quite a modest car. Even so, when you divide his chivalry in half and take away another quarter for his ignorance, he was still gallant. He immediately said we would go that minute and fetch Dad. On my word, I really did try to dissuade him. I didn't know what on earth I was going to do, but I was not insensible of the sacrifice it would entail for him. I was not certain that he knew just how much he was offering. He was adamant. We would go right then! So we did.
>
> After about a hundred miles or so he began asking how much further it was. By then it was too late to turn back, though we still had quite a way to go. At last we passed through Bakersfield. Dawn began to break and suddenly he realized

what day it now was at the studio—pay day, and he had to sign the salary cheques!

Just before we reached Pixley—our ranch was a little way outside the town—he made me promise one thing. Gently, but quite firmly, he said that no matter what news awaited us, he must make a telephone call to the studio cashier. I most meekly agreed.

An anecdote of similar charm does not exist for the other significant romantic interest of Thalberg's Universal days, Rosabelle Laemmle, the boss's spirited daughter. Rosabelle left no autobiography, but that doesn't mean she wasn't noticed, though opinions differ as to the contours of the relationship and its consequences.

Initially, as recounted by Samuel Marx, the interest was all on Thalberg's side. "He certainly enjoyed talking about her, even in a rambling sort of way, introducing her name into conversations having little to do with her," Marx remembered. "It was evident that he had her on his mind, that he liked her, but Rosabelle showed no signs of reciprocating his fondness for her, if, indeed, she was aware of it."

This dynamic started to change once Rosabelle's father made Thalberg his Los Angeles–based general manager. Not only did Rosabelle become more interested in him, but the family-oriented Carl Laemmle started to think having this gifted young man as a relative was not a bad idea. Thalberg was by this point the cooler of the pair, but according to Marx, Carl and his wife Rachel went to California in an old-school attempt to arrange things with Thalberg's mother Henrietta, to no avail: "She wasn't anxious for her Irving to marry anyone. He was a success and had no need for a wife, even a rich one. She also feared that the sexual requirements of marriage would exhaust his fragile strength." With marriage tabled, this on-and-off relationship continued for years, finally ending, according to the one anecdote we do have about Rosabelle, when Thalberg, running late at work, suggested sending a car to take her to their date instead of picking her up in person. Such was the clannishness of the largely Jewish group of Hollywood executives, despite their often-bitter rivalries, that Rosabelle became known as "Poor Rosabelle" when Thalberg eventually married a recently converted Norma Shearer. Ad Schulberg, wife of producer B. P. Schulberg, told anyone who wanted to listen that "Irving was making a terrible mistake."

Though awkwardness over the Rosabelle situation might have been a factor, Thalberg had other, more significant, reasons for discontent at Universal. Despite his key role in turning *Hunchback* into an A picture, he didn't get a raise he felt he was due, the first of many instances in his career when money became an issue. Whether or not Laemmle's displeasure at the foiled marriage plot factored into that decision, Thalberg was not pleased. Also troubling was the presence of numerous Laemmle relatives and friends on the payroll, individuals he could not fire. Estimated at more than seventy in number, they were known as "Laemmle's foreign legion." A believer in the maxim "Never remain in a job when you have everything from it you can get," Thalberg visualized something more for himself, and for film, than the haphazard way Carl Laemmle ran things. So much so that he left Universal to join Louis B. Mayer before *Hunchback* was even released and never looked back.

3

Early Days and Norma

IRVING THALBERG WAS a few months short of his twenty-fourth birthday when he signed on as vice president and production assistant at Louis B. Mayer Studios. But despite his getting the salary increase Laemmle had denied him, many must have wondered whether this was a wise career move, whether leaving a large, established studio, however dysfunctional, for a relatively new production company that supplied films to mid-level entities like First National and Metro wasn't a step down. More than that, observers like screenwriter Frances Marion couldn't see what they had in common. "Mayer insisted that he and Irving were 'brothers under the skin,'" she tartly observed. "Nobody ever skinned them to find out, but on prima facie they were opposite as the two poles." "Actually," fellow writer Lenore Coffee wrote in the same vein, "the two men were personally not at all congenial, even at the beginning."

Then, however, came an all-important caveat. "But their

talents complemented each other. Irving was not interested in money unless he made it from ideas or creations of his own. But Louis Mayer was essentially a financier. A brilliant one. He loved the complicated business of making deals. So this developed into what might be called a successful marriage."

There is more to this relationship, not to mention more to Mayer, than Coffee indicates. For one thing, congenial or not, Mayer took a strong personal liking to this young man and the regard he had for him was extraordinary. Thalberg was more than the first of several putative "sons I didn't have" for Mayer (the next, producer David O. Selznick, became a son-in-law, another, Dore Schary, ended up supplanting the older man). Because he had the unattainable gloss of German Jewishness, Thalberg was the son Mayer could never have hoped for but was delighted to have almost miraculously acquired. On Thalberg's side, with a weak father in his background, having the support of this powerful masculine figure (Mayer was fourteen years older but exuded authority, paternal and otherwise) must have been a relief. But as with any father-son relationship, especially one between an immigrant father and a native-born son, future misunderstandings and conflicts were all but inevitable.

Still, that initial sense of wonder was real, and can be experienced most vividly in an extended passage from *A Private View*, daughter Irene Mayer Selznick's elegantly written memoir.

> Then, in 1923 Irving Thalberg joined the family. My father had a son without having to raise one—wise, loving, filial. . . . My father admired both his brain and his gentle nature. Irving was ambitious and yet unspoiled, but there was a flaw in this gift from the gods. Irving wasn't really his because he was borrowed. The gods would have him back, as he had a bad heart from an attack of rheumatic fever as a boy, and his doctors had warned my father that he could go at any time, and that there was no chance of his living beyond the age of thirty.

Irving's advent was a thunderbolt. How could a fellow twenty-three possibly be much help at the studio? What was Dad so excited about? . . . My father prepared us for the introduction of Irving into our lives and he warned us we were going to see a great deal of him. . . . He said he'd almost not signed Irving because of the romantic risk to one of us. He had advised Irving not to look on his daughters with favor. He didn't want to have to cure a problem, he wanted to prevent one, and we weren't warned once, twice; we were constantly admonished.

Irving very soon came to dinner. It was hard to believe that anyone that modest and boyish could be so important. He had a most engaging manner, but we had been totally unprepared for anyone that good-looking. . . .

The evenings Irving came to dinner we found doubly exciting because at the table he and my father exchanged their opinions and ideas, exploring each other's reactions. The growing bond between them was evident. There was confidence, enthusiasm, and affection—all of it mutual. The more there was, the greater was my father's pain at the sentence which hung over Irving's head.

There seemed nothing in his background to account for his gifts or his personality. Irving was a throw-off, a mutant. . . . My father's pride and delight in Irving were overwhelming. That was an aspect of him we never saw before or after. At times he bore him an aching love. The young man with the greatest future in the motion-picture business was a man without a future.

Thalberg and Mayer were fated to occupy their lion-adjacent premises near the Selig Zoo for little more than a year before their fledgling organization was called to greater things, and the films that came out of that brief period are rarely talked about, let alone seen. But something significant for both men and their future company did happen in that span: the signing of the woman who was to become, along with Greta Garbo and Joan Crawford, one of MGM's trio of maximum-wattage star actresses, as well as the wife of Irving Thalberg, Norma Shearer.

Though she'd amassed several East Coast credits, Shearer was not a star of any kind at that point. Far from being the un-crowned queen of the MGM lot she was to become as Thal-berg's wife, she had not progressed far up the professional lad-der before she and her mother moved to Los Angeles in 1923. As writer Adela Rogers St. John observed years later, "She had the slowest rise of any star I ever knew. Sheer grit made the dif-ference."

Shearer was born in Canada (she became an American citi-zen in 1932), in Westmount, an enclave inside Montreal. En-couraged by a show-business aunt and uncle when her family faced financial difficulties, she, her sister Athole, and their de-termined mother Edith went to New York in 1920 to try their luck.

Not considered to be as attractive as her sister (who later married director Howard Hawks), according to a childhood friend "she made herself beautiful" almost by force of will. A variety of physical strikes against her, including strabismus or crossed eyes and legs considered too stocky for the fashion, caused both showman Florenz Ziegfeld and pioneer director D. W. Griffith to decide after interviews that her chances for stardom were slight. During times when parts were scarce, Shearer, who always had a classic profile, turned to modeling, working for top illustrators like Charles Dana Gibson and James Montgomery Flagg and, most notoriously, becoming known as "Miss Lotta Miles" in a series of ads for Kelly-Springfield tires.

Shearer did begin to attract some West Coast notice, ini-tially from Universal Pictures, which she said no to, and then from the Louis B. Mayer company. She accepted that offer, her first multiyear studio contract, and accompanied by her mother took the train to Los Angeles. The day after a Union Station arrival, they took a taxi from the Hollywood Hotel to Mayer's offices at the Selig Zoo studio, disconcerted not only by Los Angeles distances (new arrivals still invariably are) but by what happened when they arrived.

As Shearer details in her unpublished late-in-life memoir,

> We were sitting in the reception room waiting to see whomever we were supposed to see, when a very polite and modest young office boy came through a small swinging gate which he held open for us as he smiled quietly and said nothing. In we went and he followed us, opening another door down the hall where we found ourselves obviously in Mr. Mayer's office, very large and luxurious.
>
> To our amazement the young man went around the big desk and sat down behind it. I thought he'd better get up out of that chair before someone came in! Then he started pressing buttons on that big shiny desk and I thought, now he's playing games—he'd better stop fooling around or Mr. Mayer will come in and fire him! He looked so handsome I didn't want that to happen!
>
> Just then Mr. Mayer did come in and the young man stood up calmly and introduced us to him. . . . We realized this young man who so kindly greeted us couldn't be the office boy and we soon found out he was Mr. Irving Thalberg.

Shearer also found out almost immediately that Thalberg's default position was all business all the time. When she attempted to improve her starting salary, citing that offer from Universal as proof that others were interested in her, Thalberg revealed that the offer had originated from him while he was at the studio. "I began to suspect that he was running Mr. Mayer's studio with his permission. I didn't know he was going to run my life too and from now on I was going to spend it trying to live up to his expectations."

Reginald Barker, the director of one of her early films, took a dislike to the insecure Shearer, at one point telling her, "You don't seem to know what it's all about." A meeting with Mayer was arranged and he, as was to become his trademark style, emotionally whipsawed the young actress, starting out sympathetic and then abruptly changing tone and bawling her out. "The trouble is you're yellow," he insisted. "Here you are given a great chance, the chance of your life, and what do you do? You throw it away because maybe you don't like the director or something. I'm through with you." This tirade had the intended effect on the actress, as Shearer insisted she deserved another chance. Handed a reprieve when Thalberg delayed shooting for a few days to change cinematographers, she made the most of it. "This time," Shearer remembered, "I decided to show Mr. Barker that I wasn't afraid of him, that I could act along with the rest of the pros. I made up my mind to be as brave as the lions next door in the zoo. I could hear that roaring through the walls of my dressing room. I decided I had to learn to roar too—as loud as they did!"

While Shearer was learning to roar, other, quieter doings and stealthy meetings were taking place at Mayer's studio, and screenwriter Lenore Coffee happened by chance to be present at the creation. "In the spring of 1924 I was sitting in on a story conference with Irving Thalberg . . . and one or two others," she wrote.

> We were discussing a script being written called *Captain Applejack*, and there was a line he spoke repeatedly which became famous: "I am in a mood for dalliance."
>
> It was during this conference the buzzer of Mr. Mayer's office sounded on Thalberg's desk, and he went to answer it. He kept us all waiting for quite a long time, and when he came back he stood framed in the open doorway and said, with a great deal of ceremony, "Ladies and gentlemen, I have the pleasure to announce to you that the Metro-Goldwyn-Mayer merger is now an accomplished fact."

Now Thalberg usually didn't make jokes, but this time he did! He started toward his desk, then stopped and looked at us and said, "I think we'll do no more work today. I find myself in a mood for dalliance."

4

One Out of Many

No ONE EVER accused Louis B. Mayer of moving too slowly, and on April 26, 1924, just days after the three-way merger of his company with Metro Pictures and Goldwyn Pictures was finalized, he welcomed festive throngs to the official opening of the new Culver City home of Metro-Goldwyn as the man in charge. (When Mayer's name was officially added in January 1926, he told a switchboard operator who still answered "Hello, Metro-Goldwyn" that "It's Metro-Goldwyn-Mayer, and the next time you forget it, you won't have a job.") In physical distance the new location was miles away from East Los Angeles' Selig Zoo—diagonally across Los Angeles, in fact, and in terms of prestige and facilities it was a world apart as well.

As remembered later by Budd Schulberg, who was twelve at the time and was especially taken with the imposing "Prussian" neck of Erich von Stroheim, seated directly in front of him, the day had a kind of haphazard quality to it. The crowd included stars (Lon Chaney, John Gilbert, Lillian Gish, and others) and directors like Frank Borzage and Victor Seastrom, as well as random celebrities like the admiral of the Pacific Fleet. There was even an enormous key, with the word "Success" emblazoned on it in large letters and handed by a Goldwyn functionary to Mayer, Thalberg, and production executive Harry Rapf to symbolize the lot's change in ownership.

There was also talk, lots of talk. Telegrams were read from President Calvin Coolidge and Herbert Hoover; Will Rogers, the nominal master of ceremonies, rode in on a horse. Finally, director Marshall Nielan, who later became known for a famous crack about the new boss ("An empty taxi cab drove up and Louis B. Mayer got out"), lost patience with the slow pace of the proceedings and ostentatiously left with members of his cast and crew to return to the film he was shooting.

If this upset Mayer, he did not let it diminish his feeling of success or his determination to state his credo: "It has been my argument and practice that each picture should teach a lesson, should have a reason for existence," he said. "This is a great moment for me, I accept this solemn trust and pledge the best that I have to give."

Though in retrospect this three-way merger, masterminded by Marcus Loew, owner of the prestigious theater chain that bore his name, made complete sense, its particulars had taken Hollywood by surprise. It was the last of a series of mergers that were to reshape and strengthen other studios as well, but a felicitous combination of history, happenstance, location, and personnel, most notably Mayer and Thalberg, meant that MGM came out of this chaotic period the strongest and most successful of the lot, the gold standard of golden age Hollywood studios.

It all started, as a chunk of the earliest movie history did, with producer Thomas Ince, who way back in 1911 had created an ocean-facing working studio called Inceville in what was to become Pacific Palisades. Fledgling real estate entrepreneur

Harry C. Culver convinced Ince to start another studio farther inland fronting on Washington Boulevard in what was soon to be Culver City. In 1918, Samuel Goldwyn's company bought the lot, whose celebrated colonnade of Corinthian columns, a design element eventually to be symbolic of MGM, were said to "elevate filmmaking to the glory of ancient civilization."

While all this was happening in physical production, similar transformations were taking place on the financial side of the business. Adolph Zukor, a dynamic, influential executive, was the key player in the 1916 merger that created Paramount. Zukor is credited with pioneering the movie business's embrace of vertical integration, of combining production, distribution, and exhibition into a single corporation that would have a controlling hand in every step of the process from the making of films to the showing of them in theaters.

After Zukor put this notion into practice and started buying theater chains, his idea made Paramount the dominant film studio in the early 1920s. The swagger that came with that preeminence is evident in Paramount print advertising that dared, "Catch us if you can." Which was just what Marcus Loew intended to do.

In March 1927 successful movie producer (and father of a future American president) Joseph P. Kennedy, feeling that "the oldest of American universities should recognize the youngest of industries," persuaded the august Harvard Business School to host a series of lectures on the upstart movies. Of all the luminaries who came to speak, including Adolph Zukor, William Fox, and Harry M. Warner, only one came in defiance of his doctor's orders: Marcus Loew, president of Metro-Goldwyn-Mayer Pictures Corporation and boss of bosses for Mayer and Thalberg. In truth ill enough with heart disease that he would die in a few months, Loew had come because he was a man of his word who had promised to speak, a man who had similarly taken pains to pay off debts that had led him to bankruptcy not once but twice.

By all accounts a modest individual (*Variety*'s obituary called him "the most beloved man of all show business of all time"), Loew also came because he couldn't believe he'd been asked, opening his talk by admitting, "I cannot begin to tell you how it impresses me, coming to a great college such as this to deliver a lecture, when I have never even seen the inside of one before."

In fact, starting work as a newsboy at age six or seven, Loew had left formal education by the time he was nine. Jewish but non-Yiddish speaking, born into extreme poverty not in Europe but in New York, Loew had worked largely in the fur trade but as early as 1904 had been impressed enough by the success of penny arcades to buy into the business. Then, as he told the Harvard students, he was invited "to see a new idea in entertainment . . . and I never got such a thrill in my life." This was an early nickelodeon, known as a store show because it was an empty storefront in which chairs had been placed. "The place was packed to suffocation," he remembered, which was all Loew, instincts honed by a lifetime of struggle, had to see to know this was going to be the next big thing.

Loew believed in constructing purpose-built theaters because they soon paid for themselves. By the end of World War I, by one writer's tally, Loew "owned 112 theaters, employed ten thousand people, and owned a corporation worth $25 million." Yet though experience and serendipity played a role in his success, that, Loew cautioned the Harvard students, was not enough. "You have to have the showman's instinct with it. That is something that is undefinable, something that I really cannot explain. It is something that comes to you if it is in you, and if it is not in you you will never succeed."

Even as competitors like Paramount pushed toward a thousand theaters, Loew stayed with his strategy of fewer, larger, higher-end venues. (Loew's State, the 3,200-seat flagship of the chain with an office building on top, opened in Times Square in 1921.) But Loew also knew that with the business following Zukor's lead and becoming more vertical, and moviemakers starting to charge not a traditional flat rate but a percentage of the take, his chain had to own a production entity as well. That turned out to be more problematic than anticipated, albeit not at first.

As it happened, Metro, through which Louis B. Mayer had sometimes released, had fallen on hard times, and Loew was able to acquire it in January 1920. The first film Metro released after the sale turned out to be a huge hit and a genuine phenomenon: the World War I drama *The Four Horseman of the Apocalypse*, the film that turned Rudolph Valentino into an international star. But the good times did not continue to roll. "We used to think we made good pictures," Loew gloomily told the Harvard students about this period, "but the public would not agree with us."

Things were bad enough that Loew considered selling Metro, but while vacationing in Florida he took the advice of stage impresario Lee Shubert, a friend as well as a Loew's board member, and met with Frank Godsol, who ran Goldwyn Pictures after founder Samuel Goldwyn had been forced out, leaving his name behind. Though also in financial difficulties, Goldwyn Pictures did own that superior physical plant in Culver City and as such would combine nicely with Metro. But neither Metro nor Goldwyn had an executive considered capable enough to run the new enterprise, and it fell to J. Robert Rubin, the urbane and busy attorney, to tell client Loew about another client, Louis B. Mayer. Rubin made sure Loew met Mayer on a trip to the West Coast in 1923, and in April 1924, the merger was announced to little acclaim: Charlie Chaplin, for one, took to calling it "three weak sisters." Loew was the president of what was to eventually become MGM, Mayer was vice president and general manager, Irving Thalberg was second vice president and supervisor of production, and the indispensable middleman Rubin was secretary. In addition to salaries, these three men would divide 20 percent of the profits of the pictures they made as follows: Mayer 53 percent, Rubin 27 percent, and Thalberg 20 percent. As Mayer biographer Bosley Crowther, the first to publicize the figures, wrote, "It soon became evident that this was an underestimation of Thalberg's worth." Did this become a problem down the road? Yes, and much more than anyone could have imagined.

5

Unfinished Business

WHEN MARCUS LOEW united Metro, Goldwyn, and Mayer, he bought control of two kinds of property, intellectual as well as physical. In the earliest days of the merger, almost by default, Mayer and Thalberg became custodians of film projects begun under other executives' control, some of which caused a fuss. Marshall Neilan's version of Thomas Hardy's *Tess of the d'Urbervilles* became an early example of Mayer's zeal for happy endings, even when they flew in the face of the conclusion of celebrated novels. Unhappy with heroine Tess being hanged for murder, Mayer ordered Neilan to shoot a cheerier reprieved-from-the-gallows ending as well, and when exhibitors, not surprisingly, said they preferred that one, that's what he imposed. Neilan, in Britain for another film, complained to the disconsolate Hardy in person, with the novelist reportedly replying, "What could I do? I am an old man and have no defense against this sort of thing."

But two projects, both from Goldwyn, stand out because of their significance in film history and in the careers of the MGM leaders: Erich von Stroheim's star-crossed *Greed*, from the naturalistic fiction of Frank Norris, and the mighty epic *Ben-Hur*, celebrated for its extended, expensive chariot race that was one of the wonders of the silent age. The first became a cause célèbre for critics and other believers in complete creative freedom and threatened for a time to turn Thalberg into a whipping boy for studio interference, while the second overcame significant obstacles to become extremely successful and a high spot for the kinds of films both men wanted the new studio to be associated with.

Given the kind of furious enmity their dustup at Universal over *Merry Go Round* had created, both Thalberg and especially von Stroheim must have railed against the pitiless gods when they realized the merger had brought them together again. The director, attracted by Goldwyn's artist-friendly "the author and the play are the thing" slogan, had decamped for the studio almost immediately after his Thalberg-engineered Universal dismissal. The company had been as good as its word, allowing von Stroheim to turn *McTeague*, Norris's massive novel of lives destroyed, into the difficult, expensive *Greed*, but the merger had happened before it could be finished and released, and that was not good news.

Once shooting was over, von Stroheim labored for months on the editing, His rough cut, which he showed to friends and friendly journalists, came in at more or less nine and a half hours. By March 1924, just before the merger he feared, von Stroheim had cut the film roughly in half.

If the director thought any of this would matter to Mayer and Thalberg, he was not thinking clearly. Faced with a film they never would have approved and sure that its punishing style would not attract an audience, the MGM heads demanded further cuts, to a length of something around two and a quarter hours, which is the version most readily available today. Von Stroheim fumed that the man who did the cutting—"on whose mind was nothing but a hat"—"had never read the book nor the script," but even some viewers who had expected to like the long version, like Irene Mayer Selznick, were underwhelmed. "It was masterful in ways, and parts of it were riveting, but it was an exhausting experience; the film in conception was a considerable exercise in self-indulgence, and a testament to the incompetence of the previous regime," she wrote. "I was there—and, as it happens on von Stroheim's side in advance and prepared to do battle. When it was over, nobody said a word—including me."

Because the *Greed* imbroglio echoed what had happened with *Merry Go Round*, it would be plausible to assume that no new pictures would be forthcoming for von Stroheim from MGM, but this was not the case. Though Thalberg insisted on being in charge, he had respect for the director's gifts, and as for von Stroheim, he needed to work, as he candidly told a German film magazine, "because I do not want my family to starve." As it turned out, yet another of the projects MGM had inherited from Goldwyn was something von Stroheim had been interested in, and that was a film version of the hugely successful Franz Lehar operetta *The Merry Widow*. Making a silent film out of a stage musical sounded odd even then, and MGM admitted as much by noting in the film's souvenir book "that it was contrary to the laws of nature to attempt to bring an art designed for the ear into a newer art designed solely for the eye." But counterintuitive or not, *The Merry Widow* turned out to be one of Stroheim's greatest successes, a hit both in box office terms and with the critics. That doesn't mean it was easy.

The Merry Widow was an example of Thalberg and Mayer's pragmatism, of not only having a vision of how several not ideally matched parts could be successfully combined but also having the strength of will necessary to make it happen. Not to mention the willingness to step in when things got ugly, which they did. One element was not really their choice, and that was Mae Murray. As one of Metro's biggest stars, she was someone it was incumbent on the studio to use after she all but demanded the part of a traveling American dancer who unexpectedly inherits millions. Von Stroheim was barred from playing the villain but allowed to write the script. For the hero, MGM nixed von Stroheim's choice and went with their rising young male lead John Gilbert, open-hearted and genial as a prince of a mythical Balkan kingdom.

Von Stroheim's on-screen credit here reads "personally directed by Erich von Stroheim," and it was a title he took seriously, leading to confrontations both real and apocryphal.

The most famous of those has Thalberg asking the director why he'd shot so much footage of the villain leering at women's shoes. "The man has a fetish for feet," von Stroheim is said to have replied, with the executive shooting back, "and you have a fetish for footage!" Also legendary but vouched for by both men is a confrontation between von Stroheim and Mayer over Murray's performance, with the director insisting all women were whores and Mayer, his visceral dislike of the word combining with his willingness to get physical, knocking von Stroheim down.

The director's problems with his star, however, were quite real and came to a head when it came time to film one of *The Merry Widow*'s signature scenes, the waltz of the title. Murray, who had begun as a dancer and in fact had been a Ziegfeld headliner in 1915, had very specific ideas about how she wanted to handle this, and they were not the same as von Stroheim's. Words were exchanged, she called him "a dirty Hun," and he walked off the set with no plan to return. Mayer immediately replaced him with the sophisticated Monta Bell, but "von's Army," the informal unit of uniform-wearing ex-military extras von Stroheim kept intact from film to film, refused to work for the new man and chanted their disapproval. Mayer visited the set and, with apologies all around, a rapprochement was soon effected.

This was such a big deal that the next issue of the *Los Angeles Record* ran an eight-column front-page headline in massive type reading MAE-VON SIGN PEACE. Clearly a slow news day.

His disdain for the project notwithstanding, von Stroheim incorporated enough of his usual motifs that when the studio previewed the finished film in Pasadena, the local police stopped the screening and threatened to arrest the studio executives present for immorality. Quick thinking by Mayer, who claimed to have screened this version in Pasadena because that would be the best way to find out how far he could go, saved the day. Despite all this and von Stroheim's reputation as what Budd Schulberg called "a satanic Galahad in search of some cinematic Holy Grail, an obsessed Quixote forever tilting his lance at the hated Front Office," the man was not yet quite finished at MGM. In 1932 Greta Garbo, an admirer of his work and by then one of Hollywood's top stars, had him cast in a supporting role in her *As You Desire Me*, and three years later the studio hired him again as a technical adviser on another Garbo film, *Anna Karenina*. If Thalberg and Mayer thought you could be of use, you were hired. That would conclude his days at MGM, though von Stroheim would return to mainstream Hollywood decades later, cast by fellow iconoclast Billy Wilder as the butler/director in his scathing *Sunset Boulevard*.

Though the huge success of MGM's 1959 Charlton Heston-starring version of *Ben-Hur* tends to obscure older history, the 1925 film had a parallel success, but this was by no means the sure thing it became. In fact, it was only steely, counterintuitive decision-making by Mayer and Thalberg that saved that endeavor from being an expensive fiasco.

Also sometimes forgotten is what an across-the-board phenomenon General Lew Wallace created with his 1880 biblical novel. The plot details how Judah Ben-Hur, a wealthy Jewish prince, is betrayed by his best friend, the Roman Massala, spends years as a galley slave, but lives to take part in that celebrated chariot race and embrace Jesus Christ as the promised hope and savior of mankind.

The book had sold more than a million copies by 1913, at which point catalogue giant Sears, Roebuck bought that same number in a single transaction. A touring stage show—featuring a pair of chariots with four live horses each racing on an elaborate treadmill—was a phenomenal draw for years. In 1921 the Wallace family sold film rights to producer Abraham Erlinger, and he in turn sold them to ambitious Goldwyn Pictures for an unheard-of 50 percent of the theatrical gross. (Goldwyn's eventual owner Marcus Loew rued that deal, which was to cost MGM $4 million, almost to the day he died, unhappily telling those Harvard Business School students, "It is a contract I do not want to claim credit for.")

All this was well in the future, however, in 1924, when June Mathis, the woman who discovered Valentino, was given the *Ben-Hur* screenplay assignment and some power in the production, which, in a burst of perhaps irrational exuberance, was going to honor the novel by shooting in Rome. Long story short, very little worked out as planned. The Italian crew, divided politically between socialists and Mussolini's newly empowered fascists, did not get along, the director seemed in over his head, and everything was more expensive and took longer than expected. Both Mayer and Thalberg saw some of the Rome footage, with the latter writing, "It is almost beyond my conception that such stuff could have been passed by people of even moderate intelligence—that June Mathis, in fact any one over there, could have allowed [it] to pass, for one single day."

Mayer and Thalberg did not dither. They sent another, more assertive filmmaker, Fred Niblo, to Rome on a covert reconnaissance mission. He wrote back, like the director-in-waiting he was, "Ben Hur can be the biggest thing that has ever been done. It can also be the biggest flop." Thalberg already had experienced writers working on another script, and rising Metro star Ramon Navarro was secretly told by Thalberg he was to be the lead. (Navarro had to lie to reporters asking about his subsequent trip to Europe by claiming he was taking a vacation.) Marcus Loew went to Italy to make the changes face to face, with Mayer arriving later and, according to costar and Mayer nemesis Francis X. Bushman, finding the time to blame him when Navarro had trouble finding his feet. "He said, 'You have stolen it from him!' Bushman later claimed. 'Here you are taking every scene from him. I want you to quit it!'"

A true believer in his ability to control productions if they were close at hand, Thalberg, as well as Mayer, pushed Loew to cut his losses by allowing the production to move to Los Angeles, and in January 1925 that is what happened. Hands down the most remembered Los Angeles segment, in fact a contender for the most famous of all silent film sequences, was the grudge match chariot race between Ben-Hur and Messala in Roman Antioch's huge Circus.

This would be no surprise to Thalberg, who knew the scene's potential and saw to it that considerable thought, effort, and money were put into this spectacle, which lasted almost ten minutes on screen. Because even the MGM lot was not big enough to hold the intended structure, the studio acquired a nearby forty-five-acre tract at the corner of Venice and La Cienega boulevards and allocated $300,000 for arena construction. Eight hundred men worked in four shifts for four months to get the job done, but still Thalberg was not satisfied.

Fearing the arena did not photograph as massive as it actually was, he called for statues, "huge statues we can place the extras beside so the audience can get a sense of the scale." Understanding Thalberg completely, and not for the last time, was supervising art director Cedric Gibbons, who, according to design historian Howard Gutner, "added his own touch. Rather than gazing straight ahead, the two towering male figures at each end of the Colosseum were crouched with their heads turned sideways, as if straining to see down the long stretch of track that passed and curled around them. It was a masterstroke, intensifying the drama of the race itself."

Thalberg also paid attention to the crowd. The program claims ten thousand extras were assembled, some reportedly dragooned off nearby streets. Hollywood celebrities also attended, but Thalberg felt this was nowhere near enough to populate the massive structure. Though it was kept secret at the time, and first uncovered decades later by Kevin Brownlow, the solution, as devised by Gibbons and special effects specialist A. Arnold (Buddy) Gillespie, was the exact placement in front of the camera of an ingenious device, specially modified, called a hanging miniature. In this case it was "a model with thousands of tiny puppets that, by means of levers, could sit, stand, and wave," explains one historian. "On-screen, the dividing line between the actual set and the matte composition is impossible to discern."

With neither Mayer nor Thalberg inclined to cut corners, the camera setup for the *Ben-Hur* race is said to be one of the most elaborate in film history. A full forty-two cameras were placed in every spot imaginable: inside statues, behind shields, on towers, in airplanes, even buried in pits. Communication on that day was through signal flags (William Wyler, director of the 1959 version, was one of the thirty-some assistants) as well as telephones connected via twelve thousand feet of wire.

Even though it must have seemed to Mayer and Thalberg that opening night would never come, arrive it did on December 30, 1925, promoted by Times Square neon letters five feet high. Marcus Loew's top lieutenant Nicholas Schenck wired Thalberg the next day, "Well kid, you were repaid last night for all the hard work you put in on *Ben-Hur.* It was the most magnificent opening I ever witnessed. There was continual applause right through the picture."

Promoted by the studio as "The $4,000,000 Picture," *Ben-*

Hur went into that opening night as the most expensive film of the silent era, and it came out of its extensive multiyear run as the highest-grossing one as well and an undisputed triumph for the new MGM bosses. *Ben-Hur* played and played and played, with the manager of one New York house claiming "Ben-Hur is going to run at the Embassy until the horses get tired." The film did not go into general release "at popular prices" until late in 1927, at which point MGM ran trade ads on heavy stock grandly proclaiming to theater owners, "You will show it in October and your audience will remember it forever. By playing 'Ben-Hur' in your theatre, you are proving the greatness of your theatre. . . . Be first in the hearts of your public with Metro-Goldwyn-Mayer."

But a record $9-million-plus box office notwithstanding, distribution expenses and that 50 percent split of the gross that enraged Loew meant that *Ben-Hur* did not initially make money. Yet, as Thalberg (who felt so strongly about the film he hung its poster on his office wall) explained in a *Saturday Evening Post* by-line piece he wrote in 1933, that was not the point. Recapping the film's backstory, he explained that when the MGM team watched the first rushes from Rome, "in the cold, analytical, almost surgical atmosphere of the studio projection room, we decided that they were not getting anywhere at all. It was then that we made the decision, which was considered at the time a crossing of the Rubicon from sanity to insanity. We sent a new director and a new star to Rome. We junked the half million dollars in completed film and started all over again." The reason? "A poor picturization of Ben-Hur would have cost us in prestige far more than the half million dollars' worth of junked film. The good picturization, which we did finally make, not only earned back the huge sum of money it cost but it built up a goodwill the value of which it is almost impossible to estimate."

What Thalberg did not say is that the cascading stresses of the *Ben-Hur* and *The Merry Widow* situations took a nearly catastrophic toll on his health, leading to a 1925 heart attack so severe that, one biographer says, doctors "gave him no more than an even chance to recover." But ever a bear for work, he improved faster than anyone anticipated, even fixing up a sick room so that, recalled one visitor, he could "lie on his back and look at the rushes of *Ben-Hur* on the ceiling." Recovered enough to oversee the chariot race editing but too sick to go to the film's New York premier, he wired director Niblo that its success "has done more for me than all the doctors to make me feel better." Up to a point.

In the first appearance of a pattern that was to become familiar, when Thalberg faced a health crisis, his thoughts turned to whether he was being fairly compensated. Not a big spender—his most visible extravagance was a sporty yellow Marmon automobile—Thalberg seemed to view money both as a marker to prove he was valued and a way to make provisions for an eventual family if his often-foretold early death became a reality. Whatever the reason, it was an issue that never completely went away.

In this case, however, things were easily smoothed over, with Mayer, like a tolerant refugee father trying to deal with an American son he didn't totally understand, helping out. According to Thalberg's friend Samuel Marx, when the young man became obdurate about insisting on more money, Mayer responded with a parental, "'Listen to me, I'm older than you. I've always benefitted by listening to older men. I'll see about getting you more money, but don't go about it this way.' He illustrated with a clenched fist. 'When you do this, nothing goes out! But nothing goes in either!'"

So, with everyone grateful for the success of *Ben-Hur* and worried about Thalberg's health, a better deal soon materialized. Mayer's weekly salary rose from $1,500 to $2,000 and Thalberg for the first time equaled him, going from $650 to $2,000, with a raise for attorney J. Robert Rubin included in the package.

Mayer was still top dog, however, as his profits bonus was guaranteed at a minimum of $500,000, while Thalberg's minimum was $200,000. But as biographer Bob Thomas notes, "Thalberg was not satisfied for long. Within a year he protested to the Loew's executives that he was still not being paid enough." More money was again forthcoming, a salary of $4,000 a week and a greater profits bonus. Probably no one among Loew's New York administrators thought this was going to be the end of the story, but even corporations can dream.

6

The Right Stuff

THOUGH FILMS INHERITED from Metro and Goldwyn were what the newly formed studio attended to first, Thalberg and Mayer were beyond anxious to begin doing their own films as well, to show the rest of Hollywood what they were capable of. The first project to be both created from scratch and released by the new company, as well as the first to open with a (silent) appearance from former Goldwyn studio symbol Leo the Lion, was chosen with great care. It was 1924's *He Who Gets Slapped,* starring Lon Chaney, John Gilbert, and Norma Shearer and directed by top Swedish director Victor Seastrom.

Slapped touched a number of bases, key among them being Thalberg favorite Chaney, who was bullet-proof at the box office and provided balance to the melodramatic artiness of a Russian play about a slow-building circus tragedy given a European touch by Seastrom. Also, as became the MGM pattern, the studio cast actors on the rise like Gilbert and Shearer to help build up their profiles without having the responsibility of carrying the picture. The creation and building of stars was to be what Mayer and Thalberg's new studio was about. That and something else. A touch of class, a striving for the art in cinema, the uplifting as well as the financially rewarding, which *He Who Gets Slapped* nicely delivered. But not without, according to publicist Frank Whitbeck, last-minute editing by Thalberg, who "disappeared into the cutting room and didn't come out for two days and a night."

As it happens, all three actors went on to important MGM careers. Chaney, who by this point had starred for Universal in *The Phantom of the Opera*, the role of his career, signed with his old colleague Thalberg to become a workhorse for MGM, doing sixteen successful if often outré silents before 1930. Shearer was a hard worker as well, unswerving in her methodical rise to success. As for Gilbert, who thought his *Slapped* role too minor and had to be talked into it by Thalberg ("That part, small as it is, will do you more good than anything you've ever done"), his career was headed for one of his most celebrated roles in one of the silent era's most acclaimed films, 1925's *The Big Parade*.

The story behind this World War I–themed epic getting made shows Thalberg and Mayer working together with a single purpose, using their complementary strengths, albeit with a few hiccups, to turn what had begun humbly ("It started out as a program picture," Marcus Loew admitted) into a film that walked off with the Photoplay Medal of Honor (the precursor to the Oscars) as the year's best film.

Even *Parade*'s earliest stirrings reflect Thalberg at his most intuitive and most receptive to the ideas of creators he respected. Director King Vidor, who had moved from his native Texas to Hollywood in 1915 to pursue a film career, had progressed to being a Metro contract director by the time of the merger. According to *A Tree Is a Tree*, Vidor's engrossing autobiography, the project began with the director telling Thalberg he was "weary of making ephemeral films. They came to town, played a week or so, then went their way to comparative obscurity or complete oblivion." Vidor wanted the chance to work on something more meaningful, a story that had a shot at playing longer, and in this he and Thalberg were of the same mind. When the executive asked "if I had any ideas commensurate with this ambitious goal," Vidor told him he'd like to "make a film about any one of three subjects, steel, wheat or war." Thalberg narrowed in on the third and endorsed Vidor's central idea of "a young American who was neither overpatriotic nor a pacifist, but who went to war and reacted normally," and both men began a search for material to adapt.

That quest led Thalberg to New York, where he saw *What Price Glory?* a World War I–themed play by Laurence Stallings, a Marine captain who'd lost a leg in combat, and playwright Maxwell Anderson. Thalberg was bested in the bidding war for the rights by the more established Fox but, nothing daunted, asked Stallings whether he had any other ideas for the screen. Memories diverge a bit at this point, but it seems that Thalberg and Stallings, perhaps sitting in their underwear on a steamy train to Los Angeles, worked out an outline together, and Vidor and screenwriter Harry Behn got more out of the Marine by going along on his return train trip to Manhattan.

Given that Gilbert owed the studio another standard program picture, Thalberg's choice of the popular performer was not surprising. Some sources say neither Vidor nor Gilbert himself was initially enthusiastic about an actor not known to be multidimensional playing Jim Apperson, a rich man's son who enlists on a whim only to be transformed by the brutal realities of overseas combat, but both men were encouraged by Thalberg's fervor. Gilbert continually gave the producer credit as "the man who first realized the immense possibilities in 'The Big Parade,' and it was he, and he alone, who fired Vidor and myself with enthusiasm for the story."

Still, Vidor's instincts were key to the production's success in multiple ways, including a moment of inspiration that led to the film's most electrifying sequence.

The germ of the idea came as Vidor watched "miles and miles of government film." He noticed one company of soldiers marching "at a cadence decidedly different from the usual ones." It turned out "the men were in a funeral cortege. The thought struck me that if I could duplicate the slow, measured cadence as my American troops approached the front line, I could illustrate the proximity of death with a telling and powerful effect." Which, using a metronome to determine cadence and a bass drum to duplicate it, is exactly what was filmed.

Thalberg was so impressed by that scene that when Vidor complained that a pivotal sequence he'd had an assistant shoot on a military base in Texas lacked the long straight lines of two hundred or so bumper-to-bumper trucks jammed with men that he thought essential, Thalberg immediately said, "I guess you better go down there and shoot it yourself." As Vidor remembered, "That was typical of Thalberg. He knew instinctively when someone presented a good idea, or at least one which that person considered really important, and he didn't try to talk him out of it."

As had happened at Universal with *The Hunchback of Notre Dame*, Thalberg soon came to feel that *The Big Parade* could be a much bigger film than anyone had anticipated. He wanted more of the actual war, especially more scenes of night combat, but these would be costly, and the budget had already been spent. Mayer, who could be powerfully convincing, saw the same possibilities Thalberg did, so much so that he took a train to New York and persuaded Loew's executives that the added sequences (eventually shot by a different director because Vidor had moved on to another film) were worth the time and cost.

Mayer, however, had misgivings about the nature of Jim Apperson's injury. In Stallings's script, and in the finished film's emotional homecoming, the hero returns minus a leg. Fearful that the public would not accept a romantic star of Gilbert's stature in that state, Mayer insisted that an alternate ending be shot of Apperson merely walking with a limp. Kevin Brownlow says Vidor shot it but refused to print it. Given the strong reception the film was getting in early screenings, including from such unlikely fans as William Randolph Hearst and Marion Davies, the director's instincts were sound.

Those early screenings were prophetic. The film set records almost everywhere and, unlike the case with *Ben-Hur*, MGM got to keep all the film's $3.5 million initial profit. For Vidor, the result was mixed. He allowed Mayer and Thalberg to talk him out of a percentage of the profits that would have made him a wealthy man, but he got his next project, working with silent film superstar Lillian Gish on *La Bohème*, because of her reaction to the film. "Dear Mr. Thalberg, I have just seen all of 'The Big Parade,'" she scribbled on a small handwritten note someone thought to preserve. "There are scenes in it as fine as anything anyone has ever done."

Though Vidor in later interviews sometimes complained that Thalberg got more *Big Parade* credit than he deserved, there is no doubt, as the director acknowledged, that the executive "had a feeling for my work," an empathy that led directly to 1928's risky, much-admired *The Crowd*.

Vidor told different versions of the film's origin story over the years, but they all include a remarkable statement by Thalberg that speaks as almost nothing else does to the nature and extent of his belief in motion pictures, the art to which he was devoting his life, and the way that belief was starting to differ from Mayer's.

As Vidor tells it, *The Crowd* began as *The Big Parade* did, with a chance encounter on the MGM lot between himself and Thalberg, who wanted to know what one of his top directors had on his mind. Vidor said he was thinking about "other inter-esting environments which are dramatic for the average man, [who] walks through life and sees quite a lot of drama around him." That scenario became *The Crowd*. "I made pictures as a good employee and pictures that came from my own insides," Vidor said in a 1978 interview. "This is one that came out of my guts. There was a lot of hypocrisy in early films and I wanted to get away from it."

Thalberg's reaction was positive, but when Vidor, as an art-ist working in a commercial environment, worried that the film "probably won't make a dollar at the box office," the executive's reply was telling. "I can certainly afford a few experimental projects," Thalberg said. "It will do something for the studio, it will do something for the whole industry." Not a sentiment heard a lot then—or now, for that matter—and certainly not one shared by Louis B. Mayer.

The Crowd is the story of John, an office worker no differ-ent from hundreds of others. He falls in love and marries Mary, starts a family, and deals with the crises and heartbreaks of life, including the death of a child. No attempt is made to make this couple special, to hype their lives; rather, the emphasis, right through the ending, is on how like everyone else they are.

The Crowd was a departure from the norm in many ways, including an accurately depicted one-room apartment complete with Murphy bed and a bathroom with a graphically malfunc-tioning commode. Mayer, whose sensitivity to audience edifi-cation was violated, would always refer to the film as "that god-damned toilet picture."

Vidor's wife, Eleanor Boardman, played Mary, but the di-rector was determined to get an unknown face for the lead, and he succeeded almost beyond his expectations. He saw a young man, a studio extra, leaving the lot and chased him down in the street. His name was James Murray, and though his eventual costarring performance was everything Vidor had wanted, he was an alcoholic and sustaining a career proved beyond him. The film's afterlife, however, has been considerable: the great Italian director Vittorio De Sica told Vidor that *The Crowd* was the inspiration for his classic neorealist *Bicycle Thieves*.

The film also survived in Mayer's enmity. It was nominated for the since-discarded "best artistic quality of production" category and best director in the first Academy Awards, which in those days was picked by a five-person Board of Judges, which included Mayer. Vidor said that exhibitor "Sid Grauman called me early in the morning and said, 'I held out all night for "The Crowd" but finally I had to give in.' I found out later that Mayer wouldn't vote for it."

There is an ironic postscript to all this. In 2019 a mimeographed flyer could be found in bathrooms on the old MGM lot, at that point in time owned by Sony. Above a vintage photo of Mayer at his large and impressive desk was the following message:

> The historic Louis B. Mayer Era plumbing in this building can't handle too much toilet paper.
> If you need to, flush once before you've used too much and again if necessary.
> Mr. Mayer says Thanks!

What Mr. Mayer actually would have said can only be imagined.

7

◆◦◆◦◆

The Women

Celebrated in his later years for the best-selling *The Joys of Yiddish*, Leo Rosten in 1941 was known for writing the pioneering sociological analysis *Hollywood: The Movie Colony, the Movie Makers*. When he looked at MGM this is what he saw: "Mayer has made the entire MGM organization revolve around the hub of Personalities. The stories and production of MGM's pictures are geared to the studio's stars and, more than in any other studio in Hollywood, are subordinated to the final goal of star-appeal."

Though MGM developed its share of major male personalities, including Clark Gable and Mickey Rooney, it has always been best known for the women it made into stars, especially the lived-long-and-prospered triumvirate of Norma Shearer, Joan Crawford, and Greta Garbo. This was not by accident, as from the beginning both Mayer and Thalberg believed that stars were the essential element in film success and that in this category women counted more than men. As Lenore Coffee put it, "An interesting and revealing side of Thalberg was that he created only women stars. He developed male stars, but he didn't create them." The reason for Thalberg's feminine focus, he himself explained, was simple. "When you've got a picture women want to see, the men will have to go along. A woman can always keep a man away from a picture that attracts only him."

Developing their own female stars may have been at the top of Mayer and Thalberg's list of goals, but the Loew's theater chain's need for films was immediate and inexorable, so it was inevitable that the first two women to make an impact under the MGM banner were acquired rather than developed. Their backgrounds, their styles, and their eventual trajectories were quite different, but both Lillian Gish and Marion Davies were more than able to hold the fort until reinforcements arrived.

Starting in movies as early as 1912 and celebrated as silent film royalty for starring roles in pioneering D. W. Griffith epics like *Way Down East* and *Orphans of the Storm*, the delicate-seeming Gish was much tougher and more savvy than her damsel-in-distress image would indicate. As journalist Allene Talmey shrewdly observed in 1927, "Her fragility makes men protective, yet no woman in Hollywood needs or takes less protection."

When Gish went looking for a new studio in 1925, her quest ignited what Photoplay called "a frantic bidding war." MGM won out with an offer of $800,000 for six pictures. Clearly this was a very good deal, though Gish, ever the shrewd businessperson, wrote in her autobiography, "I would have preferred a percentage of the gross." Still, the studio "had welcomed me with great banners strung across the streets of Culver City. . . . Looking at them, I had said a silent prayer that they would be equally warm in farewell."

When Gish, Mayer, and Thalberg parted company by mutual consent just three years later with the star still owing the

Thalberg on the set of *La Bohème*, accompanied by director
King Vidor and cameraman Hendrik Sartov, all keeping
an eye on star Lillian Gish. (Photofest)

studio one more film, it was not because the relationship had
been a failure. Far from it. Gish did some of her best work in
Culver City and some of that made good money. But star and
studio turned out to have different ways of working as well as
different artistic visions, and the fit was never as good as either
side wished.

Impressed by *The Big Parade*, Gish asked Mayer and Thalberg for director King Vidor and costars John Gilbert and Renee
Adore for her first project, a version of *La Bohème*, which, due
to rights issues, could use neither the plot of Puccini's opera for
its storyline nor the opera's music for its orchestral accompani-
ment. And for a while, what was the project's biggest draw—the
love story from *Scènes de la vie de bohème*, Henri Murger's 1851

collection of stories, between the consumptive seamstress Mimi and the dashing playwright Rodolphe in the Latin Quarter of 1830 Paris—was a near thing as well.

For Gish, as everyone soon found out if they didn't already know, was a single-minded artist who defined determination. And she turned out to have very particular notions about *La Bohème*'s romantic story.

"I also had original ideas about the love scenes between Mimi and Rodolphe," she explains in her autobiography, *The Movies, Mr. Griffith, and Me.* "It seemed to me that, if we avoided showing the lovers in a physical embrace, the scenes would build up suppressed emotion and be much more effective." Convincing or not in the abstract, the resulting footage riled Mayer as well as Thalberg, who so believed in on-screen romance, according to Samuel Marx, that he told screenwriters, "I want the audience to see when the boy and girl discover they love each other or I won't make the picture." Reshoots were the order of the day, and Phyllis Moir, who was Gish's secretary (and, years later, Winston Churchill's), remembers the star archly commenting, "Oh dear, I've got to go through another day of kissing John Gilbert."

As chaste as this vehicle was, Gish's next had to be even more so, taken as it was from Nathaniel Hawthorne's drama of Puritan censure and hypocrisy, *The Scarlet Letter.* The actress was to star as Hester Prynne, a New England free spirit condemned to wear the letter A, "the brand of shame," after bearing a child conceived during her secret affair with a tormented man of God. The book, venerable though it was, was considered scandalous by church groups, and Mayer was powerfully worried.

"Mr. Mayer sat at his desk and looked across at me as if I had gone mad," Gish remembered. "Then, he stood and pointed at me. 'You?' he screamed. 'You? You? In a story like that?' Miss

Gish, would you feel comfortable making a motion picture about such a woman like Hester? How are we going to show that on the screen without running into the censors? We can't show you and that minister just holding hands and staring into each other's eyes. This isn't "Way Down East." Motion pictures have grown up. . . . How do you think the churches are going to take this film? Do you think they'll recommend it? They'll think that Lillian Gish has betrayed their trust!' "

In fact, Gish's personal assurances did mollify the church groups, and MGM's increasingly formidable creative machinery took the project on. Mayer, not always one to mix in these things, recommended that the star consider as a costar the brooding Swedish actor in *The Saga of Gösta Berling* (which featured his recent discovery Greta Garbo), and Gish remembered, "The moment Lars Hanson appeared on the screen, I knew he was the man I wanted." Thalberg for his part ensured that the script was the best possible by hiring Frances Marion for the first time in what was to become a long relationship with one of Hollywood's most respected writers, and a specialist in literary adaptation.

The most dramatic aspect of *The Scarlet Letter* happened near the end of the shoot, when Gish found out that the mother she was very close to, at that time living in London with sister Dorothy, had suffered a serious stroke. For Gish to get a train to New York in time to make the next liner across the Atlantic, the company would have to complete two weeks' worth of filming in three days. It's a measure of the esteem in which Gish was held and her value to the studio that everyone from the top down agreed to make it happen. "Irving Thalberg, on hearing the news, said 'we'll work day and night on the scenes you have to do,'" Gish remembered. "We didn't waste a moment and during those three days and nights there was very little sleep for anyone. . . . When the last scene was shot, I made a rush for the train, without stopping to change from my costume. My Mayer and Mr. Thalberg got special police on motorcycles to escort me and clear the way, so I could work to the last moment and still get the train."

Impervious to ups and downs, Gish endured. She worked for seventy-five years, winning the AFI's Life Achievement Award in 1984 and losing none of her gimlet-eyed perspective on the business in the process. Greeting Lily Tomlin from the podium at the event, she congratulated her on her success in *9 to 5*, adding coolly, "I hope you had points, and I hope they weren't net."

Though they were both essential stars for Mayer and Thalberg in their earliest days, and were on friendly enough terms, Lillian Gish and Marion Davies were not especially close. While Gish goes out of her way to thank Davies by name for being "considerate and kind . . . a great comfort," and for writing "a very beautiful letter" when *La Bohème* was released, they were driven by career and personal imperatives so different that their approaches to both acting and life had little in common.

While Gish was an intensely private person who even the secretary who lived with her called "an extraordinarily difficult person to know," Davies was applauded for her warmth and accessibility. Even Joan Crawford, who could have a sharp tongue, proclaimed her "a delightful human being who made you feel that *you* were a delightful human being." While Gish kept her personal life off-limits, it was an open secret to Hollywood (though not to the American public) that Davies was the mistress of one of the country's most powerful men, the forceful (and married) press lord William Randolph Hearst. If Gish was master of her fate as much as the studio system allowed, Davies's career was controlled by Hearst, who disregarded her exceptional gifts for screwball comedy in favor of costume dramas that did her no favors. And if Gish got to write her own story, Dorothy Comingore's portrait of talentless mistress Susan Alexander in Orson Welles's Hearst-based *Citizen Kane* left generations of viewers erroneously assuming that Davies herself was without gifts.

Hearst first met Davies when he was in his fifties and she was a teenager dancing in New York's Ziegfeld Follies, and he cofounded Cosmopolitan Pictures with an eye to creating films starring Davies. By the time of the MGM merger, Hearst was reconsidering which studio to align with when Mayer made him the proverbial offer he couldn't refuse to join his new company. According to Irene Mayer Selznick, there was a strong but inexplicable bond between the two men, and this was what Mayer shrewdly hoped to build on. "The fact that he was a yellow journalist and kept a mistress was far overshadowed for my father by what he considered Hearst's brilliance," she wrote. "The two men would walk and talk and sit and talk . . . and the affection between them was clear."

One result of all this conversation was an unusual deal offering Hearst a way to have his own movies without the onerous burdens of producing them. Mayer and MGM would finance, provide the facilities for, and distribute Hearst-controlled Cosmopolitan pictures, but profits would be split equally. There was, however, an unspoken quid-pro-quo at work. Not only would Hearst continue to use his unparalleled media empire to double down on promoting Davies's films, he would do the same for everything MGM produced. A good deal all around.

The Davies/Cosmopolitan machine was soon in full gear, and between 1924 and 1927, the actress made nine films for MGM with varying degrees of box-office success. Mayer was happy with the steady flow of star-driven product and the prestige the deal afforded, but theater owners, who wanted something easy to sell, were not always pleased, resulting in a memorable exchange at a 1927 MGM Los Angeles sales conference. Howard Dietz, an MGM executive who was there, remembers it this way.

> Bob Lynch, the fearless character who guided MGM's destiny in Philadelphia, raised his hand. "I have a suggestion,"

he said. "Why don't we stop making the Marion Davies pictures? They're a drug on the market. I know she's a blue-eyed blonde but she doesn't get us a quarter."

It was Mayer's ball. "That's a good question," said L.B., "and I'm glad you asked." The sweat came out in beads. "Marion Davies is a dear friend of William Randolph Hearst, the powerful publisher, whose good will is an enormous asset to MGM, Mr. Dietz will verify my statement."

Mayer continued vamping for as long as he could and then, Dietz reports,

> Someone gestured from the doorway. I was handed a slip of paper on which was written: "Lindberg has just landed in Paris." I eased myself to the platform and handed Mayer the note as he was delivering his peroration. . . . He glanced at the note which had been placed in front of him—"and this very moment, Charles Augustus Lindberg flying a one-engined airplane, 'The Spirit of St. Louis,' has landed at Le Bourget Field just outside Paris, the greatest and most daring achievement in all aviation!"

Summed up Samuel Marx, who also relished the story, "The convention went wild. Nothing more was said about Marion Davies. Mayer told that story as further proof that God watched over him."

Though Mayer and Thalberg were happy to have Davies's films, there was something of a problem, at least from Thalberg's perspective. As noted, Hearst envisioned his partner as a dramatic actress while Thalberg, who believed in maximizing appeal whenever possible, was the strongest advocate for her comedic talents. According to one Davies biographer, he told columnist Louella Parsons that she was "the most finished comedienne in pictures." Mr. Hearst, however, cared not what anyone else thought, and when one of Davies's pictures was in production, "Hearst bombarded Thalberg with telegraphed suggestions how to produce it. He regarded telegrams as a normal method of communication, firing them off like shrapnel. Thalberg considered them unwarranted interference. He told Mayer that if they continued, he would refuse to handle any more of Hearst's films." This never came to pass because, all this contention notwithstanding, Hearst, Davies revealed, "was crazy about Thalberg. He said, 'Oftentimes the word genius is misplaced, but in the case of Irving, it is a conceded fact.'" But that didn't mean he had to agree with him.

As far as silent film aficionados, both then and now, are concerned, the verdict goes to Thalberg, and this is in large measure because of a 1928 MGM film, *Show People*. A nifty Hollywood satire, *Show People* couldn't be bettered as a showcase for Davies and her fearless disregard for on-screen dignity. The small-town-girl-makes-good storyline, inspired by the career of Gloria Swanson (who'd gone from Mack Sennett bathing beauty to marrying her way into French nobility and becoming the Marquise de la Falaise de la Coudray) allowed for a seamless combination of comedy and emotion that still delights today.

As directed by King Vidor, one of the real treats of *Show People* is its spoof of MGM itself as "High Art Studio," including cameos of numerous real stars playing themselves. John Gilbert looks his most dashing, and Davies even does a cameo as a version of herself. But good as all this was, it came close to not getting made because it almost didn't pass muster with Davies's gatekeeper, Mr. Hearst.

As Vidor remembered it in an oral history decades later, the problem was the central place a custard pie had in the original script. "Hearst read it and saw how Marion Davies would get hit in the face with a pie, and he was adamant that it would be changed. Mayer called me in and asked me if it wouldn't be just as well if a stairway collapsed underneath her and slid her into a pool." Vidor insisted on the pie as the ne plus ultra of slapstick, and a summit was called where Vidor argued his case before Hearst, Mayer, Thalberg, and others.

> I walked up and down and I argued and explained why I wanted the pie. At the end Hearst said, "Well, King's right, but I'm right too, because I'm not going to have my Marion hit in the face with a pie." He was determined, so we settled with a bottle of water in the face.
>
> Even after that, we had to get rid of him. We had to work out a plot to have the Examiner [Hearst's Los Angeles paper] say there was an important conference and get him called from the set where we were working. The Examiner did that, and he left. When he was gone, we got out a strong hose and nozzle and squirted Marion in the face with it instead of the pie.

As Gene Kelly's Don Lockwood says in the silent film–themed *Singin' in the Rain*, also from MGM, "I've had one motto which I've always lived by. Dignity. Always Dignity."

8

Rivals

It is perhaps the most poignant unfair labor practices complaint ever voiced in Hollywood. Probably the first time it appeared in print was in Bob Thomas's 1969 biography of Thalberg, where he quotes Joan Crawford as pointedly saying, "How can I compete with Norma when she sleeps with the boss?" Thomas's interview notes record a January 24 conversation, no year indicated, at the celebrated Cock'n Bull restaurant on the Sunset Strip, where Crawford had gone into more detail. "Certainly Norma had an advantage. Any time an actress sleeps with the producer, she is bound to have an advantage. Sex is a very potent weapon."

These rivals would become twin pillars of the newly formed MGM, but that did not make them friends. Norma Shearer had had a head start on Crawford, being under contract to Mayer when he and Thalberg were still at the Selig Zoo, while Crawford was signed almost a year after the merger with Metro and

Goldwyn. Shearer was on the verge of stardom before the new-comer arrived on the lot and, as Crawford notes in her autobi-ography, her first on-screen appearance was uncredited doubling for Shearer ("our profiles did look somewhat alike") in one of the actress's giddiest vehicles, 1925's *Lady of the Night*, where she plays two radically different women, the daughter of a criminal and the daughter of a judge.

Screenwriter Frederica Sager Maas, who knew them both, claimed that "almost from the first day that they met in the commissary, Joan Crawford disliked Norma Shearer. They were complete opposites. . . . Norma was generous in spirit; Joan was calculating. She remained envious of Norma Shearer as their careers progressed."

But Crawford was as industrious as she was ambitious, which was saying a lot. "Joan tried harder than anyone else had ever tried," said Irene Mayer Selznick, and Adela Rogers St. John, seeing her very early on at a nightclub, pinpointed her "fierce and wonderful vitality." And Crawford had a particular talent that would intoxicate audiences once unleashed. She was a gifted, magnetic dancer, irresistible in motion, which is how she came to MGM in the first place.

Born in San Antonio, she told one interviewer, "We can skip childhood. I didn't have any." Determined to be a dancer, she worked hard enough to end up in the chorus at New York's Winter Garden, "third from the left in the back row," where Howard Dietz noticed her ("Her personality knocked you over") and tipped off a visiting Harry Rapf, number three at MGM after Mayer and Thalberg. The studio placed her under con-tract with a six-month option, and Crawford from her earliest days enjoyed saying, "I really danced my way into the movies." So when the opportunity of a film called *Our Dancing Daugh-ters* presented itself in 1928, Crawford, who had won so many Los Angeles nightclub dance competitions that a movement began to bar her to give amateurs a chance, seized it.

Billed below the title for one of the last times in her career, Crawford, who had "stolen the script . . . begged for it and was given it," excelled as Diana Medford, aka "Diana Dangerous," a phenomenally exuberant young woman who danced up a storm in a way that was new to the screen. The film's plot has not aged well, but Crawford's incandescent zeal for life ("It's such a pleasant thing—to be alive!") endures. *Variety* reported that during the opening run in New York's Capitol Theater "they stood five deep behind the last row with standees to the door," F. Scott Fitzgerald, who should know, called Crawford "doubtless the best example of the flapper," and, Samuel Marx recalled, Thalberg told Mayer, "We've got ourselves another star." She and Shearer, Marx added, "were the first two unknowns to achieve stardom at MGM through persistent exposure to moviegoers."

Crawford was given both a raise and some typically fatherly counsel by Mayer ("He kindly advised me to save my money") and used her on-screen pizzazz to pull even with Shearer as the silent era was coming to an unforeseen close. But her rival had a trump card of her own to play. On September 29, 1927, Norma Shearer and Irving Thalberg were married in their rented mansion at 9401 Sunset Boulevard near the Beverly Hills Hotel. Things at MGM, especially for top actresses like Crawford and Marion Davies, were never quite the same.

When the studio revealed the upcoming wedding on August 17, people in Hollywood were both surprised and not. By the time *Exhibitors Herald* columnist Ray Murray broadcast the news a few days earlier ("The engagement . . . will likely be announced soon. Both of them admit as much"), they were definitely an item, but Thalberg, his monastic demeanor notwithstanding, had had an active social life during and after his on-and-off relationship with Carl Laemmle's daughter Rosabelle, and for quite some time the notion that he would marry Shearer—or marry at all, for that matter—was far from a foregone conclusion.

As journalist Allene Talmey observed, one of the things Thalberg "delighted in" was "driving his gay car, loaded with friends at three or four in the morning." Often as not, the core of those friends was a hard-partying group known as "the three Jacks": director Jack Conway, writer John Colton, and star John Gilbert, both Jack to pals. Irene Mayer Selznick, who said that at nightclub events "the best seat, the most fun, would have been next to Irving," observed that Henrietta, Thalberg's hypervigilant mother, looked askance at this late-night carousing and was known to refer to Irving's posse, which sometimes included director Howard Hawks, his brother Kenneth, and King Vidor, as "bums."

When Thalberg got seriously interested in a particular woman, which happened from time to time, Henrietta was even more displeased. "Serious intentions were dangerous," Selznick observed. "She could not afford to put his fate in the hands of a wife." In 1924 Thalberg was briefly involved with Peggy Hopkins Joyce, whose six marriages, several to millionaires, led to a reputation as a flirtatious gold digger, "the original blonde whom gentlemen preferred." A few years later, when Thalberg told Frances Goldwyn, Sam's wife, that he was in love with Shearer, she teased him that he'd said the same about Joyce. "Oh no," he told her, "That was sex. This is love."

In between Joyce and Shearer both chronologically and in terms of seriousness was Thalberg's interest in silent film star Constance Talmadge, whose vivacious, spontaneous personality captivated him almost from day one. "This was very heady wine for Irving," remembered Irene Mayer Selznick. "Constance brought out in him an even more charming personality than we had heretofore seen. They were a magical couple with an immense delight in each other." Added Samuel Marx, "The worldliness and savoir-faire that marked his personality after the age of twenty-six was due to Connie Talmadge."

Talmadge, however, was not as single-minded in her attention as Thalberg was, and the connection inevitably frayed. In the meantime, Henrietta, and possibly Mayer as well, had advanced the idea of a Jewish bride for their young man. One non-show-business candidate, at times overlooked, was high-powered New York attorney Fanny Holtzmann, a friend of Supreme Court justices as well as a confidant of Mayer, who called her "a female Solomon." As biographer Edward O. Berkman (who was Holtzmann's nephew) relates, Mayer thought the two

> would make a splendid match. So did Thalberg's adored mother, Henrietta. . . . But the principals felt otherwise. Fanny liked the frail, soft-spoken Thalberg . . . but that was it. Thalberg in turn was clearly in love with Norma Shearer, in Fanny's eyes "a sweet, unpretentious girl who worried about his health and shared his interests."
>
> So, far from trying to break up the Thalberg-Shearer romance, Fanny lent a conspiratorial hand to it. She came to the Thalberg home as Irving's dinner guest, thereby lulling his mother's apprehensions about the actress; she did not resist Henrietta's lavish attention.
>
> Thalberg took quick advantage of the situation. Slipping away from the studio for a few hours with Norma, he would intimate to his family that he had been out with Fanny.
>
> Once the ploy nearly backfired, when Henrietta pressed Fanny for a full report on a concert she had ostensibly attended with Irving. Fanny asked her "suitor" to brief her more carefully in the future.

Given all the resistance both to her and to Thalberg getting married at all, how did Shearer prevail, how did she go from being an actress in his employ, with a relationship in which "Mr. Thalberg and I met often and spoke rarely," to the woman who became his wife? The answer is that, displaying the same steely determination that had fostered her career, Shearer both understood that she needed to play the long game and had the fortitude to execute it.

Gossip columnist Hedda Hopper, who met Shearer when both were Mayer actresses in the premerger days, remembers it beginning at the Selig Zoo. "Many stars had no time for Irving. Let it be said that he had little time for girls. He hadn't yet struck it rich, and some actresses never could see beyond their own noses. But, if you could only see it, Irving was climbing up the golden ladder and Norma had her foot on the first rung of success." According to Irene Mayer Selznick, who watched it happen, "It took Norma four or five years to get him," years that involved making sure Henrietta and her concerns about putting Thalberg's health first were satisfied. ("Oh what she had to put up with from her in-laws," Joan Crawford cracked maliciously. "I wouldn't have wished them on my worst enemy.") "She was determined . . . but non-possessive," Selznick continued. "She would say, laughingly, 'I'm Irving's spare tire. When Rosabelle and Constance are away, or someone stands him up, I'm always available. I'll break a date any time to be with him.' She said she was biding her time."

Biding her time meant putting up with jibes from the Hollywood community. The tart-tongued actress Louise Brooks remembered a party she gave where "all the place cards at dinner were books. In front of Irving Thalberg's place I put Dreiser's *Genius*. . . . In front of Norma's place I put *Serena Blandish: The Difficulty of Getting Married*—she'd been trying and trying and Irving's mother wanted him to marry a nice Jewish girl. It was so funny because Irving walked right in and saw *Genius* and sat right down. But Norma kept walking around. She wouldn't sit down in front of *The Difficulty of Getting Married*. Not at all!"

The first sign that Thalberg was himself becoming involved came in the first December on the Culver City lot; for Shearer, describing the event in her unpublished memoir, "a miracle happened, on Christmas Eve." She was working late and feeling alone and bereft in her dressing room when "the phone rang and when I lifted the receiver a shy soft voice said, 'This is Mr.

Thalberg—I just thought I would give you a jingle and wish you a Merry Christmas.' And I knew by that quiet voice that somebody in this world cared on this lonely night whether I was sad or glad or even alive. For three years I have been watching him. . . . I had waited—for this moment—never really thinking it would ever happen."

A bit later a date was made—Thalberg's secretary made the call, not the man himself—to see the opening of Charlie Chaplin's *The Gold Rush* at Grauman's Egyptian, but the couple went dancing instead at the Cocoanut Grove nightclub in the Ambassador Hotel. More dates followed, but, says Shearer, "he didn't propose, this busy Romeo—that wasn't part of the plot." She did start to call him Irving, a name she thought beautiful, although, in a classic touch, "he said I wouldn't think so if I had ever lived in Brooklyn!"

A proposal of sorts did eventually happen, "one starry night in the Cocoanut Grove. Between dances sitting at a little table under a false palm tree with a toy monkey hanging by its tail, he said with a sly twinkle, 'Don't you think it's about time we got married?'" Shearer's response has been variously reported as "I can't think of any reason we shouldn't" and "If you're proposing, you're not using the right dialogue"—she herself says she merely laughed—but verbally or otherwise, yes was understood.

While this may not sound terribly romantic, it's an improvement over a different version of the happy event, put forward by Samuel Marx and others. Shearer, he says, "was called to look in at Thalberg's office. He was standing by several trays of diamond engagement rings spread across his desk. He said, 'Why don't you pick the one you're going to wear?'"

However it happened, by the time the engagement took place, everyone had made their peace with it. Marx quotes Henrietta as claiming, "Norma has always been like a daughter to me," and Irene Mayer Selznick remembers her father fairly bursting with the news. "One night my father came home with a breathless bulletin: 'Irving's decided to marry her! There's no risk—everything will go on as it was, Henrietta's accepted the situation.'" As detailed by Selznick, that situation, once again, does not sound terribly romantic. "Norma became a live-in wife without too many prerogatives. It remained Henrietta's house; she sat at the head of the table. . . . Guests were invited by Henrietta, and she was the hostess who was thanked. The servants were hers, as were the menus. Norma and Henrietta managed, but there could never have been real peace between mother and wife." Also, when the combined family moved, Henrietta saw to it that Thalberg and Shearer's *de rigueur* separate bedrooms were at opposite ends of the house. She was not one to make things easy.

One final hurdle, again probably placed by the mother and not the groom, and approved of by Mayer, involved Shearer's conversion to Judaism. "So anxious was I to please," she writes, "that I accepted the Jewish religion knowing no less about that than my own." A press conference answer a few years after the wedding goes into more detail, linking her decision to time spent with "his people. His family are Orthodox Jews and I saw that they found peace and contentment in their religion. I wanted peace and contentment in our marriage. I decided that I had no particular religious convictions—that I could find it in the Jewish faith."

Helping with this decision was Rabbi Edgar F. Magnin, the original "rabbi to the stars," head of the oldest Jewish congregation in Los Angeles and soon to spearhead the building of the impressive Wilshire Boulevard Temple. A charismatic presence whose grandparents had founded the celebrated I. Magnin department store, he believed in "America first, Judaism second." Magnin taught Shearer enough Hebrew to get her through the marriage ceremony and maintained a presence in the couple's lives.

Thalberg and Shearer looking suitably pleased on their wedding day.
(Underwood Archives/UIG/Bridgeman Images)

The backyard wedding itself was small and very much a family affair, with key roles apportioned in ways that would cause the fewest hard feelings. The best man, for instance, was none other than Louis B. Mayer, the maid of honor was Thalberg's sister Sylvia, an aspiring screenwriter, matron of honor was Norma's sister Athol, and giving the bride away was Norma's brother Douglas, soon to be a key player in MGM's transition to sound. The bridesmaids included Marion Davies and Mayer's daughters Edith and Irene, the ushers Thalberg's nightlife pals

King Vidor and Jack Conway. Photographs from the wedding show both Henrietta and Shearer's mother Edith wearing black and looking almost forlorn, but the bride and groom, despite the fact that Thalberg, in classic work-obsessed fashion, had taken time just before the ceremony to have a story conference with writer Laurence Stallings, look quite sure of their decision. Which is no small thing.

For despite the carping about the nonromantic nature of their courtship, about Henrietta Thalberg running their lives, about the utilitarian nature of their separate bank accounts and Thalberg's wedding gift to his bride of a trailer on wheels to serve as a portable dressing room, there is ample evidence, in photographs and elsewhere, that they were truly in love. Shearer was as concerned as Henrietta that Thalberg be healthy, and having her mother-in-law run the house ("I barely knew how to boil an egg!" she wrote) helped ensure that and left her free to focus on maintaining and advancing her career, more than a full-time job.

In numerous photos, both posed and candid, Shearer and Thalberg look at each other and the camera in a way that conveys delight in finding the other person, and why not? Yes, they made a handsome couple and they knew it, but it was more than that. At a most basic level, they saw themselves in each other, recognized kindred spirits, understood the drive of steel-willed strivers whose ambition excluded all else. When Shearer said flatly, "The work came first—always," she is of course speaking for both of them. Even in a world filled with the self-created, the single-mindedness that was to make her one of Hollywood's biggest stars and him a legend among executives stood out. If their gaze at each other says anything, it's "I can't believe our luck." Each made the marriage they wanted and needed, each was able to simultaneously create and live out a romantic fantasy that was theirs alone.

9

The Two and Only

THOUGH THE IDEA of who was the dominant partner and by what percentage differed depending on who was telling the story, no one in Hollywood then or now doubted that the combination of Louis B. Mayer and Irving Thalberg was the reason for MGM's success. What the two had in common—everything from the formative role of a powerful, devoted mother to shared philosophical beliefs and a parallel understanding of the role of performance in their respective positions—was of course crucial, but the differences are often commented on as well. Given that the alchemy between these men was magical while it lasted, a look at who they were is essential.

Attempting to get a sense of Louis B. Mayer from the people who knew him can produce a kind of whiplash. For every Joan Crawford, who said, "To me, L. B. Mayer was my father; my father confessor; the *best* friend I ever had," there was, as previously noted, a B. P. Schulberg who insisted he wanted his ashes blown into Mayer's face. Well, maybe the ratio isn't exactly one to one; the detractors come out on top, and use the most vivid, vituperative language, including animal imagery. "Every time Mayer smiles at me, I feel a snake has crawled over my foot," said screenwriter Noel Langley, adding, "He was a shark that killed when it wasn't hungry." And Herman Mankiewicz, after stipulating that Mayer had both the memory and the hide of an elephant, added acidly, "The only difference is that elephants are vegetarians and Mayer's favorite diet is his fellow man."

But if you look past the invective, you hear from people who made the effort to see Mayer whole, as someone who was smart, unpredictable, and difficult to pigeonhole, as well as just plain difficult. Yes, he could be challenging to talk to, with Josef von Sternberg remembering someone "who could use his eyes, brimming over with tears, to convince an elephant that it was a kangaroo," fellow director Elia Kazan adding, "after his years of command, with not a day of self-doubt, it was useless to argue with him," and writer-director Joseph L. Mankiewicz claiming, "Louis B. Mayer would stir up rebellion even in Uncle Tom." And yes, he made mistakes, infamously turning down the chance to distribute Mickey Mouse cartoons, insisting, as Walt Disney advocate Frances Marion remembers, "Every woman is scared of a mouse, admit it. A little tiny mouse, admit it. And here you think they're going to laugh at a mouse on the screen that's ten feet high, admit it. And I'm nobody's fool." But Mayer's occasional buffoonishness disguised a shrewdness, a sense of showmanship, and an iron will, and this was noticed as well, sometimes by the same people who denigrated him.

"Louis B. Mayer knew that the coin he dealt with was talent. He would husband it and be very patient with it and put up with an awful lot of nonsense if he really believed in it. Of course, he was tough, and he could be ruthless and very disagreeable, but [books that] represent the great showmen simply as monsters—that's stupid," said director George Cukor, who worked on numerous MGM films. "I think people don't understand how a place like MGM had to be fed, sustained and organized every day." Producer David Lewis struck a similar note, writing, "To the naked eye he was a fascinating monster," but adding, "He was a very impetuous man—given to sudden infatuations, temper outbursts, emotional moments. . . . His magnetism could not be missed. He was a spellbinder and a hypnotist. By reputation he could charm anyone. . . . He was an extraordinary man—my God how extraordinary." This back-and-forth, often from the same person and sometimes in the same interview, underscores the ambivalent feelings, simultaneously admiring and aggrieved, Mayer elicited. Screenwriter Langley, who compared him to a shark, also said, "He was a giant compared to the cigar-store Indians who came after him," and even Herman Mankiewicz had to allow, "Louis B. Mayer may be a shit, but not every shit is Louis B. Mayer."

While opinions diverged about the totality of Mayer's personality, two aspects of it were beyond dispute, and they reinforced each other. If there was a single trait that ruled the day with him, it was emotion in all its forms, from anger to those eyes brimming with tears. His feelings could be, and often were, all over the map, but no matter what they were, he rarely modulated them. And, as often as not, their paradoxical aim was to buttress his stated goal of the studio as one big happy family with himself as the titular head. Putting this dream into words was MGM's insider nickname of *Mayer's Ganza Misphoche*, Yiddish for Mayer's entire extended family, one forged out of many.

Though, as actress Ann Richards pointed out, "You never knew if he was going to cry or roar"; that roar, Mayer's legendary temper, was by far the hardest emotion to experience. Not even his children were exempt, his daughter Edith remembering, "The resonance of that voice! 'God damn you!' That's it. I'd hear it and I'd run." Though Edith's sister Irene believed that had her father "not been as emotional as he was, I don't believe he would have been so drawn to, or have succeeded so well in, the picture business," it was a stiff price for those around him to pay.

Mayer's emotionalism presented itself most dramatically in the fainting spells/heart attacks that would afflict him at the precise moments when situations in his office weren't going his way. As related by Budd Schulberg, "L.B. would groan, roll his eyes, clutch his heart, and crumple to the floor. His loyal secretary was so used to this phenomenon that she kept a bowl of water and a towel handy." Initially, daughter Irene said, these attacks were genuine responses to low blood pressure, and some friends, like Schulberg's mother Ad, felt they were always legitimate. "'He was a very emotional man, so intense he might be described as on the borderline of insanity,'" she told her son. "So, in a crisis . . . L.B. would faint. He was always an extremist."

Myrna Loy was among those who were more skeptical. She tells of a contentious meeting with Mayer and Joseph L. Mankiewicz. "All of a sudden Mayer got up and rushed out," and in a moment an assistant rushed in and said, 'He's fainted! God help us, L.B. has fainted!' . . . He was sprawled on a couch, hands folded over his chest, eyes closed, his face drained of color. I'd heard about the phony fainting spells he pulled to get his way, but I thought My God, he really is having a fit." When the actress left for her dressing room, however, she got an immediate phone call which made her realize, "That son of a gun must have leapt off the couch to get to the phone. He'd been fully conscious, aware of everything." Mankiewicz adds the coup de grâce to the story, reporting that "the moment she closed the door, Mayer leaped off the couch and briskly inquired of his secretary, 'O.K., who's next?'"

No matter who that was, Mayer treated them like family.

Sometimes they literally were blood relations, as Mayer (like Thalberg, who employed his sister Sylvia as a screenwriter) had no compunction about hiring his literal *misphoche*. His brother

Jerry became an executive at the studio, and his nephew Jack Cummings was a producer whom Mayer invariably needled, sarcastically using the Yiddish word *macher*, big shot, to greet him. But usually they were the employees that Mayer wanted to buy into his vision of MGM as the classic American home where everyone pulled for everyone else, and the welcome mat was always out. As Samuel Marx noted, echoing the party line, "When other studios—Warner Brothers, for instance—were very much more stringent with their people, MGM had a very paternal atmosphere. . . . 'People who do their jobs have one for life' was one of Mayer's repeated statements. . . . Many would remain the full span of their careers and weld the studio into a family organization." Not that any of this was necessarily easy.

While some writers have written skeptically of Mayer's "cloak of paternalism," it seems to have been real to him, though it occasionally baffled others. Surrealist director Luis Buñuel, of all people briefly on the MGM payroll, attended a Mayer speech to hundreds of employees in which the studio head vowed to reveal the secret of MGM's success. "An expectant hush had fallen; the tension was positively palpable. Mayer turned around, picked up a piece of chalk, and slowly and deliberately wrote on the blackboard in huge capital letters: COOPERATION. Then he sat down to a burst of wild, and apparently sincere, applause. I was beside myself; the whole scene was beyond me." And screenwriter Lenore Coffee, when she returned to work years after leaving MGM because Mayer had subjected her to "the ugliest scene I've ever experienced," was stunned to have the studio head greet her with open arms, a wide smile, and the words "So you had to come home!"

If, as screenwriter Walter Reisch put it, "we were all soldiers of the great army of MGM," some soldiers were smiled on more than others. Mayer told actor Robert Taylor, "If I had a son . . . I can't think of anything I would have wanted than that son to be exactly like you," and sent the young man to his own tailor to be fitted for four new suits and evening wear, all paid for by Mayer. (Another, probably apocryphal version has Taylor's agent asking, "Did you get the raise?" and the actor replying, "No, but I got a father.")

When costume designer Irene, universally known by her first name, developed a serious drinking problem, Mayer made numerous personal visits to her home to bolster her attempts to stop, with the designer telling one of her staff, "I know Mr. Mayer really cares about me." And then there was the case of actor Wallace Beery, a notoriously sour individual who had a proclivity for stealing props and other MGM property that caught his fancy. Mayer, however, would not hear a bad word about the star. "Yes, Beery's a son of a bitch," he would say. "But he's *our* son of a bitch." The generosity was always on Mayer's terms, but if you were in favor that was not a bad thing.

Not surprisingly the Mayer family's actual home was also a center of studio-as-family activity. Built on what is now Pacific Coast Highway (known then as Ocean Front or Palisades Beach Road), a seaside Gold Coast where Douglas Fairbanks, Marion Davies, and even Irving Thalberg and Norma Shearer had homes, it was designed by MGM's Cedric Gibbons and built with a healthy dose of studio labor. It also housed Mayer's aging father Jacob, whom Mayer, perhaps still hoping for a good word from this perennially withholding parent, moved out to Los Angeles once he was successful. The two had not gotten along when L.B. was young, and did not necessarily now, but he was the father and in Mayer's family-centric worldview attention must be paid. Jacob insisted on and received strictly kosher meals and mostly spent his days in Torah study, his presence in the home invariably surprising guests and visitors.

Attorney Fanny Holtzmann, a friend of Mayer's, remembers the father as "shrunken and dour under a black *yarmulkah* [skullcap]" and told her biographer, "But he was always there, always treated with respect. No matter who came to dinner—

and over the years that included prime ministers, generals, scientific geniuses . . . the old man alone presided at the head of the table, *yarmulkah* on his head. 'I don't give a damn who is being honored,' Louis used to say. 'If he doesn't like it, he can leave!'"

Though he considered everyone on the lot as his family, Mayer paid special attention to MGM's actual children, with Elizabeth Taylor, whose Hollywood career took off with the studio's *Lassie Come Home* and *National Velvet*, remembering annual mandatory celebrations of the studio head's birthday: "All we kids would stand and sing 'Happy Birthday.' Then he would address the assemblage with, 'You must think of me as your father. You must come to me, any of you, with any of your problems no matter how slight they may seem to you, because you are all my children.'" A similar sense of obligation centered on Mayer's at-home events. There were weekend pool parties for the younger set, with actress Bonita Granville remembering, "All the MGM kids were invited and attendance was mandatory, if one wanted to keep working on the lot." Similarly compulsory were Mayer's Sunday brunches, with only serious illness or a mother's birthday allowing one to stay away. Comic Phil Silvers likened them to meeting the pope, noting, "Of course, it wasn't His Highness's ring you kissed."

Given that family in all its forms was Mayer's guiding light, it's unsurprising that he found time for another entity that can be viewed as a family on a larger scale even than the studio: the Republican Party. Like many another poor boy who made good, Mayer was a shamelessly partisan conservative to the core of his being. His journey to becoming the most prominent Republican in Hollywood began with Herbert Hoover, whom Mayer met when Hoover was secretary of commerce in Calvin Coolidge's administration. Mayer became a California delegate to the 1928 Republican national convention that nominated Hoover for president, assiduously raised money for him, and along with his

Mayer starting a race at his Santa Monica beach home, with participants including Mickey Rooney and Judy Garland, whose birthday it was.
(Marc Wanamaker/Bison Archives)

family became the first overnight guests in the Hoover White House. Rumors of an appointment to the ambassadorship to Turkey remained just that, rumors, but Mayer stayed true to the faith. He became chairman of California's Republican State Central Committee, even asking every studio employee to contribute a day's salary to the Hoover campaign when he ran against Franklin D. Roosevelt in 1932.

Mayer became increasingly conservative over time, taking meetings with Mussolini's son Vittorio and telling Harry Rapf's son Maurice that his radical leftist activities were "bad for the Jews." When Mayer visited England in 1936 in connection with MGM producing films there, novelist Graham Greene, then a film critic, reported with more than a touch of condescension hearing "the little level Jewish voice" and characterized it as "the voice of American capital itself: a touch of religion, a touch of the family, the mixture goes smoothly down." A long way for the small boy from St. John to have traveled, a long way indeed.

The key player in making the Hoover connection that started Mayer's Republican ascent was an exceptionally capable woman who also became central to Mayer's modus operandi at MGM and almost the definition of a gatekeeping power behind the throne. That would be Ida "Kay" Koverman, whose official title was executive secretary to Mayer but who for twenty-five years, working with her own secretary and two assistants, had a hand in much more than who got in to see the studio chief. Jimmy Fidler called her "one of the most powerful personages in the entire motion picture industry; when she pulls the strings, world-famous stars dance like puppets." Fellow Hollywood columnist Hedda Hopper added, "I never saw him take orders from anyone else."

Hopper was referring to Koverman helping Mayer deliver his speeches ("L.B. had a tendency to get carried away and stray from the script, so Ida had a signal worked out to stop him"), but that was just the beginning. An associate of Hoover's before he entered politics and a force in both his and Coolidge's presidential campaigns, she had become, by the time journalist Beth Day knew her, "official studio hostess, mistress of protocol, and self-styled talent scout. . . . An adroit politician, public speaker, lobbyist, and expediter . . . L.B. looked to her for cues on everything from the proper greeting to the Ambassador from Japan to what fork to use at a banquet." Depending on the situation, she either frightened or consoled those who came in contact with her. One executive remembered "She was everyone's aunt, and she knew everyone's troubles," but actress Evie Johnson saw things differently. "We called her Mount Ida. . . . She was dictatorial, unbending and unyielding. She was *not* a nice old grandmother." Though Mayer eventually fell out with Koverman, perhaps feeling he'd ceded her too much power, he probably would have agreed with Lillian Gish, a force in her own right, who simply called her "one of the most formidable women I've ever seen in my life."

There was no Ida Koverman in Irving Thalberg's life, though perhaps he could have used one. The difficulty of getting into his office, of seeing him face to face, became the stuff of legend, with almost everyone who made the attempt commenting on the enormity of the task. Only the frequency of new acquaintances from his early days mistaking him for an office boy is commented on quite so much.

In fact, the practice of people having to wait was not something Thalberg adopted on his rise in stature at MGM; it had been part of his modus operandi as far back as his hectic days at Universal. "His secretary, Dorothy Howell, was forced to bring continuous complaints from waiting men and women," Samuel Marx reported, "but he refused to be distracted and concentrated his attention only on matters before him." At MGM, this proclivity only worsened (a University of Southern California professor who introduced him at a campus talk noted that unless you had been at the studio and "observed how difficult it is for people to talk with Mr. Thalberg, you cannot fully appreciate this privilege"), and if his high rank curtailed complaints, it also raised the importance of those who were forced to wait.

As King Vidor described it in his autobiography, "In Thalberg's outer office there was a piece of furniture known as the Million Dollar Bench because stars, producers, and directors often cooled their heels there." Barbara Stanwyck, for one, reported a forty-five-minute wait, but most of those biding their time were writers, and since many of them were wits, their responses have a certain bite. George S. Kaufman, for example, cracked, "On a clear day you can see Thalberg," and, on finally meeting the executive, asked him, "Do you want it Wednesday or do you want it good?" Anita Loos, who did needlework during the interminable waits, gave Thalberg the resulting scarf and reported telling him, "Well, Irving, I think this is probably the most expensive gift you'll ever get, because I'm crocheting it for your Christmas present and so far it's cost MGM studios $20,000." And one possibly apocryphal story claims that when Dorothy Parker gave up and left the studio for a romantic rendezvous, she excused her absence when finally summoned by writing "I can only offer the explanation that I was too fucking busy and vice versa."

It wasn't only Loos who responded with something tangible. S. J. Perelman had perhaps the most extended reaction, writing "And Did You Once See Irving Plain," a frequently anthologized 1957 memoir about the experience. Calling Thalberg "a producer whose name was uttered only in cathedral whispers, universally acknowledged the top genius of celluloid," Perelman had such difficulty seeing the man that "my wife and I seriously began to question whether Thalberg even existed, whether he might not be a solar myth or a deity concocted by the front office to garner prestige." A meeting eventually took place with "a frail gentleman with intense eyes which he kept fixed unwinkingly on us," but the conference ended abruptly when "word arrived from Miss Garbo that Western civilization would collapse unless Thalberg hastened on the double to Stage 9." It may have come twenty years after Thalberg's death, but Perelman finally got a measure of revenge.

Opinions differ on the reason almost everyone waited almost all the time. Vidor says Thalberg once told him, "I get a kick out of looking out there and seeing people like Von Stroheim, Seastrom and Niblo waiting to see me," and Perelman noted that "power is the ability to purchase people and make them wait for you." But it is also plausible that the waiting was not a Thalberg stratagem but a function of what mattered most in his life. He was a man on a mission, someone who lived for, was even obsessed by, his work to the exclusion of almost everything else, including the niceties of time management or even basic consideration. To Howard Dietz, who'd had the experience of waiting ten hours in that outer office ("I got saddle sores from sitting on leather") only to realize "when you were ushered into his presence, he forgot that he had called you," Thalberg was a man "who had hardly brushed up against the real world. . . . He was thoughtful when he thought of you, but he rarely thought of you unless you were useful to a picture project." Similarly, Ben Hecht saw him as "a genius [who] hadn't the faintest idea of what was going on anywhere in the world except his office. . . . He lived two-thirds of the time in the projection room. He saw only movies, he never saw life . . . but he knew what shadows could do."

For as it turned out, one of the defining qualities of Thalberg as an executive and an individual was that no matter how irritating the extended wait had been, once you crossed that elusive threshold, the combination of the man's presence and perceptions completely changed everyone's mood. No one enjoyed the wait (how could they?) but almost no one felt that the resulting meeting had wasted their time. As director Clarence Brown related, "You would be working with your writer and you would come to this scene in the script. It didn't click. It just didn't jell. The scene was no goddamn good. You would make a date with Irving, talk to him for thirty minutes, and you'd come away from his office with the best scene in the picture."

A more potent example of the effects this connection could produce is this extended reminiscence by actress Myrna Loy. Signed by MGM in 1931, she was called into a meeting with Thalberg two years later. "He kept me waiting interminably in his outer office," she, of course, remembered.

> When I finally got in, he turned his back on me, looked out
> the window, and started talking. Well, my back went up. That
> was *Miss* Loy, you know. As I started to walk out, he swiveled

his chair back toward me. "Thank you," I said rather pompously. "I was brought up to look at people when I talk to them."

"What?" he replied, startled but not displeased. Although always a little bit ill, with shoulders that hunched forward slightly, he was an attractive man, really beautiful, I thought, with a great face and deep, penetrating eyes. "Myrna," he observed, despite my outburst, "you're terribly shy. There's no reason you should be. It's hurting you, putting a veil between you and the audience. You've got to cut through the veil and take hold of that audience. Make it yours. It's there and they like you. They adore you. You're beautiful enough for the movies, you're making good progress here"—both of which I myself had doubted—"so make it work for you."

Well, my shyness was nothing new to me, but I hadn't realized it affected my work. It's interesting that Thalberg discovered it. He didn't know me at all—oh we met at parties and things like that, but we never had spent any time together. Yet he discerned this. . . . After that meeting with Irving Thalberg, I felt for the first time that M-G-M had plans for me,

a confidence that soon bore fruit in *The Thin Man* and its sequels, films that were landmark successes for both the actress and the studio.

Though journalist Allene Talmey half-dismissively described him as "nervous, skinny, mostly dark eyes and no body," even she had to acknowledge that Thalberg was possessed of "a fluent quality from within," a kind of self-possession that was innate. Various physical characteristics were noted as part of his appeal, with Jim Tully writing about fingers that were "long, sensitive, and delicate, the fingers of a Richelieu or a Machiavelli," and producer Walter Wanger emphasizing those "terrific eyes. . . . You thought that you were talking to an Indian savant. He could cast a spell on anybody." Asked to differentiate him from other producers, Lenore Coffee came up with a striking image: "Well, if you were going to have a knife stuck in your back Thalberg would not only hold the knife correctly but would use it with a certain elegance."

While much of the way Thalberg presented himself was instinctual, he was not averse to heightening the effect with attention-grabbing props of various sorts. Just one prop, really, because although mention is made of a pocket watch ("I'll never forget the way Irving used to swing his watch when he was thinking," Mayer told writer Lillian Ross) and even a cane ("kind of a power symbol," said David Lewis), his one consistent accessory was a coin. Anita Loos remembers him "boyishly flipping a big silver dollar," while others talk about a $20 gold piece, with Joan Crawford remembering that he "tossed it and tossed it, with such concentration that you never dared speak to him." Once, according to Samuel Marx, he flipped it so high it disappeared into a chandelier. After that, he'd bounce the coin off a glass-topped desk, but the noise so "distracted everyone who worked with him" that, by pre-arranged plan, his associates simultaneously did the same thing, causing such a racket that Thalberg, not slow to take a hint, "never did it again."

One of the ironies of Thalberg's life is that though he was largely self-educated, the noun applied to him with regularity was "genius." Not just in the glib "Boy Genius" way that came to irritate him, but as an example of sincere belief in his creative powers. Frank Capra, for example, wrote, "It has often been said that Hollywood had produced only three true geniuses: Chaplin, Disney and Thalberg," and Mervyn LeRoy narrowed it down further: "I think he and Walt Disney are the only two who really deserve that word."

What the "genius" designation meant in Hollywood terms was not just that Thalberg the autodidact was the rare studio executive who, from his invalid childhood onward, loved books and could be considered, as Budd Schulberg grudgingly admitted, "Hollywood's resident intellectual." He didn't just drop Freud into conversations, he actually read him. And he was not just one of those who, as producer Pandro Berman put it, engaged in heedlessly "buying great thick books and Broadway plays and making movies out of them." He knew, to a remarkable extent, why he was spending the studio's money. "When it came to pictures," Helen Hayes says flatly, "Irving's judgement was infallible. He picked good properties, and spared no expense on buying them, on adapting scripts, on casting, and his productions were lavish."

His taste and interests, however, were surprisingly catholic, extending to the kinds of films that he felt were wrong for MGM. Fritz Lang related that Thalberg had told a group of his writers to study and learn from *M*, Lang's German early sound thriller centered on a child murderer. But when someone asked, "'Mr. Thalberg, what would you have said if I had brought you the script of this picture?' Thalberg answered, 'I probably would have said, 'Go to hell.''"

Thalberg's decisions about material, it's important to clarify, were grounded not in some platonic ideal of what was worthy but in his intuitive sense of what the public was willing to pay for in the here and now. Although both Thalberg and Mayer (though especially Thalberg) believed in the medium's artistic potential, in elevating and uplifting what film could do, they also did not want to get too far ahead of their audience. Acutely aware that "there is no medium of today that so universally must please as great a number of people" as the movies, Thalberg took pride in having an innate sense of what all those people would respond to, a satisfaction which made him appear to Allen Rivkin as "an immense egomaniac." A screenwriter brought in to write physical gags for an MGM movie, Rivkin never got over the way "Thalberg leaned far over the desk and tapped the following out slowly: 'Listen, young man, when I say a gag won't play it won't play. I, more than any single person in Hollywood, have my finger on the pulse of America. I *know* what people will do and what they won't.'"

Another story, this one involving art director Cedric Gibbons, makes a similar point. The film involved was a 1926 romance set in and called *Paris*, which contained a Thalberg-suggested love scene to be shot with a moonlit ocean behind it. Gibbons objected that there was no ocean anywhere near Paris and Thalberg confidently replied, "We can't cater to a handful of people who know Paris. . . . Audiences only see about ten per cent of what's on screen anyway, and if they are watching your backgrounds instead of my actors the scene will be useless. Whatever you put there, they'll believe it." To prove his point, Thalberg later asked Gibbons if there had been any complaining letters about the scene. There had been none.

When Thalberg addressed USC students in 1929's Introduction to the Photoplay class, the first ever course given in what was to become the School of Cinematic Arts, he emphasized the same point in a more elegant way. "One of my chief functions is to be an observer and sense and feel the moods of the public," he told the students. "When I am asked to pass on the expenditure of huge sums of money and decide whether one kind of picture should be made or another kind, the greatest problem to be settled is that of judging whether or not the subject matter of the story is topical. What is accepted by the public today may not be accepted tomorrow."

Because his power on the lot was so considerable, Thalberg tried, not always successfully, to treat others judiciously and strove to be treated that way in return. Those vouching for his fairness include director W. S. "Woody" Van Dyke, who insisted, "Irving Thalberg has given me a squarer deal than anyone I ever worked for." When screenwriter Coffee reported a difficult salary dispute, she took pains to minimize it, noting, "I had a difference of opinion . . . not a quarrel." And while Thalberg told Cedric Gibbons, "The last thing I need is flattery!" it was inevitable that his presence altered the dynamics of a situation. "I think he was rather frightening," Maureen O'Hara remembered.

"He didn't talk much and when he spoke it had meaning. I found him intimidating. He was a little awe-inspiring. . . . He was a remote figure, and when he came on a set, there was really silence."

While partisans like Anita Loos (who insisted to biographer Bob Thomas, "He wasn't St. Irving") never pretended Thalberg was without flaws, there were of course those, like gag writer Rivkin, who did not connect at all to aspects of the man's personality and did not hesitate to say so. It was a situation David Lewis approached with resignation. "I can only present the Irving Thalberg I knew," he wrote. "Many others saw him differently, and all sorts of pictures have been painted of him. I do not deify or sanctify him—he was most of all human, with human qualities and faults."

Those who did not share that view mostly commented on the remoteness and lack of connection they wished had been forthcoming. Director Joseph Newman, for example, said, "Thalberg was a brilliant man, but he was a little cold. It took a long time to know him, and he didn't have the personal warmth that I found in Mayer." Perhaps unsurprisingly, given that he did not usually deal with them, it was actors who had the most difficulty with Thalberg, who rarely conveyed the intuitive understanding of their craft that screenwriters invariably commented on. Mickey Rooney barely mentions Thalberg in his autobiography and then only to make disparaging comments like "he produced as many flops as hits, and it seemed to me that he went out of his way to put his wife in films she didn't need and wasn't right for." Lynn Fontanne, with husband Alfred Lunt the great theatrical couple of the age, was also dismissive. "Thalberg was, in his way, a clever man," she told biographer Maurice Zolotow, "and he had taste and intelligence and he seriously wanted to make good movies, we both felt. But he wanted slaves, not actors, and we couldn't be any person's slaves."

Feeling similarly, and if anything, more violently, was Edward G. Robinson, in 1930 a successful New York stage actor with hardly any screen credits whom Thalberg wanted to sign to a contract paying $1 million for six pictures over three years. The executive, Robinson reported in his autobiography, "couldn't have been more gracious—or tougher," insisting on an exclusive deal with no time off to do theater.

> M.G.M. would have to make all the career decisions, don't you see. I did not see.
>
> Visions of sugar plums and a million dollars danced in one part of my head; in the other was icy rage that this young man, whose credentials I considered inferior, would dare suggest that all decision would be taken from me, that I was some article to be packaged and merchandised. . . . Thalberg compromised on nothing; he sat there, stern and immovable—the godhead.
>
> I disliked him thoroughly. His eyes showed me that an actor was beneath contempt. . . . It was High Noon. Thalberg's way or no way. Robinson's way or no way.
>
> No way.
>
> My agent and I abruptly left Thalberg's office. Then, trying to hide myself from the extras and executives in front of his building, I vomited.

Of all the accounts actors and others have left of interacting with Thalberg, perhaps the most compelling, because it's both the most detailed and apparently written without a collaborator, comes in Charles Bickford's *Bulls, Balls, Bicycles, and Actors*. Given that it's an actor's story, its unhappiness with the studio boss fits the overall pattern, but it excels at describing how Thalberg's great ability to project creative understanding persuaded people to go along with his ideas despite their own reservations and, at times, their own experience.

Bickford was a New York stage success when he was signed by MGM in 1929, but he didn't meet with the studio's top executives until he was chosen for the big-deal assignment of costarring with Greta Garbo in her *Anna Christie* sound debut the following year. His view of Mayer ("the glibness of a self-taught evangelist . . . mantled in the arrogance of success") was not promising, but Thalberg made a different impression: "a personable young man who had somehow fallen in with bad companions. Frail, unhealthy-looking (his skin had a bluish tinge), his eyes revealed intelligence and sensitivity. I liked him on sight and tabbed him as someone I could probably talk to on my own level."

When Bickford was invited to lunch with Thalberg he was "pleased to discover that my first impression of him endured. We were quite compatible. He confessed his predilection for actors and seemed to have a sympathetic understanding of our problems." When Bickford said he wasn't sold on costarring with Garbo, Thalberg was able to win him over, and the actor left the meal confident that "my next picture under the MGM banner would be 'Anna Christie.'"

Then the other shoe dropped, and Bickford was informed his next project would be a loan-out to Universal for an indifferent film. "The following afternoon found me cooling my heels in Thalberg's outer office. My stormy mood was not eased by a two-hour wait and when my turn to enter the sanctum came, I ignored his genial greeting and got right to the point. 'What are you people trying to do to me?'" Thalberg expressed ignorance of the situation and "after hearing me out, he said thoughtfully, 'So that's what's eating you. I don't blame you for feeling sore. I didn't know anything about this, Charlie. I'll look into it. Come back in the morning and we'll talk.'"

When Bickford returned, "I saw instantly that Thalberg's attitude had changed. There was no genial greeting, nor did he ask me to sit down. He remained seated at his desk and his manner was that of a stern executive whose unpleasant duty it was to keep a recalcitrant employee in line." There followed a back-and-forth that included Bickford claiming that the mistress of an MGM executive was to be in the Universal film.

"No important executive could be expected to accept this brand of positive defiance sitting down and Thalberg rose to the occasion. He didn't speak, he yelled; and his voice was strident with anger. 'Where do you get off coming in here and telling me what you will and will not do. You're under contract to this studio and you'll do as you're told.' I out-roared him. 'The hell I will.'" After further back-and-forth, including a heated conversation with another executive, "Thalberg intervened. 'There's no occasion for anyone to get tough,' he said sharply. . . . 'The studio has seen fit to loan you out to Universal for a picture. If I had known about it, I would have been against it. But I didn't, and the deal was made and we're on a spot.'"

The same situation recurred with another questionable loan-out, this time to Fox. "I took my beef to Thalberg. I gravitated to him partly, I think, because I liked him but mostly because of his own seeming dedication to the making of worth-while pictures. . . . I stormed into his office and plunked the offending script down on his desk." After yet another back-and-forth, Thalberg said "You feel that I'm on your side. Isn't that right?" and when Bickford agreed, Thalberg came back with, "Now, will you for Christ's sake give me credit for knowing what I'm talking about?" Bickford's response on the page: "He was a very persuasive little guy."

This was not the end of things, not even close. Bickford was then cast in "a dreadful piece of clap-trap." He complains to Thalberg, who tells him that he "mustn't jeopardize the big plans that were being made for me by refusing to do it. I should have told him to shove the big plans, and walked. But my trust in Thalberg prevailed and once again I was outsmarted." And then comes a long and complex battle over something called *The Sea Bat*, which begins with Bickford describing how he "crashed into Thalberg's office, only to be immediately disarmed by his appearance. . . . He had lost considerable weight, his color was ghastly and he looked very tired. My anger melted into concern," but soon enough the atmosphere changed, with Thalberg saying, "Don't get sarcastic with me, Charlie. I only work here too, you know." The interchange ended with Thalberg insisting, "Everything will work out if you'll have a little patience. . . . I think you can be one of the biggest stars on the screen. Just have a little faith in me." Bickford: "Once again I allowed the Thalberg charm to overcome my own judgement."

After the actor takes his frustration with *The Sea Bat* to Mayer, Thalberg tells him, "When are you going to smarten up? You can't tangle with men like Mayer and Hearst and get away with it. A man of your intelligence should know that, for Christ's sake." But when he did not get a crack at a promised major film, Bickford finally reached his limit. "What about Thalberg?" he asks rhetorically. "Was he really championing my cause against great odds, or was he a blue-faced little Machiavelli lulling me with soft words so he could destroy me piecemeal? Of one thing I was sure. No longer would I fall for the soft-sell. No one would con me into playing this latest insult to my ability as an actor. For me, Thalberg's charm had lost its potency." Without Thalberg's side of the story, the sincerity of his belief in Bickford, who had obvious star power and went on to a trio of Oscar nominations and a continuing reputation for rebelliousness, is open to debate, but what is sure is that within days of his final talk with Thalberg, the actor got the release he was seeking from his MGM contract.

Putting Thalberg's modus operandi into a broader perspective than Bickford's tale of serial betrayal (which is conveyed in even greater detail in his book) was director George Cukor, who had just started shooting the 1936 Garbo-starring *Camille* when the executive died. "In his own way he was an artist himself," Cukor told author Gavin Lambert. "He was very friendly with a great many talented people. He admired them, and at the same time he was very demanding of them. He wouldn't stop until he felt everything was as good as it could possibly be.

Metro was really built on that attitude. You might not always agree with what they did, but they did it so well!"

Given how different they were on the surface in terms of personality and presentation, it's important to emphasize that Mayer and Thalberg had underlying values in common, values that for a time made their partnership at MGM more seamless than casual observers imagined it would be. One value both shared was a belief in morality, something that was visible as early as their 1922 introductory meeting at the Los Angeles home of attorney Edwin Loeb. As Samuel Marx tells the story, Mayer spent a chunk of time fulminating against a film his company was committed to that he nevertheless wanted to stop. It was called *Pleasure Mad*, it involved artists cavorting with unclothed models, and as a husband and father of two young girls Mayer would have none of it. Asked for his opinion, Thalberg agreed the film should be stopped, and though that position has mostly been viewed as reflecting his belief in studio authority, it also has a whiff of morality about it.

Though Mayer's belief in moral order was the very visible cornerstone of his personality, both public and private, Thalberg shared it in ways that were not always apparent because of his corporate responsibilities. For as long as he lived, Thalberg was the studio's front man in MGM's battles with various Hays office entities that attempted to regulate what could and could not be seen on screen, which meant that he pushed for the measure of license that box office receipts proved audiences favored. "People influence pictures," he believed, "far more than pictures influence people."

Though his presentation was unmistakably cultured and sophisticated, Thalberg could exhibit an unbending sense of morality in his private life as well. One of the best examples of this is provided by actress Helen Hayes, who along with her husband, the writer Charles MacArthur, were close friends and frequent traveling companions of Thalberg and Norma Shearer. "We took a cruise through the Panama Canal and spent a few days in Panama," she wrote later.

> At our hotel someone told Charlie and Irving that in the red-light district the prostitutes used the names of their favorite movie stars. The brothels displayed signs bearing these well-known names as a lure to customers.
>
> Naturally, the men had to see that titillating sight, and the ladies went along. We drove in a hired car through the heat and dust to the red-light district. The driver knew where "Norma Shearer" worked, and he took us to a ramshackle house; there on the front was a sign with Norma's name in big bold letters.
>
> We all thought it was very funny, except Irving, who found it offensive. He would often get serious about things that no one else thought important. He said he was going to demand that the brothel's owner take that sign down immediately. The madder he got, the more we laughed at him. But Norma, who was so refined on screen and off, seemed flattered by this tribute to her name.

Parenthetically, Thalberg's prominence in matters of suitability, as well as the overall predominance of Jews in Hollywood, stoked the antisemitism that was never far from the surface in the religious/nativist anti-Hollywood screeds of the day. Los Angeles' Catholic Bishop John J. Cantwell wrote a 1933 article decrying immorality in movie houses and claiming, historian Frank Walsh relates, "The Jewish studio owners were partially to blame because the filth was created by the directors and writers, 75 percent of whom were pagans." And Joseph Breen, Thalberg's primary antagonist as administrator of the revitalized Production Code Administration from 1934 to 1954, was given to unashamedly antisemitic rants in his letters to fellow Catholics, writing to one colleague, "The fact is these damn Jews are a dirty, filthy lot. Their only standard is the box-office. To attempt to talk ethical value to them is time worse than wasted."

Even more critical to the job at hand than a moral code, Mayer and Thalberg shared a passionate belief in the ever-increasing artistic value of film. This conviction is so much a given today, so much a part of the framework in which cinema operates, that it's almost shocking to realize that it was far from the case in years not so far past. To take but one example, the Los Angeles program for the 1923 run of *The Hunchback of Notre Dame* includes director Wallace Worsley decrying an anticinema declaration by celebrated newspaperman William Allen White, the "Sage of Emporia" having declared that the movies "attract as habitues only cripplewits, lamebrains and half heads."

It was not only Worsley ("I guess Mr. White has been sticking too close to his own home town to know what is going on") who was upset at this line of thought; these were fighting words to Mayer and Thalberg as well. Both were driven to add respectability to film, to take the medium seriously in part because the question kept coming up. Legitimization was an issue not only because of the form's youth but also because of its vaudeville and penny arcade origins. In the introduction to his *The Best Moving Pictures of 1922–23*, future Pulitzer Prize– and Oscar-winning writer Robert E. Sherwood feels he has to devote his preface to "that painfully moot question, 'Do the movies constitute an art?'" (His answer is a qualified yes.) And as late as those 1927 lectures on film given to the Harvard Business School, film producer Joseph P. Kennedy expresses undisguised pleasure that "those at the university accepted the motion picture as something more than an inferior kind of drama."

Like the flip side of the quest for morality, which had Mayer in the leading role with Thalberg offering support, the quest for legitimacy was more Thalberg's area, though Mayer certainly shared the younger man's zeal for film and belief in its power.

Grandson Danny Selznick told Neal Gabler, "He adored movies with a relish that, I suspect, may have been unique. I mean,
I wonder whether Jack Warner or Harry Cohn loved movies
the way Mayer loved movies, [took] the incredible pleasure he
took in the movies he'd made." As to Thalberg, his passion for
the medium was of such a particularly intense nature that more
than one colleague referred to it in religious terms. Budd Schulberg called him "a young pope" who "burned with a Jesuitical
faith in the world religion of motion pictures," while his friend
screenwriter Charles MacArthur went one step further. "Entertainment is his God," he said. "He's satisfied to serve him without billing, like a priest at an altar, or a rabbi under the Scrolls."

Thalberg had to battle not only the scorn of outsiders like
William Allen White but also people inside the industry. Screenwriter Anita Loos, one of Thalberg's favorite collaborators, is
quoted by Helen Hayes as saying that "we never thought filmmaking was an art. It was just a job, and we worked hard at it."
Against this tide, Thalberg swam tirelessly. Believing that film
"could be an artistic as well as a commercial success," he told
one reporter, "The time has come when the ridicule of motion
pictures must stop. If a picture can move audiences, it must be
praised. The motion picture is a new art in America, and there
is need that it be respected here. No matter how many bad ones
are made, the important thing is to point out the good ones."

Perhaps Thalberg comes across most clearly as a true believer in cinema in his remarks to that USC film class, when
he began by stating that film "satisfies the emotional needs of
the people and the satisfaction of those needs is perhaps one of
the most vital problems of our civilization. I do not know what
would happen if pictures were taken away from the world. It
would not make much difference for a week or a month, but if
they were completely and permanently taken away, think what
everybody would lose—those in rural communities and those

piled on top of one another in the cities—without the motion picture theatres to go to."

In addition, Thalberg helped pioneer the concept of the prestige picture, a production that did not have to make money to redound to the studio's credit. It was in fact, as shall be seen, just such a high production value, heavily promoted vehicle, 1936's *Romeo and Juliet*, that finally caused the country's highbrow cultural establishment to admit they had underestimated film. As to Thalberg's fellow ambitious producers, they more than anyone knew what he'd achieved in that area. David O. Selznick called Thalberg "beyond any question the greatest individual force for fine pictures," with Darryl F. Zanuck agreeing that "more than any other man he raised the industry to its present world prestige." And, as we have seen, the *New York Times*, a crucial cultural arbiter, said on his death, "He helped, perhaps more than any other man in Hollywood, to make the motion picture a medium of adult entertainment."

Mission accomplished.

10

Garbo

NOTHING IS AS transitory in Hollywood as fame. In but a few decades, its biggest names are one with Nineveh and Tyre, and this axiom has held true even for the much-publicized pride of MGM. If Joan Crawford is remembered by non–film buffs, it's likely in connection with her adopted daughter Christina Crawford's controversial *Mommie Dearest* memoir and its lurid film version. The last time Norma Shearer was on the cover of a book was in connection with an essay entitled "'What Price Widowhood?': The Faded Stardom of Norma Shearer," which lamented "her current relative obscurity." Only Greta Garbo endures. Only Garbo could still truly say, as Norma Desmond proclaims, "I am big. It's the pictures that got small." Desmond herself reinforces that notion, saying later in *Sunset Boulevard*, "We had faces. There just aren't any faces like that anymore. Only one: Garbo."

And this attention is not a case of appreciating someone

who was undervalued in her prime. Quite the opposite. Garbo has always been in a category apart, someone critic Kenneth Tynan characterized with the often-quoted line, "What when drunk, one sees in other women, one sees in Garbo sober." And, far from being blasé, it was fellow film professionals who were most impressed. Even as competitive an observer as Bette Davis called her "pure witchcraft. I cannot analyze this woman's acting. I only know that no one else so effectively worked in front of a camera."

Not always remembered in all this deserved fuss is that unlike most stars, Garbo's entire Hollywood output, twenty-four films from 1926 to 1941, was for one studio, and that was MGM. Her career was perhaps the most successful specific example of the intuitive collaboration between Mayer, who signed her and negotiated her contracts, and Thalberg, who guided her career and gained her guarded trust. As Samuel Marx noted, "Thalberg was loyal but rarely emotional; Mayer was emotional but rarely loyal."

Though it was indisputably Mayer, in Europe to deal with the "Ben-Hur" fiasco, who signed the nineteen-year-old Garbo in Berlin in 1924, aspects of the event are complex. For one thing, Garbo was hardly an unknown who needed to be discovered, at least in Sweden. She had been a student in the prestigious Royal Dramatic Theater Academy and appeared in filmed commercials for a Stockholm department store when she was but fifteen, though a cast member complained, Garbo biographer Barry Paris reports, "You're not going to have that fat girl in the picture, are you? She won't fit the screen." Slimmed down, she had been cast at age seventeen in a key role in 1924's epic *The Saga of Gösta Berling*, the longest and most expensive film in Sweden's history.

The film was directed by Garbo's mentor, Mauritz Stiller, and though it's been said that Stiller was Mayer's main target and Garbo was the movie equivalent of a player to be named later, this turns out to be inaccurate. Mayer, nothing if not tenacious in his pursuit of acting talent, had screened *Gösta Berling* before signing Garbo and, according to Irene Mayer Selznick, was immediately enthusiastic about the actress. "Miss Garbo overcame him in the first reel. It was her eyes . . . the capacity to convey feeling through the eyes. Dad said, 'I'll take Stiller, all right. As for the girl, I want her even more than Stiller. I can make a star out of her. I'll take them both.'" As Louise Brooks put it with a bit more pizzazz, "Looking at Greta Garbo in the Swedish picture *Gösta Berling*, in Berlin, he knew as sure as he was alive that he had found a sexual symbol beyond his or anyone else's imagining."

Whatever big future plans Mayer and Thalberg had for Garbo, they had here-and-now difficulty deciding on a first project for her. She began to learn English, preferable but not essential for Hollywood silent filmmaking; had some Thalberg-suggested cosmetic dentistry; and posed for publicity shots with Leo the Lion. To help her pass the time, Stiller would frequently park her on the set of the Lillian Gish–starring *The Scarlet Letter*, directed by fellow Swede Victor Seastrom and costarring her *Gösta Berling* costar Lars Hanson. "Garbo would sit there, watching," Gish remembered. "She was treated shabbily in her first weeks at Metro, subjected to all kinds of publicity gimmickry, and she is reputed to have said emphatically that, when she was 'beeg like Mees Geesh,' she would no longer tolerate it. 'No more publicity like this; no more posing in bathing suits,' she vowed."

Garbo's first starring role turned out to be 1926's *Torrent*, adapted from a Vicente Blasco Ibáñez novel about the romantic complications of a poor girl turned legendary opera diva. *Torrent*'s director, however, was not Stiller, as both Garbo and he had hoped, but MGM favorite Monta Bell. Garbo, who even at this early stage had an independent streak, considered turning it down, but Stiller convinced her it would be better to forge ahead. He also gave her some pointed advice that, decades later, she repeated verbatim to journalist Sven Broman: "Don't take

A young Garbo posing warily with MGM's Leo the Lion in 1926.
Once she became a star, the actress refused all such publicity requests.
(Private Collection; © Classic Picture Library/Bridgeman Images)

any notice of other people. Be yourself. Don't try and be like anyone else. Every person is unique. Don't try and be like Norma
Shearer."

Torrent also marked the first time Garbo was photographed
by cinematographer William Daniels, who ended up shooting
nineteen of her films. With Daniels's help, Garbo became "Garbo"
almost at once, vaulting with apparent ease into the iconic status she would never relinquish. Thalberg, for his part, never had
any doubts, predicting to *Variety* that the film would make her
a star. "Louis B. Mayer," the trade publication continued, "can
hand himself a few pats on the back for having brought this girl
over from the other side."

Though not averse to pats on the back, Mayer always had his mind fixed on the main chance, and even before *Torrent* was released he pushed its star to extend her three-year contract to five. Not for the last time in his business discussions with Garbo, this was not a meeting of the minds. As she herself candidly wrote, "I could never understand what he meant by it. We never said anything about money. He just said he couldn't afford to advertise my pictures and put money into me if I would not sign for five years with them. I had already signed for three years, and why should I sign again when I had not yet a picture—and then when I had only *Torrent*."

Making things worse was the situation with Stiller. He was to be the director of the star's next film, *The Temptress*, but his slow, idiosyncratic method of working soon ran afoul of MGM's increasingly assembly-line-oriented production methods, and after a few weeks the always budget conscious Thalberg had him replaced. "Mr. Stiller is an artist, he does not understand about the American factories," Garbo recounted laconically. "How I was broken to pieces, nobody knows."

At that pivotal point, John Gilbert entered Garbo's personal and professional life. Performances like *The Big Parade* were making him the country's preeminent romantic lead, and it was not surprising that Thalberg, the prime mover in deciding Garbo's roles, was eager to costar them in something provocatively titled *Flesh and the Devil*. The property was unremarkable, and there are reports that Thalberg once again leaned on his friendship with Gilbert to get him to agree, but what happened between its two stars was incendiary.

Garbo, as it happened, tiring of nonstop vamp roles, was no more enthusiastic than Gilbert was. As Norma Shearer recalled in her memoir, "Miss Garbo at first didn't approve of playing the sophisticate, the exotic woman of the world. She used to complain, 'Mr. Thalberg, I am yust a joong gur-rl!'" Upset as well by the sudden death of her sister, she tried to turn this production down or at least postpone it, but Mayer insisted that everything proceed on schedule. Stories inevitably differ on how the established star and the rising young talent, eight years apart in age, actually met—one has him enthusiastically shouting out a "Hello Greta" on the MGM lot and she insisting on "Miss Garbo"—but whatever that truth is, once filming began, passion took over.

Flesh and the Devil is yet another bleak romantic yarn about a femme fatale who comes between two best friends though in truth nothing that happens in the plot department registers compared to what transpires early on, when Garbo and Gilbert meet on screen and in real life. Director Clarence Brown, nominally in charge, remembers the scene vividly: "It was the damnedest thing you ever saw. It was the sort of thing Elinor Glyn used to write about. When they got into that first love scene . . . well, nobody else was even there. Those two were alone in a world of their own. It seemed like an intrusion to yell 'cut!' I used to just motion the crew over to another part of the set and let them finish what they were doing. It was embarrassing."

These scenes have long been celebrated for their erotic frankness, and we can still feel the powerful chemistry between Garbo's languid sensuality and Gilbert's dynamism that rewarded Thalberg's decision to pair them. As the actor's daughter Leatrice Gilbert Fountain accurately summed up, "You can actually see these two terribly attractive people falling in love with each other on the screen."

It was on this film, director Brown told Kevin Brownlow, that he became aware of what made Garbo one of a kind to him. "I would take a scene with Garbo—pretty good. I would take it three or four times. It was pretty good, but I was never quite satisfied. When I saw that same scene on the screen, however, it had something that it just didn't have on the set. Garbo had something behind the eyes that you couldn't see until you photographed it in close-up. You could see thought. . . . For me, Garbo starts where they all leave off."

Garbo and Gilbert were a couple off-screen as well as on for some months, which provided a publicity and box-office coup for Mayer and Thalberg's studio, which modestly advertised them as "the most sensational pair of screen lovers the world has known" and reaped the benefits. In the exhibitor-written column "What the Picture Did for Me" in *Exhibitors Herald*, the positive response had one caveat: "Greta Garbo does splendid work," wrote a theater in Scottsboro, Georgia, "but she is a bit too hot for the elder people."

The poignant final chapters of the Garbo/Gilbert story do not play out until the sound era, but they were about to become key players in a celebrated contretemps silent film historians still disagree about. Gilbert was apparently given to asking Garbo to marry him, and she was given to refusing. But when Gilbert's friend and *Big Parade* director King Vidor was set to marry actress Eleanor Boardman on September 8, 1926, shortly before *Flesh and the Devil* was to be released, Garbo was apparently persuaded to agree to a double-ring ceremony, "apparently" being the key word.

Aside from the fact that Vidor and Boardman did wed that day in Marion Davies's Beverly Hills home, with Thalberg and Mayer among those present, there is little agreement about what else happened. Gilbert was not in Mayer's favor, having recently proclaimed to the executive that his own mother had been a whore, at which point, according to Samuel Marx, "Mayer leaped at him and knocked him down. Gilbert was lucky to get off the floor intact." In Eleanor Boardman's version of the wedding day, related to Kevin Brownlow, when Garbo did not show up, "Gilbert was getting very nervous, he was getting rather violent. It seems that Mayer was in the men's room with Gilbert and Gilbert was crying about this situation, and Mayer said, 'Sleep with her, don't marry her.' Gilbert socked him and knocked him down and he hit his head on a tile." Added Gilbert's daughter, "After Jack had knocked him down and drawn blood, Mayer said, 'I'll destroy you.'" Enticing as this story is, Irene Mayer Selznick, among others, says it did not happen and, for a variety of reasons, including Mayer's imposing physicality, could not have happened. Samuel Marx takes a middle ground, reporting that Mayer only "tried to commiserate. But Gilbert was in no mood for kind words and told the studio boss off in explicit terms that Mayer would never forget."

No matter what the cause, Gilbert was indisputably in Mayer's bad graces, not a promising place to be. As for Garbo, increasingly shrewd about contracts and money after, on the advice of Gilbert, retaining the services of his agent/business manager Harry Edington, her next step was to go on strike, an unheard-of activity in an era of increasing studio power.

Unhappy with her roles in addition to her salary, Garbo refused to report for work and Mayer refused to pay her. Her salary maxed out at $750 a week, and Edington, knowing that Gilbert was earning $10,000 per week, asked for $5,000 for Garbo. As the grosses for *Flesh and the Devil* began to mount, so did the pressure on Mayer, the studio's usually unflappable salary negotiator. After seven months, he gave in and Garbo's return was announced in a film she wanted to do, a Frances Marion–written version of Leo Tolstoy's story of passion and sacrifice, *Anna Karenina*, that was called *Love*. It's a tribute to Garbo's power even this early on that a previous version of the picture, then being shot on the MGM lot with different costars and a different director, was scrapped by Thalberg and begun anew with Gilbert as Anna's lover Count Vronsky. (Marion biographer Cari Beauchamp relates the studio wanted to call it "Heat" until Marion pointed out that "Greta Garbo in Heat" was not a good tagline.) "They were tough," Garbo told her grand-nephew Scott Reisberg. "But so was I."

As he had done previously, Mayer insisted that two endings for the story be filmed, one directly from Tolstoy, of Anna ending her life by stepping in front of a train, and a happier one of

Anna and Vronsky reunited after her husband's convenient death. Critics couldn't be bothered to object, and in fact, with few exceptions, nothing Garbo did in her seven succeeding silent films upset them. But though no one realized it, the most cataclysmic of cinematic changes was close by. A little less than two months before *Love*'s 1927 premier, Al Jolson's *The Jazz Singer* opened at New York's Warners' Theatre. Like an unwelcome guest at a lavish banquet, sound had arrived.

11

Sound Makes Some Noise

WHEN IT COMES to the advent of talking pictures, much of what we think we know about it is wrong. Maybe not everything, but a lot. But this is not a cause for despair. The movie studios themselves, even the farseeing ones that pioneered sound, initially misunderstood what its attraction was and stayed with outmoded technology longer than they should. Even MGM, on its way to becoming the industry's leader, was very late embracing the new, and this includes the ordinarily perceptive Irving Thalberg, who flatly told *Motion Picture* magazine, "I do not believe the talking motion picture will ever replace the silent drama." Taking the same tack, Garbo director and Mayer favorite Clarence Brown insisted, "There is so much money invested in present-day equipment that there is no danger of the companies throwing out everything and beginning again on a talking picture basis. Millions of dollars in investments would be worthless." With a change this epochal, confusion was par for the course.

If MGM was late off the mark where sound was concerned, and it was, there were several reasons the studio and its executives had their minds elsewhere. Thalberg, for example, had to be tracked down on his honeymoon for a reaction when Al Jolson's *The Jazz Singer* had its celebrated October 6, 1927, New York premiere. "Novelty is always welcome, but talking pictures are just a passing fad," he said, and Mayer was similarly circumspect: "Let them develop it if they can. Then we'll see about it."

Part of this prudence came from how well MGM had done with silent film in its first few years. Initially known for its elongated name ("'Metro-Goldwyn-Mayer' takes too long to say in busy Movieland, so one shortens it to M.G.M.," reported visiting writer Alice M. Williamson), the studio in its first full year of operation, from April 1924 to April 1925, made more profit ($4.7 million) than anyone but industry leader Fox. By the end of 1926, MGM had claimed the top spot, more than $6.38 million in the black, and its trade ads mirrored the youthful exuberance Mayer and Thalberg must have felt. In the July 9, 1927, *Exhibitor Herald*, the studio ran an eight-page color advertising supplement on heavy stock that emphasized its newness: "LINE UP AND SIGN UP WITH YOUNG BLOOD. The most aggressive bunch of boys in the business." No wonder that another trade, *Hollywood Vagabond*, headlined, "Will M-G-M Keep Up Its Great Pace?" or that this success created some jealousy. One journalist complained in print that Mayer spent Sunday mornings "on horseback parading through the streets of Beverly Hills, puffed up like a pouter pigeon, and inviting eyes to look at him, the handsome Prince Charming."

Also Mayer and Thalberg had more pressing worries to contend with closer at hand than jealousy or even sound. On the Labor Day weekend, just a month before *The Jazz Singer* debut, Marcus Loew, founder of Loew's theaters and the man who made the Metro-Goldwyn-Mayer merger happen, died at just fifty-seven. Born in poverty, he died a millionaire many times over at Pembroke, the thirty-five-room, forty-six-acre estate in Glen Cove on the Long Island Sound he never fully felt at home in. He was the first of the moving picture moguls to die and perhaps the most genuinely liked, and in his memory theaters nationwide both closed until 2 p.m. the day of his funeral and started their opening shows with a rendition of "Lead Kindly Light," said to be his favorite hymn since he'd first heard it at, of all places, President McKinley's funeral.

Loew had been ill with heart disease for three years, and Nicholas Schenck, the man who'd been in charge during that time, was now officially president of Loew's Inc. and MGM's boss. The division of power and influence between Schenck in New York and Mayer and Thalberg in California was to be a troubling dynamic off and on for decades. It was still an issue for Dore Schary, Mayer's successor years later, who as late as a 1959 interview compared it to "like having a chief of staff 3,000 miles removed from a battlefield." It was a recipe for discord, and discord was what everyone got.

It didn't help that Schenck, who liked to be called the General, had a manner to match. "The undisputed boss of the whole shebang" according to *Fortune*, he had, wrote John Huston, "the reputation of having blood of a hyperborean temperature. He scared people to death." Like so many of the early film executives, Schenck and his brother Joseph (who independently produced Buster Keaton and married star Norma Talmadge) had stumbled into the film business, starting when they became partners with Loew in an amusement park in 1907 and going along for the ride. While Thalberg, producer David O. Selznick pointed out, had "never been subject to the word or approval of Nicholas Schenck," the situation was different with Mayer. The pair spoke at least once a week by transcontinental phone, not the usual procedure in those days, and Schenck, said Michael Korda (whose producer uncle Alexander knew both men), was engaged in "a lifelong struggle to destroy Mayer." This antipathy was in part due, according to Dore Schary, to a radical difference in personal style: "if seriously challenged, L.B. would maul you to death—Nick would do you in with a cyanide cocktail."

This aversion notwithstanding, Mayer and Schenck shared a similar caution in sound's early days. Schenck was quoted in 1928 as feeling "the novelty of sound has upset all reason," adding in a *Film Daily* byline piece a year later that "my personal opinion is that silent film will never be eliminated." But if MGM was conservative where sound was concerned, that didn't mean they were doing nothing. As sound authority Douglas Gomery observed, the transition across the board was "a gradual *evolution* not a rapid revolution." So as dubious as Mayer and Thalberg were, they also had a can-do attitude based not only on their life experience but on their success to date. Thalberg pragmatically told associates, "We know as much about this as anybody does," and two-time Oscar-winning editor (including for the 1959 *Ben-Hur*) Ralph Winters remembered the day "Louis B. Mayer called a meeting of the editorial department."

> Gee! It wasn't that often that the big boss came around. We convened in the open space outside "cutting alley" in front of the Washington Street bathroom.
>
> "We're going to make 'talkies,'" he announced to the thirty-five editors and assistants gathered before him.
>
> This was an exciting proposition, but then he said, "How are you going to cut them?"
>
> Danny Gray got up and said, "Mr. Mayer, if you can shoot them, we can cut them."

And so it turned out to be.

That transition happened quite rapidly. In 1927, only 157 theaters had sound capacity, but by the end of 1929 the total had risen to more than 5,200, with theatrical attendance more than doubling during that span. Mayer and Thalberg may have moved slowly at MGM, but parent company Loew's, by contrast, fully wired its theaters before most of its competitors.

Thalberg, already interested in New York theater, was soon importing folks who knew their way around spoken dialogue, including writers as well as actors and directors from the Broadway stage. As the veteran Lenore Coffee put it, "A silent film was like writing a novel, and a script for a talking picture was like writing a play." A voice teacher brought over from Italy had so much importance that Mayer went to the train station personally to meet him. The search for an in-house sound guru, however, ended closer to home. Much closer to home.

Douglas Shearer, Thalberg's brother-in-law, a machinist by trade with a strong interest in engineering, had come to Hollywood to visit his sister and gotten involved working on odds and ends with MGM, including putting radio broadcast sound into theaters. Eddie Mannix, the studio's general manager, knew about these experiments, and as Shearer remembered it, "When sound came in, Mannix said, 'We've got a fellow down here in the special-effects department who does camerawork and trick stuff. Why not throw the sound problem in his lap?' Overnight I was the one-man sound department. They ordered me to do the job, they didn't just give it to me. . . . At any rate I had to learn a whole lot about electronics." Shearer learned enough to work on some fourteen hundred pictures, winning twelve Oscars during his forty-one years at the studio.

As a stopgap measure until the first dialogue films came out, MGM, like other studios, oversaw a synchronized musical score and a soundtrack for a film that had been shot silent. This was 1928's *White Shadows in the South Seas*, a part-travelogue, part-morality-play potboiler about the pernicious influence the greed of white exploiters has on a previously unspoiled Tahitian island. As much as anything else, *White Shadows* is also remembered as the first time studio symbol Leo the Lion was heard as well as seen: one short roar followed by two long ones shattering the silence.

White Shadows is also known as the first of multiple turning points in the complex and consequential relationship between David O. Selznick (future husband of Irene Mayer but for now son to Louis J. Selznick, one of Mayer's most implacable rivals) and MGM. Even though Mayer held an ancient grudge against David's producing pioneer father and had decreed, Irene Mayer Selznick relates, that "no Selznick could work in the studio, nor could one even cross the threshold," the young man, as was to become his pattern, was nothing daunted by obstacles. A few years earlier, he'd done Nicholas Schenck a good turn, and when the Loew's head was in town, Selznick asked in person for a two-week trial and, Mayer's previous objections notwithstanding, was hired on the spot.

Selznick, the future producer of *Gone With the Wind*, even then had his trademark energy and feel for story and soon worked himself up to a position where he supervised MGM's inexpensive Western programmers starring Colonel Tim McCoy. Not only that, Irene Mayer Selznick recalled, "by taking along on location a different script, another leading lady, and a few extra actors, he turned out two Westerns for slightly more than the cost of one. He was on his way." There were, however, bumps in the road.

Assigned to work on *White Shadows*, he got into a dispute with supervisor Hunt Stromberg, who was producing under Thalberg, about the direction the as-yet-unmade film was going to take. "So I went to see Thalberg," Selznick remembered years later, and had "a very acrimonious discussion in which Thalberg agreed with Stromberg. I told Thalberg in the rather strong language of youth that he didn't know what he was talking about, and I was fired. He gave me a chance to apologize for having disagreed with him, which I refused to do, and I was out of a job." Thalberg, typically, remained on good terms with Selznick and his ideas, letting him go simply because from an executive point of view he believed, "We must have authority here." Selznick was promptly hired by Paramount and went on to take charge of production at RKO, where he backed *King Kong* and was the first to sign Fred Astaire and Katharine Hepburn, but his dealings with Thalberg and Mayer were far from over.

While all this was going on, MGM, like other studios, was building sound stages as quickly as it could, altering the country-club face of the landscape. By August 1928, work everywhere was so extensive that the *Los Angeles Times*, under the headline "Studios Spend Millions In Talkie Construction," visited several lots, including MGM, where it poetically observed, "Silent drama is about to be silenced forever." Being built at the Culver City location were structures almost frighteningly massive. "Four hundred tons of structural steel, more than 1200 cubic yards of concrete, doors that weigh more than two tons each, and apparatus so delicate that it can register the footsteps of a fly—these are some of the things that go into giving a voice to the movies at that studio."

The next question was what kind of sound films were going to be made on these stages, what did this newly ravenous public want? Following on *The Jazz Singer*'s lead, and because song and dance were entertaining in and of themselves, musicals were high on Mayer and Thalberg's list, and MGM managed to leapfrog its rivals, filming what is often considered the very first Hollywood musical, *The Broadway Melody*. Released in early 1929 and promoted as "All Talking! All Singing! All Dancing!," it got excellent reviews and went on to win that year's best-picture Oscar.

Conscious of not exactly being a sound pioneer, MGM had made a virtue of necessity, boasting in the film's souvenir program of "months of painstaking preparation under expert supervision" undertaken because "the futility of a 'haste-makes-waste' policy was recognized at the start." As Mayer had written in a memo to Thalberg, and clearly believed, "What matters is that M-G-M becomes identified with the quality talking picture!"

It was Thalberg's idea to make a musical of Edmund Goulding's story of vaudevillian sisters Bessie Love and Anita Page coming to New York looking for their big break and having a charismatic songwriter (stage actor Charles King) come between them. Thalberg hired another writer, James Gleason, to pep up the dialogue with hip Broadway slang (the program helpfully provides a glossary) and took on the untried song-writing team of Nacio Herb Brown and Arthur Freed (in later years the head of MGM's powerhouse musical Freed Unit). They rewarded him with classics like "You Were Meant for Me" and "Broadway Melody" ("A million lights, they flicker there,/A million hearts beat quicker there"). When Florenz Ziegfeld usurped the story's original title, "Whoopee," Thalberg named the project after one of their songs. "I remember he visited the set every day," Page recalled, "something he never did with other pictures."

Page also remembers the difficulty of figuring out how to make sound films as they went along. Sometimes necessity led to innovation: when Thalberg asked for reshoots of the "Wedding of the Painted Doll" dance number he considered too static, sound man Douglas Shearer suggested, "We've got a perfectly good recording of the music. Why not just play the record and have the dancers go through the number? Then we can combine the film and the sound track in the lab." Thalberg thought it was worth trying, and, with exceptions, musicals have used that system ever since.

Most fascinating from a modern point of view was the contemporary worry whether audiences would accept the sudden appearance of music without a visible source, for instance when the stars broke into song in a hotel room. Thalberg addressed that very issue when he admitted in a speech, "We were aware of the possibility that the playing of an orchestra in connection with a scene where no orchestra was present might shock the audience. We observed the reactions of the first audiences with interest and were prepared, if necessary, to recall the picture." This proved unnecessary because, as Thalberg well knew, "Entertain them and they will not be critical of details of technique." These were words he would live by his entire career.

Following up quickly on the success of *Broadway Melody*, Mayer and Thalberg put out *The Hollywood Review of 1929*, more or less a straight variety show in which many of the people the studio employed did a range of bits. The film was notable for the debut of the Nacio Herb Brown/Arthur Freed "Singin' in the Rain" and for its promotion as democratizing access to top musical talent. "A front seat at a Broadway review," the printed program boasted, "is no longer just a fantastic hope for the small-town dweller."

Since sound was brand new, *Hollywood Review* was the first time audiences heard MGM's top stars speak, and some of them were quite nervous at the prospect. Joan Crawford breezed through both a song and a rousing Charleston and seemed not to have a care in the world, but she did say later, "In 1929 everybody panicked at Metro, but I mean everybody—stars, producers, directors—everybody but starlets. Starlets didn't know enough to be scared."

Marion Davies was in a particularly precarious position. She stuttered in real life, so much so that she cried when she saw *The Jazz Singer*. Not out of any empathy with the protagonist's plight but because "when I heard the voice of Al Jolson, I thought, No. This can't be. There can't be talkies. I'm ruined. I'm wrecked." Thalberg, often sensitive to talent anxiety, had Davies take a screen test in which, much to everyone's amazement, she ad-libbed her way through without stuttering. She handled her number in "Hollywood Review" flawlessly and years later she wrote to Robert Ripley of "Ripley's Believe It or Not" that she had stuttered all her life, but once talking pictures came in "I stopped stuttering—I suppose because I had to."

Most interesting from a film history point of view is *Hollywood Review*'s two-strip Technicolor pairing of two of MGM's biggest stars, each with a connection to Thalberg: his wife Norma Shearer and his former "Three Jacks" fellow carouser John Gilbert. They were teamed doing two versions of the balcony scene from *Romeo and Juliet*: the way Shakespeare wrote it and, in response to a fictious studio directive, in slangy modern language. (Though you have to listen closely to catch it, there is a joking reference to "Uncle Irving" in their banter.) Both actors' vocal performances were as they should be, but their very different journeys through the perils of the transition to sound were just beginning.

Norma Shearer provides an example of a career path the coming of sound put a damper on: she became a major star without spending any time on stage. The experiences that theatrical performers, even amateur and collegiate ones, took for granted—the ability to memorize lines, to use voice as a key to creating character—she had done without. With that kind of a handicap, could she make the leap to sound stardom? Despite her inside track to Thalberg, Shearer, being a striver and a perfectionist, worried as much as anyone.

In fact, never one to shirk a task, Shearer had seen to it that she appeared in MGM's first all-talking dramatic film, released three months before *Hollywood Review*. *The Trial of Mary Dugan*, written and directed by Bayard Veiller, was adapted from Veiller's play, something of a popular sensation at the time.

Along with musicals, courtroom dramas were a popular source of early sound films because all information is neatly imparted via dialogue, and having most of the action in a single set simplified recording. Shearer and Thalberg had enjoyed the play in New York, and once MGM purchased it at his suggestion, the actress reports in her memoir seeing the author "crossing the lot one day and told him how much I admired his play and would he give me a chance to read the part for him."

It's safe to say that neither Thalberg nor anyone else thought the elegant Shearer was the best choice to play a chorus girl accused of murdering the millionaire whose mistress she had been. According to Veiller, whose charming autobiography *The Fun I've Had* deals with the situation in some detail, the main thing on the ever-pragmatic Thalberg's mind was "his fear for his wife. . . . He wanted me to be very sure she was the woman for it. . . . Irving said to me, 'Go on, talk to Norma about it. She wants to play it. If you want her to play it, you can have her. That's up to you.' Then he looked at me with that funny little twisted grin of his and said, 'You can have stage No. 23 for your rehearsal.'"

Writer/director and actress met at the stage and Veiller immediately saw that Shearer "was pretty badly frightened." They went right into a scene, "and there in front of my eyes on that awful empty stage grew into being a girl on trial for her life, frightened, fighting and distraught—exactly what I wanted. So after four or five minutes of this I said, 'Come on, let's go back,'" at which point a remarkable scene, rich in insecurity and misunderstanding, occurred.

> Together we went back to Thalberg's office. Norma wouldn't speak to me—not a word could I get out of her on the way back. She burst into her husband's office. I followed her. Norma was mad.
>
> The minute she saw her husband she said: "Irving, it isn't fair. I haven't had a fair chance with Bayard—just one speech, that's all he'd let me say. I think I ought to have another chance at it."
>
> I don't suppose anyone in the world was more surprised than I was. Irving looked at me and said: "Don't you like her? You don't have to have her, I've told you that."
>
> I said: "Irving, somebody's gone stark, raving crazy and

it isn't me. Norma has given me exactly what I wanted. I don't know any moving-picture actress who can approach her in the part."

"Well I'll be damned!" said Norma. "I thought you didn't like me."

Veiller had immediately realized that because "Norma was playing her first starring part in a 'talkie,' failure would have been a terrible thing for her," and he came to understand intuitively the best way to direct the type of instinctive actors the movies often turned into stars. "She was extremely easy to direct, once I realized she couldn't be coached," he wrote. "I soon discovered that the way to get results from her was to leave her alone. The other members of the company I rehearsed time after time, hour after hour, to get their timing right, to get their readings right. But I didn't do anything of the sort with Norma. She went through the scene once, possibly twice, and then she played it with great reality and great power and great honesty. But she wasn't acting—that was the trick—she was living it, she wasn't acting it." Much of Shearer's acting turned out to be silent, sitting at the defense table reacting to other witnesses, but when she took the stand in her own defense, wrote the *New York Times'* Mordaunt Hall, "she reveals herself quite able to meet the requirements of that temperamental device—the microphone."

The sound trajectory of John Gilbert, Shearer's MGM partner in that *Romeo and Juliet* snippet, is both sadder and more complex than her career. Why his robust livelihood went south the way it did is one of the silent era's eternally vexing questions, probably because the reasons for it were multiple and involved his fractious relationship with Mayer. The fact that he became the poster boy for stars who could not transition to sound is as unfortunate in its own way as Marion Davies's being unjustly pilloried in *Citizen Kane*.

Even as late as 1928, when Mayer and Thalberg were trying to figure out whether sound was a fad, Gilbert could accu-

rately tell the *Kansas City Star,* "I'm sitting on top of the heap.
. . . Right now, I'm the public's favorite dish." Still, as the star of
The Big Parade and the lover of Garbo presciently acknowledged
in the same interview, "every actor carries the nightmare of becoming a 'has been' in the back of his head." Given that, Gilbert
must have been gratified when his agent Harry Edington, whom
he'd recommended to Garbo, concluded an unprecedented contract for him with MGM. The star was to be paid $250,000 per
picture with a two-films-per-year guarantee over three years,
making for a whopping $1.5 million in all. The contract was
worked out not with Mayer, who took pride in his negotiating skills, but with newly installed Loew's president Nicholas
Schenck (who, it shall be seen, had his own corporate reasons
for agreeing to the terms), which turned out to be a mixed
blessing. Whether Gilbert did or didn't knock Mayer down at
King Vidor's wedding, the actor was already on the studio head's
enemies list, and going around him to Schenck, while it may
have been sound business, earned Gilbert Mayer's unbridled
enmity, never a good thing.

All this came to a head with MGM's 1929 release of Gilbert's first talking feature, *His Glorious Night.* Even though it
ended up "a modest boxoffice success," anecdotal evidence was
widespread that audiences laughed at the star's usual Great Lover
performance. Was a subpar voice the problem or was it something else?

Heard today, Gilbert's voice in that film, while not exactly
glorious, sounds perfectly acceptable. His daughter and biographer Leatrice Gilbert Fountain compares it to David Niven, "a
rather light baritone" and historian Donald Crafton, after re-
viewing most of Gilbert's ten talkies, describes a voice that is
"intelligent, appropriate for his physical stature." Though there
are dark theories that Mayer had technicians sabotage the recording devices or leaned on director Lionel Barrymore to mess
things up ("I watched Jack Gilbert being destroyed on the sound

stage by one man, Lionel Barrymore," costar and future columnist Hedda Hopper dramatically claimed), reality is more
nuanced.

The heart of Gilbert's problem was that sound changed more
about the movies than was initially realized. Both the largeness
of the actor's melodramatic acting style and the over-the-top
nature of his dialogue ("Oh, beauteous maiden, my arms are waiting to enfold you. I love you. I love you. I love you") though
acceptable via intertitles in the silent world, came off as florid,
out of date, and, yes, risible when actually heard in a theater.
Explained actress Colleen Moore, that kind of intimate spoken
language "disconcerted and embarrassed all the women in the
audience. . . . In their embarrassment they giggled." Added director King Vidor, "The literal content of his scenes, which in
silent films had been imagined, was too intense to be put into
spoken words."

Whatever the reason, public displeasure with a star of this
magnitude was big news in Hollywood. Samuel Marx remembers that the same October 30, 1929, issue of *Variety* that reported the stock market crash with the celebrated banner "Wall
Street Lays an Egg" also had a headline reading "Audiences
Laughing at Gilbert." With a studio united behind him, Gilbert
might have weathered this storm, but this was not the case. Irene
Mayer Selznick, for one, remembers her father bringing home
the bad reviews and gleefully announcing to the family, "That
should take care of Mr. Gilbert."

For Thalberg, long a friend, the situation was more complicated. A series of sound roles were offered Gilbert and accepted, and though contemporary critics thought he was im-
proving ("At last he has mastered the talkies idiom," wrote one),
the public humiliation had taken some of the essential vitality
out of the man. "He was like mercury," King Vidor told Kevin
Brownlow. "Touch him and he vanished." Though Thalberg had
hoped to cast Gilbert in both *Grand Hotel* and *Red Dust*, the ex-

ecutive was always attuned to public reaction. In a crisis he often put business considerations first, and with Gilbert's broken spirit likely to affect those films, the roles went instead to John Barrymore and Clark Gable. Even Norma Shearer wasn't sure what had gone wrong. "Irving was known for salvaging careers," she wrote. "The renaissance of personalities was his specialty. He held out his frail hand to many, and many found strength in it, but not Jack Gilbert." There was, as it turned out, one more bright moment to come, but it was not enough.

Though they had little else in common aside from strong relationships with Thalberg, two of MGM's most significant stars ended up dealing with the transition to sound the same way: they waited. Both Lon Chaney and Greta Garbo, confident in their theatrical backgrounds, had enough clout to escape being rushed to appear in *The Hollywood Review of 1929* or anything else. With popular yet quite specific silent personas, they had the assurance to hang back and, with Thalberg and Mayer's acquiescence, avoid being stampeded into roles that didn't suit them. As Mayer reportedly said when the actress's sound prospects were raised, "Maybe I'll never win a fortune at the race track but that won't keep me from betting. I'll take a chance on Garbo."

Several factors played into Garbo's being the next to last MGM star to turn to sound. She needed more time to improve her English, and Thalberg pursued George Bernard Shaw's *St. Joan* as a vehicle for her until Shaw decided he was not interested in selling. Thalberg's eventual pick, an adaptation of Eugene O'Neill's *Anna Christie*, written by Frances Marion and directed by *Flesh and the Devil*'s Clarence Brown, was a shrewd choice for several reasons. As a Pulitzer Prize winner, it was a prestige item; a 1923 silent version had proven its viability as a film project; and, with a protagonist who was Swedish-American, it was ideal for Garbo's accented English.

The story of a former prostitute who reconciles with her father and finds love with a castaway, *Anna Christie* was essentially a chamber drama, and two of the roles, Anna's alcoholic drinking pal Marthy and her sailor beau Matt Burke, were problematic and involved some Thalberg intervention.

Screenwriter Marion was a longtime close friend of Marie Dressler, a veteran comedienne from the earliest days of silent films. How Marion had masterminded her friend's return to Hollywood is a story for a later chapter, but Marion thought Dressler would be ideal for a rare dramatic role as *Anna Christie*'s Marthy. Director Brown was resistant, but a screen test convinced him, and he in turn convinced Thalberg. The consequences for both Dressler and MGM were to be considerable.

For the key role of Matt, Charles Bickford was cast, but the iconoclastic actor, who'd just made a film with Cecil B. DeMille, was a difficult fit for the increasingly regimented studio system. As noted, Bickford related in his autobiography, *Bulls, Balls, Bicycles, and Actors*, he had reservations about costarring with Garbo, and had no difficulty telling Thalberg what was on his mind. "He was genuinely surprised by my attitude," the actor remembered, before providing a concise, candid glimpse of the producer at his most convincing. "Nor did Thalberg press the point. He was too clever for that. Instead, he readily admitted that the role was a supporting one; then proceeded quietly to brief me on the importance of the picture to MGM—the eminence of Garbo as a star, the extensive advertising campaign planned to exploit the world-shaking revelation that Garbo could talk, and finally, the undeniable fact that the picture would expose me to millions of Garbo fans throughout the world thereby materially aiding the studio to create the following necessary before I could be rated as an important motion-picture star." Almost against his better judgement, Bickford found himself persuaded.

In contrast to many of her silent roles, Garbo doesn't even

enter the film until a quarter of an hour in, and her direct-from-the-play first line ("Gimme a whiskey—ginger ale on the side. And don't be stingy, baby") has become a classic. But it wasn't her lines that mattered in *Anna Christie*, it was how Garbo said them, and in this she was given high marks. A few professionals like George Cukor felt "her voice wasn't flexible at all. . . . She wasn't in command of it," but most reviewers followed the lead of the *New York Herald Tribune*'s Richard Watts Jr., who raved that Garbo's voice is "revealed as a deep, husky, throaty contralto" that perfectly complemented "the outstanding actress of the motion picture world." Thalberg's plan had paid off.

Anna Christie's success was helped by one of the most famous taglines in film history. Credit, relates journalist Beth Day, should go to marketer Frank Whitbeck, who, at the end of a long session with Thalberg,

> picked up a used envelope from Thalberg's desk, sketched on the back of it the proportions of a 24-sheet billboard, six blocks long and four blocks high, then penciled in a couple of words and handed it to the producer.
>
> Thalberg stared at the envelope. In the billboard space indicated by the lines were just two words in king-size lettering:
>
> GARBO TALKS
>
> "That's it!" Thalberg cried, slapping Frank's shoulder in approval. "Now get the hell out of here!"

That line had exceptionally wide circulation. Just how widely it penetrated is demonstrated by an anecdote told by longtime MGM costume designer Adrian. During a long session in which he described a particular Garbo outfit in detail, the actress had remained silent. Finally, "she just said, 'Yes.' And then with a look of surprise, she said 'Garbo talks!' " (Known for a deadpan sense of humor, the actress reportedly said to marketer Whitbeck when they were introduced, "Aren't you ashamed?")

As for Chaney, whose 1930 talkie debut came a few months

after Garbo's, an additional complication was that he was negotiating a new contract with MGM specifically for sound pictures. To read the back-and-forth between the actor's attorneys and Mayer as detailed by Michael Blake is to feel how enthusiastically Mayer threw himself into the minutia of dealmaking. This was not a chore; this was what he lived for. Things got so convoluted that Thalberg, whose relationship with Chaney went back to their Universal days, made a rare contract talks appearance, presumably with Mayer's approval, and ironed out the differences.

For Chaney's sound debut Thalberg decided on a remake of one of Chaney's silent hits, *The Unholy Three*, in which the actor played Echo, the ventriloquist ringleader of a trio of con men. The plot allowed Chaney to speak in not just his voice but also as the ventriloquist's dummy, an elderly woman named Mrs. O'Grady, a parrot, and a girl in a sideshow audience. Sensing a publicity opportunity, the studio had the actor sign a notarized affidavit that all five voices were his. Having road-tested the campaign with Garbo, MGM unhesitatingly promoted the film in posters and ads with "Lon Chaney Talks!"

The vibrant sound career everyone expected for the actor, however, did not materialize. Though it had been kept secret, Chaney had been ill for some time. When the public was finally told he had anemia, writer Adela Rogers St. John remembered that "outside Metro's grilled gates stood long lines of workingmen, many of them still in their overalls, stagehands in whose union Lon Chaney still carried his card, carpenters, grips, electricians, grim and silent, came to offer their blood." On August 26, 1930, the actor died at age forty-seven of a pulmonary hemorrhage brought on by bronchial cancer. Mayer sent out a memo asking for "a period of silence" on the lot to coincide with the burial service. Fated though he was to die young, Thalberg was not to be spared the pain of close colleagues who passed on before he did.

12

◆·◆·◆

Threats and Opportunities

It's DIFFICULT TO overstate how completely the change from silent to sound upended behavior and expectations all across the Hollywood spectrum. It was especially disorienting because, as film royalty Mary Pickford put it, "It would have been more logical if silent pictures had grown out of the talking instead of the other way around." Initially, like a dark power suddenly liberated and run amok, this atmosphere of uncertainty fostered across-the-board opportunities for chaos that Mayer and Thalberg were forced to deal with, crises of various types that they labored to both counter and turn to their advantage.

One situation both men considered a threat had a response with a surprisingly vibrant afterlife. Paralleling the time sound came in, moves were being made by the Actors Equity Association and IATSE (International Alliance of Theatrical Stage Employees) to organize actors and film technicians, respectively. Always an enemy of unions and not averse to some industry self-promotion, Mayer, according to Nancy Lynn Schwartz's *The Hollywood Writers' Wars*, looked up from playing solitaire at his Santa Monica beach house to encourage guests who were discussing the formation of an industry-wide organization and said, "Why don't you get together, then, and try it out."

The result in short order was the formation in 1927 of the Academy of Motion Picture Arts and Sciences, which at its founding had but five branches: actors, directors, producers, technicians, and writers. Yes, the organization gave out awards, soon to be called Oscars, and was officially intended to be geared toward "development of artistry and effective quality." But it was also intended to arbitrate disputes, in effect to become a company union that could forestall the entrance of more aggressive entities, which it did successfully until the Depression changed the economic equation. Sometimes one aspect of the Academy reinforced the other, as Mayer himself admitted in a posthumously published interview tinged with the bitterness of being out of power. Asked how he controlled a studio full of talent he said, "I found the best way to handle them was to hang medals all over them. If I got them cups and awards they'll kill themselves to produce what I wanted. That's why the Academy Award was created. Creative brains will do anything to win that little gold Oscar."

The most existential and unexpected threat Mayer and Thalberg faced came from fellow founding mogul William Fox, yet another ambitious child of penniless immigrants, the man who started the Fox studio and who in early 1929 consummated a coup that one of the Hollywood trades called "the biggest deal in motion picture history." Or so he thought.

Motivated to grow his studio into the undisputed largest in the world, Fox had heard that the family of the late Marcus Loew, founder of MGM's parent company Loew's Inc., was interested in getting out of the business and was willing to sell its stock if the profit was right. Under the code of strictest secrecy, Fox enlisted the help of Nicholas Schenck, Marcus Loew's successor, and what resulted was a $50 million deal for 400,000 shares of Loew's stock, the $125 share price being considerably more than the going rate. Though still a relatively young studio, MGM was well enough established that a takeover of this sort was, as Bosley Crowther put it, "almost as hard to imagine as that the United States should fall into the hands of Mexico."

Though the deal caused universal shock when it was announced on March 3, 1929, Crowther further believed that "probably the most amazed men in the whole amazed motion picture world" were Mayer, Thalberg, and their attorney J. Robert Rubin, all of whom had been kept completely in the dark. Amazement turned to anger when the trio realized that Schenck had managed to maneuver the transaction so that he ended up with a bonus estimated at between $8 million and $10 million.

The agreement certainly looked ironclad, with Fox going to the trouble of getting a clean bill of health from Washington about potential antitrust violations, but a triple whammy of events derailed it. The first was a serious July 17 automobile accident when the chauffeured green Rolls-Royce that was taking Fox to a golf game with Schenck and Paramount head Adolph Zukor was hit by another car and spun into a ditch. The chauffeur was killed, and Fox was so seriously injured that he was incapacitated for months.

Event two was Black Thursday, October 24, 1929, the start of a tumultuous stock market crash that left Fox extremely vulnerable financially. Finally, newly elected president Herbert Hoover turned out to have different feelings about the merger than his predecessor, and when his Department of Justice filed an antitrust suit against the deal, that was the end of the line. It's likely that Mayer, who had become close to the new president, had a hand in this change, but Fox preferred to see the situation in more cosmic terms: "I think," he told biographer Upton Sinclair, "the thing that plays the greatest pranks in our lives is Fate."

The Fox takeover threat may have been stopped, but its implications lingered, some for decades. The relationship between Mayer and Thalberg on the West Coast and Schenck on the East, never very good, now curdled into permanent distrust. And though their mutual sense of aggrievement initially brought Mayer and Thalberg closer, it amplified the financial issues that contributed to their eventual split.

By an unfortunate coincidence, Thalberg in 1929 had specific needs for a cash influx. For one thing, unlike Mayer, who believed in the value of real estate, Thalberg invested heavily in the stock market and took a substantial hit in the crash. Almost simultaneously, he found himself the subject of an IRS investigation for fraud because of, among other things, stock transfers he had made to his mother. "He was informed that if he was judged guilty, it would result in a jail sentence," his friend Samuel Marx reported. "The matter hung like a dark cloud over him."

Much as he was unwilling to do so, Thalberg turned to Mayer for help and the studio head, whose Washington contacts had helped terminate the Fox merger, was able to mitigate the charges. But a $100,000 penalty remained, which is probably the reason Thalberg took a $250,000 peace offering from Schenck for keeping him in the dark about the Fox deal. That payment led to an especially revelatory comment from Eddie Mannix, one of MGM's top executives. When Thalberg left for New York to confront Schenck, he told his team, "Whatever I get, I'll split with you fellows." Even though he returned with that quarter of a million, Mannix recalled, "we never saw a dime," and reminding Thalberg of his promise was not in the cards. As Mannix explained to Samuel Marx, "'What would that accomplish? After all, it wasn't something that would simply slip his mind. Irving was a sweet guy, but he could piss ice water.'"

Beyond this cash payment, Thalberg also felt he deserved a bigger percentage of the studio's profits than he was getting. Yes, the possibility of a family loomed ever larger now that he was married, but as always to Thalberg money was the proof that his work was valued. So, in 1930, a new deal was negotiated that give him a greater share of the studio's profits. Stating unequivocally that "his value was incalculable," Irene Mayer Selznick says she personally "found Irving's demands understandable. No one else was a saint about money; there was no reason for him to be." But she also noted "my father yielded repeatedly, if unhappily, by whittling down his share of the profits in Irving's behalf. It was never enough." Compensation continued to be a bone of contention between the two men that even the passage of time and Thalberg's death did not temper. As late as 1948, in the midst of hiring Dore Schary to be MGM's executive vice president in charge of production, Mayer talked to the new man about "his inability to work with Thalberg, who 'believe me, was a genius but he was money mad. That was his problem. Money—money—that ruined him.'"

As long as film has existed, the movies and morality have gotten on each other's nerves. During the silent era, state and local censorship boards multiplied, and in an attempt to keep regulation in house the studios formed the Motion Picture Producers and Distributors of America and brought in rock-ribbed conservative Republican Will Hays to run it.

Though Thalberg was an opponent of censorship, preferring to let audiences decide what was too much, he chose to take an active role in the process, heading an industry committee that drew up 1927 guidelines colorfully entitled "Don'ts and Be Carefuls," which were "a codification of the most common city, state and foreign rules for elimination." The Don'ts, for example, included "profanity, white slavery, sex hygiene, sex perversion," while the "Be Carefuls" included "crime methods, rape, and wedding-night scenes which were to be handled with special care."

The arrival of sound amplified these battles, so to speak, as what audiences could hear became a critical factor. Not one to shirk responsibility or onerous work, Thalberg then chaired another committee which produced a revised, stricter Production Code in 1930. This was laxly enforced until Joseph Breen took over the revamped Production Code Administration in 1934, ending four years of racy, boundary-pushing films known generically today as pre-Code.

For the entirety of his time at MGM until his death in 1936, Thalberg was the studio's point person in dealing with the various iterations of the Code. Thalberg probably took this on because he was good at it, understanding how the game was played and willing to fuss over tiny details in an almost Talmudic fashion. As one of his frequent Code adversaries, Jason Joy, wrote in reluctant off-the-record admiration, Thalberg "rarely fails to catch the fine line of distinction." In one memorable situation, related in a letter from Code executive Lamar Trotti to Hays, he and Thalberg "went into a session which lasted literally far into the night while my wife and his wife sat outside in the anteroom and starved. Thalberg, of course, is a man of persuasive powers and he used the usual high pressure salesmanship methods on me."

Thalberg was persuasive because he both believed what he said and had the goal of final approval always before him. He was willing to give up lines of dialogue like "losing a mistress is a private misfortune" in 1931's Joan Crawford/Clark Gable *Possessed*, a film the Code eventually approved but had initial misgivings about, as an unsigned internal memo reveals: "We were considerably worried about this picture which deals with a kept-woman, and so expressed that view to Mr. Thalberg. It is his belief that this theme is usable when handled in good taste, which it unquestionably is in this picture which hasn't any sex scenes in it."

The MGM actress who gave the Code the most difficulty, fully as much as the risqué Mae West did over at Paramount, was a young woman who'd been a classmate of Irene Mayer Selznick's at the tony Hollywood School for Girls. Someone of whom Mayer's daughter remembered, "There was something spectacular about her even in the school uniform, which was seductive only on her." She was Harlean Carpenter at the time, but the movies knew her as Jean Harlow.

Harlow as a presence remains alive in popular culture decades after her shockingly early death of kidney failure at age twenty-six in 1937. Partly this is because of her beauty, especially "platinum blonde" hair, an expression reportedly coined by a publicist for her. Partly it was the air of relaxed, natural, unapologetic sexuality her characters projected. But it was also a quality director George Cukor noticed, "a tough girl yet very feminine, like Mae West. They both wisecrack, but they have something vulnerable, and it makes them attractive. Jean Harlow was very soft about her toughness."

Initially uninterested in the movies but controlled by an ambitious mother who was, Harlow was what one fan magazine called "The One Star Who Has No Enemies." Myrna Loy echoes the consensus that off-screen the young actress was "far from the raucous sexpot of her films," and the keen Howard Dietz pegged her as "an unpretentious personality who wore her success casually."

All this was far in the future in 1929 when Howard Hughes cast Harlow as a free-spirited young woman involved with two brothers in *Hell's Angels*. But how did someone whose career hadn't thrived as expected after that moment and whose screen personality did not radiate family wholesomeness end up at a studio where that was becoming the reigning philosophy?

Given that Harlow became a major star for them, it's surprising that it's unclear whether Thalberg or Mayer was the prime mover in MGM's buying her contract from Hughes for $60,000. The likeliest instigator was another man, Paul Bern. Bern was a top MGM executive and one of Thalberg's most

The power and the glory. Mayer the patriarchal studio chief
with one of MGM's most glamorous stars, Jean Harlow, in 1933.
(Bettmann/Getty Images)

trusted associates who often offered friendship to actresses and
others who felt adrift. Irene Mayer Selznick, for one, considered
him "probably the single most beloved figure in Hollywood."
He was steadfastly in Harlow's corner and when a project named
Red-Headed Woman materialized, it's likely he saw to it that the
actress was considered.

The 1932 film was a sensation before, during, and after its
filming. Though it almost didn't get made, it ended up catapult-
ing Harlow to stardom and creating a moralistic outcry that
led eventually to a strengthened Production Code ensuring that
that kind of material was headed out of style, something neither
Thalberg nor even Mayer wanted.

Based on a *Saturday Evening Post*–serialized novel by Katharine Brush, *Red-Headed Woman* was purchased by MGM before
Brush had even figured out the ending. That didn't stop Thalberg and story editor Samuel Marx from assigning it to F. Scott
Fitzgerald, who had been gone from Hollywood for five years.

This was not fated to be a triumphal return, however, as Fitzgerald, for a variety of reasons, probably including nervousness and a disappointing collaborator, attempted, as Thalberg claimed to screenwriter Anita Loos, "to turn the silly book into a tone poem."

It is possibly Fitzgerald's work that Production Code executive Jason Joy was referring to when he wrote to his boss Will Hays that the script was "utterly impossible in every way. In fact, I think it is the worst script I have ever read, both in major theme and in details." What stoked Joy's ire was the journey of title character Lil "Red" Andrews, a self-aware and determined young woman whose motto is "When I kiss them, they stay kissed for a long time." Lil embarks on a string of seductions that move her up the social ladder at a remarkable clip, but the film's consequence-free ending was especially problematic. Though he thought the chances of achieving this were slim, Joy allowed that "if they get into it a feeling of satire and make the girl a gold-digger rather than an out-and-out strumpet, it may be all right." Which was precisely what Thalberg set out to do.

Thalberg's first tactic was to change screenwriters, replacing Fitzgerald with Loos, whose writing career was nearly as old as the movies themselves. She was still a teenager when D. W. Griffith hired her in 1912, and though she had been away from screenwriting since the silent days, her reputation as the author of the insouciant *Gentlemen Prefer Blondes* made her just the person Thalberg was looking for to "make fun of its sex elements." She in turn became one of many writers who enjoyed working with the executive. "One always wrote *with* him," she explained to John Kobal. "You would take your material in and go over it with him and his suggestions always became part of the script." One of the things Loos learned was that "to Irving Thalberg every film had to be a love story. It wasn't at all necessary for the affair to concern people of the opposite sex. . . . Irving could spot sublimated sex in any human relationship." In this case, once

Thalberg hit upon the notion that in this particular story "our heroine must be deeply in love with herself," everything fell into place for Loos.

Tactic two was to cast the notoriously blonde Harlow, who'd been thought of as a dramatic actress, as the comedic redhead Lil. Though so many MGM actresses auditioned for the part that a gag publicity photo was snapped of sixty-something Marie Dressler in a red wig, both Thalberg and Loos were taken with Harlow after a meeting that Loos recounts.

> "Do you think you can make an audience laugh," asked Irving.
>
> "*With* me or *at* me?"
>
> "*At* you!"
>
> "Why not? People have been laughing at me all my life."

The final tactic was convincing audiences and Production Code executives that *Red-Headed Woman* was being played for laughs. After a tepid preview in Glendale, Thalberg, as was invariably the case, knew what the problem was. He told Loos, "I'd like you to contrive a prologue which will tip the audience off that the movie's a comedy." What resulted was a pair of quick takes—Harlow looking at a mirror and chortling, "So gentlemen prefer blondes, do they?" followed by her announcing to a shocked saleswoman that she would be buying a see-through skirt. Message delivered, and not only to the audience. "In the cold projection room," Jason Joy wrote to his boss, "it seemed to be entirely contrary to the Code. . . . However, when seeing it with an audience, it took on an entirely different flavor. So farcical did it seem that I was convinced that it was not contrary to the Code." Though he passed the film for release, Joy added an anguished afterthought: "My chief worry is not whether this picture is just over the line or under the line but because it is too close to the line. . . . It and several other pictures will serve to force a new understanding of our purpose."

Joy's worry proved to be prophetic. Moralists were outraged by the film, the head of the Atlanta board of censors, for instance, announcing, "We have been working for years for clean decent pictures, and here in 1932 we have THIS. . . . Sex! Sex! Sex! The picture just reeks with it until one is positively nauseated." Other studios, as Joy predicted, put out incendiary films of their own, and MGM itself followed up with another gleeful Harlow provocation, *Red Dust*, the same year. But the handwriting was on the wall for pre-Code movies, and when Joseph Breen took over the strengthened Production Code Administration in 1934, one of his first acts was to ban rereleases of *Red-Headed Woman*. The next glimpse U.S. audiences got of it in any form was when it was released for home viewing in 1988, its place in film history by then secured.

13

New Beginnings

WHEN WE THINK about film's transition from silence to sound, we inevitably think first of the beleaguered actors, forced to submit to the tyrannical verdict of the unfeeling microphone. But in truth directors and writers felt the change every bit as much. The very first Academy Awards, covering the years 1927–28, included an Oscar for title writing that was never to be given again. But though title writing became obsolete, silent screenwriters who adapted to sound were able to use the understanding of the business that years on the ground had given them to flourish in the new medium. Foremost among these, and the prime example of how and why writers found working with Thalberg satisfying (as well as the often unexpected good things that resulted from the collaboration) was Frances Marion.

With hundreds of screen credits in a career dating back to 1915, Marion was a force in Hollywood well before coming to MGM, having written the best of silent superstar Mary Pickford's films, including *Rebecca of Sunnybrook Farm* and *Pollyanna*. But it was while she worked with Thalberg at MGM that she became the only woman to win two screenwriting Oscars (for *The Big House* and *The Champ*), and when she came to publish *How to Write and Sell Film Scripts* in 1937, she dedicated it to "the memory of Irving Thalberg as a tribute to his vision and genius."

Marion met the future executive in 1921, when he was still working for Carl Laemmle at Universal, and later remembered him as someone with "a sensitive face, a frail body and the dark searching restless eyes of the ambitious." According to Cari Beauchamp's definitive biography, *Without Lying Down*, "What fascinated Frances was Irving's breadth of knowledge and his comfort in discussing almost any subject. He moved from movies to art to philosophy with equal ease and, unlike most men she met in the business, was obviously very well read. Their mutual respect was seeded that day." After her success with Lillian Gish's 1926 *The Scarlet Letter*, MGM wanted to put her under contract. and it was her connection with Thalberg—what she described as her belief in his "power of incisive analysis" and his rare "flair for human dignity"—that led her to sign.

After safely shepherding Garbo into the realm of sound with her adaptation of O'Neill's *Anna Christie*, Marion took off on an adventure of her own when she wrote the original screenplay for 1930's groundbreaking early sound prison movie *The Big House*.

Marion's script follows the intertwined fates of three archetypal inmates. Recently married new guy on the yard Kent (Robert Montgomery) is doing time for drunk driving manslaughter, but he shares a cell with a pair of hardened cons: Machine Gun Butch, as lawless as his name (Wallace Beery), and Morgan (Chester Morris), described by a jailer as "the slickest crook we've ever had here."

The idea to do a prison picture came from director George Hill, soon to become (briefly) Marion's husband and someone with an interest in prison reform. Thalberg liked the outline, but his uncertainty about the effect of sound on audiences ("Right now, with everything in flux, we had better see what catches the public's eye") made him delay. In the interim, Marion managed a tour of San Quentin to absorb atmosphere, even though the warden was not keen on a woman taking on this kind of assignment. "Everywhere we went," Marion reported, "I became an object of repressed ridicule."

None of this affected MGM's gradual belief in the project. When J. J. Cohn, the head of physical production, asked Thalberg, "'How do we want to make this?' he said, 'I think it ought to be an important picture, Joe.'" That led to large and impressive sets for three-tier cell blocks, mess hall, and prison yard. In another kerfuffle, Thalberg, who was the last word on things production, had to be called to the set when Cohn and the director disagreed on how many extras were needed for a big prison yard scene. Cohn thought they had enough, the director wanted more; Thalberg looked around and "told Hill not to worry about it." That's how hands-on his job could be.

But Thalberg's real strength, as had been the case with *Red-Headed Woman*, was as nuts-and-bolts counterpuncher to a preview audience's responses. As Howard Dietz and others noted, "His was the most valuable skill on the lot. His main talent was his editing and cutting." When a first preview in San Bernardino was soft, Thalberg was puzzled. Unsure why, he scheduled another preview but, according to biographer Bob Thomas, "this time he went alone. He shifted his seat from one part of the house to another, trying to fathom the reason for the audience's failure to accept the film." As he subsequently told his staff, he soon found out what was wrong. "When Morris gets out of prison, he goes to see Montgomery's wife and gets into a romance with her. Women flinch at that; they don't like it. Now supposing we make the girl Montgomery's sister instead . . ." The change was easily made with voice-over adjustments, and the film became a hit. *Big House* won an Oscar for sound man

Douglas Shearer as well for as Marion, and Thalberg went on to his next plot dilemma. Which involved Frances Marion's next Oscar-winning original.

The very origins of *The Champ* speak to the instinctive trust that existed between Thalberg and Marion. Noting the success of Westerns like *Cimarron*, which won the 1930–31 best-picture Academy Award, and eager to put *Big House* star Beery into one, he suggested to Marion, "Why don't you drive down to the Mexican border and sop up some atmosphere?" Marion did as suggested, but what she saw was very different than anticipated. "Suddenly the door of a saloon was flung open, and a big drunkard staggered out," followed by a protective small boy and his friends. "'Git outa the way, you sons o' bitches!' the kid yelled. 'Can't you see the Champ needs air!' . . . I watched them until they were out of sight . . . and I knew that here was the springboard for a story." Thalberg was initially dubious about what Marion herself characterized as "a tear-jerker," but after he read a long synopsis, he sent for her. "'I'd like to own the handkerchief concession on your soap opera,' he said, 'but I have to admit it's a great role for Beery and little Jackie Cooper,'" and under King Vidor's polished direction so it proved to be.

Though they did not get along in real life, the veteran Beery and the ten-year-old who had already been Oscar nominated were a magnetic combination on screen in this love story between a boy and the alcoholic ex-boxer father doing his best to raise him. The film culminates in a fight that, against all reason, the Champ wins, only to be felled by a heart attack in the dressing room afterward.

None of the film's success, including the Oscar for Marion and a shared one with Fredric March's *Dr. Jekyll and Mr. Hyde* for Beery, might have happened had not Thalberg had one of his ideas. As Samuel Marx related, "Much of *The Champ* had been warmly received in its sneak preview but near the end, audience interest faded." That version of the film, as it turned out, had followed logic and had the Champ lose the fight before dying. "The lights came up in the projection room and Thalberg shook his head in disbelief. 'We're chumps not champs,' he said. 'Let him *win the fight*, not lose it. That's what the audience wants to see.' The ring scene was reshot and at its second preview the audience cheered the film."

There was one further example of the collaborative synergy between Marion and Thalberg that is as unlikely and as ultimately significant as any specific film the studio made. It concerns the saving of an individual, not a movie, and its effects were so unexpected and so widespread that even Mayer was drawn into its orbit. The actress at the center of it was no svelte ingénue but a woman of advanced years and unashamed bulk, a woman who, a New Orleans critic wrote in 1932, "can lay claim to neither beauty, grace nor physical allure." A woman named Marie Dressler.

Dressler got her start in vaudeville well before movies were invented, going on stage at age fourteen in 1882. She made her motion picture debut with Charlie Chaplin and Mabel Normand supporting her starring role in Mack Sennett's 1914 slapstick epic *Tillie's Punctured Romance*. According to Marion's memoir, *Off with Their Heads!*, the two became friends even earlier, in 1911, when Marion was a cub reporter for the *San Francisco Examiner*.

Vaudeville went out of style, Dressler found no film work between 1918 and 1927, and Marion, who kept in sporadic touch with the actress, was shocked when a letter came from a mutual friend saying, "Don't believe Marie's bluff that she's on the 'up and up.' . . . Can't you do something for her in Hollywood?" (Dressler wrote in her own autobiography that after "nine years of marking time; of humiliation; of beating my head against a stone wall of managerial indifference and prejudice," she was "a tired, discouraged old woman.")

Marion found a property MGM already owned and turned

it into *The Callahans and the Murphys*, a comedy of feuding families she tailored to the combination of Dressler and MGM actress Polly Moran. Now all she had to do was persuade Thalberg, who, Marion related, initially replied, "I haven't heard of her in years." The screenwriter tried to bluff her way past this obstacle, but "I stopped short, Irving's dark, solemn eyes were focused upon me. 'Irving,' I finished lamely, 'Marie's a friend of mine. She needs a job desperately.'" It took Thalberg only a moment to make up his mind. "'My theory is that anybody who once hits the bulls-eye, it doesn't matter in what profession, has the brains and stamina to stage a comeback.' . . . He paused and a twinkle came into his eyes. 'Send for Miss Dressler. We'll start the picture as soon as she gets here.'" But though this story had begun like a fantasy, fate still had multiple twists in store, and the tide did not fully turn for her until Frances Marion once again pleaded with Thalberg on Dressler's behalf for an unconventional role: costarring with Greta Garbo in the star's *Anna Christie* sound debut.

In typecasting contrast to Jean Harlow, Dressler had never been known as anything but a comic actress, but Marion thought the dramatic part of waterfront habitue and eventual Anna pal Marthy was exactly suited to her. Dressler proved to be the revelation of the production, and her insights into her costar are compelling. "She is a great artist, but it is both her supreme glory and her supreme tragedy that art is to her the only reality," Dressler wrote. "It is only when she breathes the breath of life into a part . . . that she herself is fully awake, fully alive."

What happened next to Dressler was even more unanticipated. Unbeknownst to anyone at the studio, Marion had written another script, this time pairing the actress with big lug Wallace Beery. A friend of the writer's, a tubercular MGM screenwriter named Lorna Moon, had published a grim novel titled *Dark Star* that she hoped to sell to the studio for money needed for a sanatorium stay. Knowing that the novel was too bleak for

MGM, Marion, with some help from friends in the story department, pretended her Dressler/Beery script was adapted from *Dark Star*. No executive, apparently not even Thalberg, bothered to look at the book, the ruse worked, the novel was purchased, and to this day the credits on the DVD package read, "Suggested from the book 'Dark Star' by Lorna Moon."

That Marion script became *Min and Bill*, released in 1930 to indifferent reviews but phenomenal box office. Described by the writer as "a rip roaring comedy about two old water front toughs, set on the docks of San Pedro," it stars Dressler as the proprietor of a waterfront hotel and Beery as, naturally, a fishing captain. Not only did audiences eat this up, making *Min and Bill* the highest-grossing film of the year, but the Academy did as well: Dressler won the best-actress award for 1930–31.

So, at age sixty-something, the actress no one had wanted became, according to a *Motion Picture Herald* poll of twelve thousand exhibitors, the number one box-office attraction in America two years running, besting Crawford, Garbo, Shearer, and all the rest. Though Dressler had come to the studio through the Marion-Thalberg connection, Mayer, who looked on the handling of actors as one of his prerogatives, came not only to value and appreciate Dressler but also to back his words up with action when she became ill with the cancer that was to end her life.

The nature of Dressler's illness was kept from her for quite some time, and, ever the workhorse, she did not cut down on her productivity, with Mayer, who encouraged her efforts, reportedly giving her a $100,000 bonus for her exertions. The most successful of her final films was 1933's *Tugboat Annie*, something of a reprise of the *Min and Bill* lovable riff-raff scenario, with Beery costarring again. Though parts of the shoot were physically demanding, Mayer tried to make things easier, mandating no more than three-hour workdays and an on-set sofa for Dressler to rest on between takes. Most unexpected is what happened after the actress was asked to choose between nearby houses for living quarters during location work.

"I added purely in fun that what I really should like would be a little vine-covered cottage we had passed on our way to location. The next thing I knew, there was the cottage with a blue bow of ribbon tied to the handle of the front door and a card which said, 'Welcome Home, Marie!' Mr. Mayer had bought it, vines and all, and had had it moved for me." *Tugboat Annie* validated everyone's work, with *Time* magazine putting Dressler on its cover, the first to feature a film actress. Mayer also mandated a huge sixty-second birthday party for her on an MGM sound stage in November 1933, attended by a guest list of eight hundred and boasting an eight-foot-tall cake. It was to be the last birthday Dressler was to celebrate. She died in July 1934, then and now the unlikeliest number one star Thalberg and Mayer ever produced.

For Crawford, Garbo, and Shearer, the MGM actresses who unexpectedly toiled in Dressler's wake, the early sound years proceeded apace. With everyone on the lot still struggling to master the new medium, their films were solid but uneventful. That is, until an actor named Clark Gable entered their professional lives with an impact that was both unforeseen and substantial. Each of the three had a film with Gable that was released in 1931, with Crawford managing three. The speed of filmmaking in the early sound days was lightning fast.

A high school dropout from Cadiz, Ohio, Gable had been stagestruck as a teenager and most of his early acting experience had been in small touring theatrical troupes. In Hollywood he managed extra work in the silent era, but it was sound that was the making of him. His resonant voice and the appealing, unselfconscious male swagger it conveyed—one fan magazine characterized him as "a lumberjack in evening clothes"—were made for the talkies. It was only a matter of time before Mayer and

Thalberg, on the lookout for leading men after John Gilbert's uncertain sound work, noticed and pounced.

Perhaps fittingly for a man who came to be known as the King of Hollywood, it was women connected to MGM who were central to Gable's signing. Physical drawbacks, mainly unusually large ears, were initially a negative for more than one male executive, with the actor as late as 1957 vividly remembering that decades earlier "Irving Thalberg said, 'Not for my money he won't be all right. Look at his big, batlike ears.'" But women had no trouble seeing past them to Gable's quintessential masculinity. Frances Marion tells of watching the actor in a play in New York in 1928 and being convinced "he'll rise to stardom like bread in a warm oven," but no one male was listening. Equally convinced was Ida Koverman, Mayer's influential secretary. She organized a screening for MGM female employees, and they reacted as she did. "That's the trouble with this business," Koverman noted. "It's the men who pick stars— and the women who react to them!"

Gable was eighth-billed in MGM's *The Easiest Way*, the film that finally got him seriously noticed, but it mattered not. With a forceful, casually sexual presence that was new to the screen, his ambitious laundry truck driver dominates every scene he's in though his role is by nature peripheral. As Samuel Marx remembered the preview crowd, "Gable electrified the audience. It was a tangible thing. Everything that was wrong about his appearance suddenly seemed right. Thalberg stood in the patio when the picture was over, asking men and women leaving the theater how they liked 'that new fellow who plays the brother-in-law.' Then he drew the studio executives to a corner of the parking lot and said, 'We've got ourselves a new star!'"

As became MGM policy, Thalberg and Mayer began pairing the newcomer with the studio's more established stars. Crawford was the first and most frequent collaborator, making eight films with Gable all told, including those three 1931 efforts, and

Crawford acknowledged in her autobiography that the chemistry between them immediately became personal as well as professional. "His nearness had such impact, my knees buckled," she wrote. "This magnetic man had more sheer male magic than anyone in the world and every woman knew it, every woman looked at him with desire."

If MGM publicity is to be believed, one of those who desired him professionally was Garbo, who was cast opposite Gable for the only time in their careers in the oddly named romantic drama *Susan Lennox: Her Fall and Rise*. The title comes from a novel that Thalberg apparently acquired only after taking an informal poll of women in his office to learn whether they'd heard of it. (They had.) It took a long time for multiple studio writers (one source cites fifteen, another twenty-two) to come up with an acceptable script, Thalberg telling one unsuccessful team, "No, you've missed it. Entirely. The formula we're after is this: love *conquers in the end!* We're not interested in defeat—no one is! You've got this girl *down*, but there is no *rise*. Try again."

If Gable had played a rough-edged character before, he doubled down on that aspect in *A Free Soul*, his 1931 film starring Norma Shearer. It was taken from a novel Hollywood writer Adela Rogers St. John had based on her earlier life with her father, a celebrated San Francisco criminal attorney.

Joan Crawford was in the mix, but Thalberg was looking for a role to make a splash for his wife in her first outing since giving birth to their son Irving Jr. in 1930, and this was to be the one. As Crawford later remembered it, "There were several roles I wanted very badly. One was *A Free Soul*. I was dying to do it. And Adela wanted me to. But Norma got it anyway."

Shearer plays Jan, the free soul of the title. She falls fast for Gable's Ace Wilfong, a charismatic gambler whom she prophetically calls "a new kind of man in a new kind of world." "Their love scenes," columnist Hedda Hopper remembered, "were like hot fat on an iron griddle."

Though *A Free Soul* was promoted as a Norma Shearer vehicle, Gable stole the show. His electrifying attitude toward
Shearer's character, roughly pushing her into a chair not once
but twice and all but snarling, "Sit down, take it and like it" had
the most lasting impact on contemporary moviegoers. As novelist Rogers St. John wrote, "After *A Free Soul* was released,
Clark Gable's stardom was as instant and total as an explosion,
as definite and complete as an Act of Nature—which actually I
suppose it was."

Always looking for new variations for his stars to help ensure longevity, Thalberg turned up a play turned silent film that
became the sound hit for Crawford and Gable, *Possessed*. "Joan
Crawford needs a change of pace," Lenore Coffee reports Thalberg told her as he handed her a copy of the play. "She's outgrown
all those flapper roles and needs to get her teeth into something.
Perhaps you can develop this so that it will be suitable for her,
yet be quite different from anything she's done."

Though Coffee, who was returning to the MGM staff after
time away, came to feel that Thalberg, who could be coldly pragmatic, had deceived her about her new salary, she nevertheless
delivered what he asked for. *Possessed* focused on the relationship between a wealthy man and his mistress and was such a hit
that, according to Samuel Marx, Mayer pushed for a sequel,
often his default position, until Thalberg squelched the idea
with a deadpan "Very good, L.B. We'll call it *Repossessed!*"

As far as the purported Gable/Crawford romance, though
there are reports that as studio arbiter of morality Mayer read
them the riot act and broke them up, neither ever admitted to
a physical affair. Adela Rogers St. John, however, related a vivid
memory of "the night I stumbled on them behind the band-
stand at the Cocoanut Grove, with *his* wife and *her* husband sitting out at the tables. . . . That these two were as mad about
each other as any pair I ever saw, I *know*."

Though Gable's multiple 1931 films with Crawford, Shearer,

and Garbo caused a stir, it was a 1932 picture without him that
fully involved all of Thalberg's producing gifts and become an
underrecognized landmark in Hollywood history: *Grand Hotel*.

For a film so significant, *Grand Hotel* came to MGM in a
particularly convoluted way that speaks to the thoroughness and
tenacity that were becoming two of the hallmarks of the studio
Mayer and Thalberg were putting together. Samuel Marx, a prolific memoirist, thought it so significant he wrote about the process in three books, and it is quite a tale.

It starts with Kate Corbaley, whose title of assistant story
editor only hints at her key position at the studio. Corbaley noticed an item datelined Berlin in the *New York Times*' theatrical
news about the failed dramatization of a Vicki Baum novel called
Menschen im Hotel (People in a hotel). As the title indicates, "the
play dealt with different forms of humanity passing through
thirty-six hours in a modern hotel. Mrs. Corbaley thought that,
in spite of its failure, this was an interesting movie idea and we
ought to read the play." The work was duly acquired, translated,
and read with interest. But when the studio was ready to purchase the rights, it turned out that they had somehow been acquired by a New York underwear manufacturer who had given
them as a silver wedding anniversary present to his aspiring actress wife, who in turn had her eye on the central role of prima
ballerina Grusinskaya.

But theatrical presentation can be expensive, and soon
enough the film rights to what was now known as *Grand Hotel*
were sold to MGM for half of the $27,000 needed to mount
the stage production. The wife exited the company, Broadway
professionals became involved, and in November 1930 the play
that had flopped in Berlin became a hit in New York.

In May 1931 Thalberg finally saw *Grand Hotel* on stage during a New York stopover on the way to a European trip. He also
found time for an interview with the *New York Times* in which
he predicted that "the technique and tempo of 'Grand Hotel'

. . . the swift-moving, episodic character of the play will probably serve as a pattern for many films. . . . The general idea will
be that of drama induced by the chance meeting of a group of
conflicting and interesting personalities." What Thalberg didn't
say was that, in a move unprecedented for Hollywood, he would
fill those roles with a group of major stars. While parsimonious
studios had heretofore used only one or two stars per film, *Grand
Hotel* would topline five, creating a model that would influence
everything from MGM's own *Dinner at Eight* to the classic 1939
Western *Stagecoach* to action films like *The Great Escape* decades
later.

While the film would basically follow the plot of the play,
that didn't mean the scenario was preordained. Though it's not
widely known, Thalberg had a stenographer record many of his
story conferences, and reading the transcripts of the multiple
Grand Hotel meetings Thalberg, director Edmund Goulding,
and producer Paul Bern held over four months is a revelation
for what it shows us about how Thalberg thought and acted, as
well as the verbatim in-the-moment language he used.

Not surprisingly, given the amount of time spent in these
story conferences, Thalberg comes across as exceptionally detail oriented, willing to go over the script line by line and, in
later conferences, footage almost angle by angle. No specific
was too small for him. He wanted, for instance, to open a scene
with Grusinskaya "sweeping into the lobby, flowers preceding
her," so the audience knows she's had a triumph. And having, in
his own words, "played a lot of chemin de fer," he had several
ideas as to how the card game should be portrayed in the film,
including the tart observation that it's "one game you can't play
with friends."

Again and again, it's clear that Thalberg lived for the ins
and outs of sentence structure and story construction in a way
that is unexpected for an executive and was crucial to the strong
bonds he formed with writers. More than just story, Thalberg

believed in the audience as the ultimate arbiter of what was before it. "Nothing in the world could make me do that," he begins one response, "unless I saw it on the screen and was convinced." Having seen *Grand Hotel* on Broadway, he had strong memories of what had worked, and he didn't hesitate to reference them. When he talks about getting "the audience to the point where they say: 'Jesus!' " he is offering his highest praise.

Given that as the executive in charge of production Thalberg was supposed to care about how much money was being spent by the studio, it's a bit of a surprise to see him make the point again and again that as long as the film was a go, it should try to be the best no matter what the cost. "If you could get things over by a lot of extra people walking out with golf bags, pictures would cost about twenty-five thousand dollars apiece," he says at one point, adding at another, "I don't think there is any argument: if it's good it's good, if it isn't it isn't. The way to save a lot of money is not to make it."

Perhaps the greatest pleasure of the story conference transcripts is that they reveal how totally in charge Thalberg was and how much he relished that situation. He could hedge his bets ("my slight one tenth of one percent preference"), but mostly his comments are of the "I'll bet any amount of money" and "Well, what of it?" variety. When he is at his most vivid and colloquial, saying at one point "Over my dead body you'll cut that scene. . . . Don't destroy what is right," he's at his most convincing.

With Greta Garbo and Joan Crawford running virtually unopposed for their roles, one person there was no room for was Thalberg's competitive wife Norma Shearer, who candidly blurted out at the film's Grauman's Chinese premier, "I just wish I'd been in it myself. You can't have all the luck, can you?"

The plot has its five guests at the Berlin hotel wending in and out of each other's lives like the weave of the "painted carpet on which the figures walk" that Thalberg referenced in one of those conferences. Garbo toplined as emotionally spent ballerina Grusinskaya, fully inhabiting what was to become her signature line: "I want to be alone." Baron von Gaigern (John Barrymore) is a gentleman jewel thief who plans to rob the diva but ends up stealing only her heart. Flaemmchen is an ambitious young woman with a flexible moral code; Crawford in her autobiography dismissively called her "the little whore-stenographer." Flaemmchen goes to work for General Director Preysing (Wallace Beery, the only actor allowed a German accent), a textile magnate facing a financial crisis. (Thalberg, a frequenter of German spas due to his health, insisted on the designation in conference, noting, "In Germany everyone is called by their title.") Rounding out the group is Otto Kringelein (Lionel Barrymore), an employee of Preysing's with only a short time to live who has come to Berlin to enjoy life while he can.

Aware of how much *Grand Hotel* meant to Thalberg, the actors were well behaved. According to John Barrymore's friend and biographer Gene Fowler, at the end of a difficult scene "Miss Garbo electrified the director and the camera crew, *and* Barrymore, by impulsively kissing the actor. 'You have no idea,' she said in the presence of others on the set, 'what it means to me to play opposite so perfect an artist.'" Still, juggling all the film's egos was a challenge, as Thalberg admitted a year later when he parenthetically noted in a bylined magazine article, "If picture making were as easy as that, we'd be making Grand Hotels every week of the year."

Grand Hotel repaid the faith the studio had in it by becoming a major success, the first MGM film since *Ben-Hur* and *The Big Parade* to have the juice to tour as a road show. Some journalists did not embrace Thalberg's all-star cast idea, with one New York critic calling the film "an opulent zoo harboring an impressively high-priced menagerie," but most agreed with *Motion Picture Herald*'s approval of "a galaxy of stars that just have made the Milky Way sit up and keel over."

Thalberg, ever Mr. Inside, can be glimpsed in newsreel footage of the premiere schmoozing in the background, while Mayer, Mr. Outside, came to the microphone to both bang the drum for the studio ("Our fans are entitled to the best and I'm thankful we can supply what we consider fine pictures") and single out one particular individual by name: "I'm proud of my associate Irving Thalberg, who was able to make this picture himself."

Grand Hotel went on to win the best-picture Oscar, but it was also the only picture in Academy Award history to win that award without getting so much as a single other nomination. Similarly, though no one knew it at the time, the success of *Grand Hotel* proved to be something of a high-water mark in the Thalberg-Mayer relationship, a moment when their dreams and desires were still satisfyingly in sync. As the rest of 1932 unfolded, unforeseen events and circumstances created rifts that would prove increasingly difficult to paper over.

14

To Each His Own

By THAT PIVOTAL year of 1932, MGM had both achieved and begun to solidify a position as the most envied of the Hollywood powerhouses. And, not incidentally, it also made the most money. The Depression was difficult throughout Hollywood, with receipts down across the board, but MGM's parent company Loew's was the only film company to pay dividends all through the bleak years. Historian Tino Balio reports, "Of the twenty-four films that made it to *Variety*'s annual list of top-grossing films from 1930 to 1933, MGM produced nine, or more than a third." Making sure that the world was aware of its success, the studio ran exuberant trade ads, like one in the April 13, 1932, edition of *Film Daily* headlined "MERRILY WE ROLL ALONG!" Illustrated with a cartoon of an ancient exhibitor circa 1972 telling his grandson he survived the Great Depression because "I played Metro-Goldwyn-Mayer Pictures," the text proper

began "GOOD pictures sock depression RIGHT on the schnoz-
zola" and jauntily concluded, "The Hell With Depression!"

More than earning all this money, in an era when studios
had the kinds of definable personalities that have all but disappeared, MGM was coming to be known, says Dore Schary,
who eventually ran the place, as "the richest, most prestigious
and certainly the most publicized studio in history." Even director John Huston, not a fan, allowed that it was "the holiest
of the cathedrals." Helen Hayes, who won an Oscar there, saw
it in absolute terms: "It was *the* greatest film studio of the world.
Not just of America or of Hollywood, but of the world."

If the world knew all about MGM, and it did, it was because of the work of two men who were with the studio almost
from the beginning. Howard Dietz, general publicity and advertising director based in New York, and Howard Strickling,
director of studio publicity based in Los Angeles, were separate
and, if not quite equal (Dietz ranked higher), were pretty much
masters of all they surveyed on their respective coasts. Though
Dietz wrote a memoir and had a parallel career apart from the
studio and Strickling remained a keeper of secrets to the end,
both were unapologetic studio loyalists intent on promoting the
notion that the tireless efforts of Mayer and Thalberg had made
Metro-Goldwyn-Mayer the greatest movie studio on the face
of the earth.

While Strickling tended to the needs of stars ("If there was
bad publicity or something coming up," remembered Maureen
O'Sullivan, "You took it up with Howard Strickling"), Dietz,
who had a successful career as a writer of musical theater lyrics,
took on other tasks. He wrote both of MGM's celebrated mot-
tos, "More Stars Than There Are in Heaven" as well as the Latin
"Ars Gratia Artis" (Art for art's sake), which put the loftiest aspirations of both Thalberg and Mayer into words. Often mor-
dant in his personal sensibility, Dietz claimed to have borrowed

a sign from the office of *New Yorker* editor Harold Ross to hang in his own. It read: "Don't Be Famous Around Here."

The most lasting impact Dietz had at MGM was that Leo the Lion trademark, which was also his idea. He thought it up as a drawn logo at Goldwyn, probably because his alma mater Columbia had used it as well, and though Mayer apparently wanted to bring his company's American eagle trademark to the new venture, a flesh and blood king of beasts won out. Though the lion's roar could not be heard in the silent era, that did not stop in-house discussion of what should be shown. Finally, Samuel Marx remembers, Mayer himself "decided on two fast roars, a pause, then a third," and so it was. As a symbol, Leo, considered to be perhaps the most widely recognized trademark in the world, was also the rare studio logo that got applause in theaters when it appeared. MGM executive Eddie Mannix got perhaps the best use out of the animal. Perhaps inspired by Dietz, he had a sign placed near his desk, but this one read "THE ONLY STAR AT MGM IS LEO THE LION."

Given the universal agreement that it was the Mayer/Thalberg partnership that took the newly minted MGM to the pinnacle of Hollywood success ("Athens in Greece under Pericles" said one dazzled participant), it is remarkable that anecdotes of the two men together are thin on the ground.

How they roughly divided responsibilities was commonly agreed upon, with veteran editor Margaret Booth summing it up economically (if too broadly) as "Mr. Mayer did all the money thing, and Irving did all the creative work." They had nearby offices in the old MGM executive structure (star Ramon Novarro claimed a secret panel connected them), when they conferred it was often one on one, and the few tales about their being in the same room vary widely in emotional tone, from the innocuous to the incendiary.

On the innocent, even sweet side is this account from writer Adela Rogers St. John, who says, "I can remember sitting there in Irving's office and there would be a pitter-patter of feet and Mr. Mayer's head would come around the side, and he'd say, 'Irvie, do you have time for me?' He called him 'Irvie.' And Irving would say, 'No, Mr. Mayer, not now.' And Mr. Mayer would say 'All right,' and go back to his own office. I can always remember his head peeking around the side of that door."

Set against this warm, almost Andy Hardy moment, is a quite different anecdote taken from an unpublished memoir by Rowland V. Lee, an independent director who recalled sitting in Thalberg's office relating a story idea he'd had.

Suddenly Mayer burst open the door in a wild fury. Paying no attention to my presence he lashed out at Thalberg—called him a stupid, blundering fool and many unprintable things—wheeled and left the room violently slamming the door behind him.

Thalberg said not one thing in his defense. After L.B. had made his exit, Thalberg calmly turned to me, "You were saying the train was wrecked . . ." I shortened my telling of the story. Thalberg said he thought the story was not MGM material and thanked me for coming in. He couldn't have been more gracious.

There's no doubt Mayer and Thalberg were contrasting personalities in a way one longtime employee characterized with the pithy "Thalberg did the brain work, but Mayer mingled with the people." Screenwriter Donald Ogden Stewart went a little deeper, saying, "L. B. Mayer wanted to be liked, but Irving never tried to be popular. He was too busy getting his own way."

Yet extremes of behavior aside, there were also, as there had to be, especially in the earlier, less problematic years, more balanced interactions, times when reasoned joint decisions were made and these men with common values and exceptionally complementary gifts set about dividing the moviemaking work at hand into interconnected areas of expertise. Thalberg's first biographer Bob Thomas reported that "Mayer rarely made an important decision unilaterally. When a business proposal was made to him in his office, he generally said, 'Wait a minute— I'll see what Irving thinks,' and he discussed the matter on the intercom." The men also apparently took turns being a restraining influence on each other. Actor Conrad Nagle recalled, "Mayer would sometimes get hot and abusive, Thalberg would sit with him and calm him down by saying, 'Now, Louis,'" while Mayer told Lillian Ross, "That was Irving and I working together. He'd get mad. He'd come back. Then he'd start again. He'd always come back." Sometimes a wonderful piece of encouragement would be transmitted between the two men, as happened when Thalberg was in New York deciding whether director Edmund Goulding should be hired for *Grand Hotel*, and Mayer cabled him, "Close deals whenever it is good for us. You will make mistakes, so will I. We worry together on our mistakes and glory together in our wonderful accomplishments."

When it came to assessing their collaboration, while some observers engaged in backhanded denigration of Mayer ("He never made pictures, he made contracts," one employee said, while Hedda Hopper wrote in 1952, "Louis was always the clever politician—still is—but Irving was the little creative giant"), the more thoughtful understood what each man contributed. Lenore Coffee said, "Mayer was smart enough to know that he himself did not have any great creative ability. He had a remarkable head for making financial deals but he knew he needed a man of talent and imagination." Silent star Rod La Rocque was even more specific. "By an act of absolute magic, Mr. Mayer organized a company out of these three failures: the Goldwyn, the Metro, and the Mayer enterprises. . . . Thalberg had an innate understanding of tempo, timing, character, philosophy, psychology. Why? That's like asking why does Heifetz play the violin so expertly. . . . Thalberg and that very different man, Mr. Mayer, made a team . . . each displaying an uncanny acumen for his craft."

From the point of view of director King Vidor, generally thought of as a Thalberg man, "Mayer held the whole thing together and persuaded stars to stay. His greatest talent was to keep all those stars and actors satisfied, to keep the organization going. If you started to leave he'd practically break down and cry. He would say, 'You're walking out on your home.'"

"Thalberg was a great creative artist, but without Mayer he could not have operated," Adela Rogers St. John summed up for Kevin Brownlow. "If you think of the British War Office and the commander in the field, you have a correct parallel. Whatever the commander may achieve, he does so because the War Office supplied him with the troops and ammunition to do it with." David O. Selznick, who worked closely with both, said it best: "Between them they created MGM. I don't think either of them could have created it without the other."

Mayer was far from alone among the original moguls in coming to Hollywood with a background in business, but it's worth remembering, as daughter Irene Mayer Selznick related, that his childhood entry into that world was starker than most. The young Mayer journeyed "well across Canada, to bid at auctions on discarded bridges and burned-down factories . . . hardly suspected of being able to pay cash."

Mayer's domain at MGM was the business of the business, including studio administration, hiring and firing, negotiating contracts, and dealing with the ever-difficult Loew's corporate overlords in New York. But it's important to note that a substantial amount of his West Coast negotiating time was spent with the studio's central creative group, the actors. Hard as it is not to feel empathy for these overmatched performers and their agents, face to face in contract talks with the man who as a small child had outfoxed hardened salvage negotiators, the reality is that these folks (with exceptions like Charles Laughton, who considered Thalberg "the most brilliant producer in the world today") by and large preferred dealing with the blustery Mayer than the sometimes distant Thalberg.

The reason is no mystery: Mayer in his unrestrained way was a kindred spirit, considered by more than one observer to be the best actor on the lot, someone whose very initials were jokingly said to refer to Lionel Barrymore and who was compared by his own loyal wife to the ultratheatrical Yiddish actor Maurice Schwartz. Screenwriter S. N. Behrman remembered him as someone who was "incorrigibly histrionic and put on a great show. Sometimes it slipped his mind what role he was playing: whether the benevolent autocrat, the humanitarian concerned for the well-being of everyone except his enemies, the emotional sentimentalist, the religious leader." Echoing many others, screenwriter Casey Robinson said flatly, "The scenes in Mayer's office would win Academy Awards. He'd cry, he'd weep, he'd beg, he'd kiss, he'd love, he'd hate, he'd scream—he'd do anything!"

Examples of what Mayer would say and do when actors were present are manifold and eye-widening. Selecting the highlights from across his career is challenging but these stand out:

Greer Garson already had an Oscar nomination for 1939's *Goodbye, Mr. Chips* to her credit when Mayer approached her to star in *Mrs. Miniver*. She was reluctant, fearing she was too young to play a mother whose son goes off to war, but then "Louis B. Mayer called me into his office and pleaded with me to play the role. I said no. He said, 'I brought you to America. Do it for me.' Still no. Finally, to prove the opportunities afforded me in the role, he began to read aloud from the script, acting out all the parts. When I couldn't take it any longer, I cried out, 'All right! All right! I'll play Mrs. Miniver.'" Garson won an Oscar but she always claimed, "I still think Louis Mayer played it better than I did."

Vouched for not once but twice over is a meeting between

Mayer and the studio's 1930s musical star Jeanette MacDonald, who had story approval and was not eager to do Mayer's choice for her next film, the venerable *Naughty Marietta*. As related to Bosley Crowther by Herbert Stothart, MGM's musical director, who was in the room, Mayer offered MacDonald "courteous suggestions as to how she should strive for an emotional quality in her singing style. Suddenly, to her astonishment, he got down on his knees and began singing the Jewish lament, Eli, Eli, in a most serious and tremulous way. [Mayer was probably familiar with the legendary cantor Yossele Rosenblatt's recorded version.] Miss MacDonald was genuinely affected by the uninhibited sentiment of the man. . . . The experience disarmed her completely. *Naughty Marietta* it would be."

This story unexpectedly reappears more than a dozen years later in John Huston's autobiography, in which Mayer is referred to as trying to persuade the director to do a proposed version of the Roman epic *Quo Vadis*. Mayer asked Huston to breakfast at his home and told him the story of instructing Jeanette MacDonald how to emote

> by singing the Jewish "Eli, Eli" for her. She was so moved, he said, that she wept. Yes, wept! She who had the reputation of pissing icewater!
>
> He sang the same song for me by way of demonstration. Then he said that if I could make *Quo Vadis* into that kind of picture, he would crawl to me on his knees and kiss my hands . . . which he then proceeded to do. I sat there and thought, "This is not happening to me. I've nothing to do with any of this!" L.B. pressed me for an answer. I told him I wasn't at all sure I could give him what he wanted. He said, "You can only try! Try, John! Try!"

Needless to say, someone other than Huston made the picture.

Mayer not only instinctively understood acting, but he also revered it in his own *paterfamilias* way, telling an associate, "Don't ever say anything bad about actors. If it weren't for actors, I wouldn't be where I am." And he was inexorably drawn to it, hell bent to possess the best of it for the studio. True, as journalist Ezra Goodman found out when MGM killed his *Saturday Evening Post* story on studio casting director Billy Grady, Mayer did not want anyone but himself to get credit for any discovery, but, starting with his signing of Garbo, he did have what studio drama coach Lillian Burns called "a smell for talent," as well as the zeal for acquiring it. "L. B. Mayer ransacked the world for fresh, young talent," said Arthur Mayer, publicity director at rival Paramount, with producer Pandro Berman saying bluntly, "If anybody was good, he wanted them." And if that talent wasn't his, that didn't necessarily stand in his way. "I can't prove this," director Clarence Brown said, "but I think Mayer had set up a spy system—certain employees at other studios were paid to tell him when an actor was being dropped. And if he were interested, he'd get in there and start negotiations before even the agent knew his client was about to be out of a job." Whether the correct version of his often-quoted phrase was "I'll go down on my knees and kiss the ground talent walks on" or "I'll go down on my knees to talent" or even both, Mayer clearly meant it.

Actors, almost uniformly, returned the favor, though sometimes with caveats. Joan Crawford, perhaps his biggest booster, wrote, "In the many years he guided my career I valued his judgement, his patience and the fact that he never played games." Ava Gardner was more mixed in her analysis, saying, "I never liked him very much, but at least you knew where you stood."

Perhaps Mayer's most unlikely supporter was Katharine Hepburn, who conveyed her admiration to multiple writers. "I always called him Mr. Mayer, never Louie or L.B.," she told biographer Gary Carey. "People say he could be wicked, but he was an angel as far as I was concerned." To writer A. Scott Berg, she characterized him as "the most honest man I ever met in

Hollywood. A straight shooter . . . [one of the] romantics and gamblers [who] weren't afraid to express their opinions and put their money where their mouths were." And, as Irene Mayer Selznick reports, that regard was more than mutual. "To him she was proof that one could have talent without temperament. 'Now there's someone I like to do business with. She gives you her word, that's enough, you don't need a contract.' Nor did they ever have one; they relied on a handshake and pretended there was nothing unusual in that. She found my father the most reasonable of men. . . . His regard for her was total."

If Thalberg was often cited for his quasi-religious devotion to film, Mayer was referred to with equal frequency as the deity itself. Writer S. N. Behrman observed tartly that Mayer's "relationship with God was intimate and confidential; he spoke for Him as well as for himself; they thought along the same lines," and his actors always got the message. "I don't think I ever put my foot in Mr. Mayer's office," said Ingrid Bergman, who starred at MGM in the 1940s. "That was God himself up there." Added Mickey Rooney, "In that total MGM culture in which I lived, when Mr. Mayer disapproved, could God's own disapproval be any different?" Viewing the proceedings in the most positive light, as many of MGM's stars did, Ann Rutherford felt "from the time you were signed at MGM, you just felt you were in God's hands. Somebody was looking after you."

If MGM's actors considered Mayer a kindred spirit, the studio's writers held Thalberg in similar regard. Though he never put pen to paper, so to speak, never turned in a polished script in the same way that Mayer put on memorable performances, writers almost uniformly felt he had an intuitive understanding of and appreciation for what it was they did. In an industry that devalued writers almost from its inception, he made them feel seen. And because of that, his approval was widely sought but not easily given. "There was a father-and-child feeling at MGM when Thalberg was around," said Donald Ogden Stewart, one of his key writers. "You wanted to please Daddy."

Yet this aloofness aside, there was a paradox to Thalberg's relationship with writers. He truly appreciated their work but only up to a point; he valued their ability but had limited room for the individuality of genius. Matching writers to projects was important to Thalberg, but he had a system for using his employees, and a system by definition mandates a kind of interchangeability and willingness to be a team player that meant people were sometimes not treated with the consideration they would have liked. Writer Curt Siodmak put it this way: "Irving Thalberg once said: 'The most important man in the motion picture business is the writer. Don't give him any power!'" There was a tradeoff in working at MGM and if you were not comfortable with that—and most writers were—you would not be happy at the studio.

A good indication of the overall acceptance of Thalberg's system is the great number of writers, more than at any other studio, who found employment there. Numbers fluctuated over the years, with the coming of sound leading to an influx of theater-savvy folks familiar with spoken dialogue. *Fortune* magazine grandly reported in 1932 that "more members of the literati worked [at MGM] than it took to produce the King James Version of the Bible." Eighty-eight were reported in 1936, and Lenore Coffee put the maximum in the studio's 1940s heyday at 108.

If Thalberg took pride in believing "If it isn't for the writing, we've got nothing," this proliferation of writers did not sit well with Mayer, who felt Thalberg was "too tolerant for his own good" and himself had a factory owner's obsession with visible productivity. Prolific screenwriter John Lee Mahin reported that Mayer once went to Thalberg and complained. "'Oh, these writers! Some of these writers are getting drunk, and they have three-hour lunches in the Derby. We ought to put our foot down.

Jack Warner over there runs a tight ship!' Irving said, 'No Louis, they're signed for fifty-two weeks. If I get forty-two weeks a year out of them, that's fine with me. It's worth it. Let them alone, they're doing fine.' He had no kicks about the product." Anita Loos, always one for dramatic effect, phrased it even more starkly, claiming, "The studio's product was actually supplied by only about ten per cent of its writing staff."

Thalberg's system was a complicated one and it was grounded in his belief, unexpectedly shared with numerous sports coaches, that a victory for the studio was a victory for all concerned, no matter what each individual's role. There is no record of Thalberg ever uttering the nostrum "There is no 'I' in 'team,'" but he surely believed it and acted on it. He expected his screenwriters to do extra work, seeing the newest MGM films and reporting their thoughts to him at weekly staff meetings. Even weekends were requisitioned, with Lenore Coffee reporting, "Irving had a great habit which continued over many, many years . . . of expecting writers to read any scripts sent to them for comment, criticism or help. . . . Almost invariably on a Saturday evening or the day before a holiday we would hear a motorcycle coming up the hill then the clang of our gates and my husband would say, 'A script from Thalberg for you to read over Sunday,' and more often than not, it was." As Howard Dietz acknowledged, "Thalberg worked every minute of the day and he expected every creative person on his studio staff to do the same."

Thalberg's almost obsessive fixation with letting nothing get in the way of fixing plotlines led to story conferences taking place in the most unlikely situations. Not only did Thalberg take extensive notes and make phone calls during the USC football games he regularly attended, but he also held a story conference with Laurence Stallings while he was getting dressed for his own wedding. Two of the most celebrated story situations involved director King Vidor, who reported that he not only drove in a studio car to the Santa Fe station with Thalberg, he boarded the New York–bound train with him and stayed on it until Albuquerque. Best known is the day when, as related in Vidor's autobiography, he and screenwriter Stallings (who were working on a Billy the Kid script) were summoned for a limousine ride with Thalberg to parts unknown. When the destination was reached, "the doorman who stepped up to our car wore white gloves and a dark suit. I realized that we had stopped at the main entrance of a funeral parlor. Apparently we were late for a funeral! Whose funeral? I wondered." The answer, it turned out, was silent film star Mabel Normand, shockingly dead at age thirty-six. Even though their dress was inappropriate, the executive insisted the two writers join him inside. In the midst of the service, Vidor relates, "Thalberg leaned toward me."

> "Too many murders," he whispered.
> Had she been murdered? I was stunned.
> "The public won't accept it," he added, and I suddenly realized he was talking about Billy the Kid.

The most vivid description of the various ways the system played out for individual writers comes from Irene Mayer Selznick, who observed from a distance. "Sometimes writers worked in succession. Sometimes they worked in teams—or several writers worked separately on the same script, and each one thought he was alone on it. Sometimes one writer did the outline, someone else did the synopsis, someone did the dialogue, someone did the revision, someone did a complete rewrite. Who the hell knew who wrote anything?"

Contrasting to this jaundiced view is the more admiring and specific memory of David Lewis, who as one of Thalberg's intimates saw how things worked from the inside. "Thalberg had a system for constructing a script. He would start with what he later called the 'ditch diggers.' . . . When they had broken down the elements of a story, he would bring a playwright in: George S. Kaufman, S. N. 'Sam' Behrman, Donald Ogden Stewart, Charles

MacArthur and Talbot Jennings all worked for Thalberg. He also used short story writers and novelists. . . . Then, if he felt he needed some added sparkle, he would call in a dialogue specialist like Anita Loos or Robert Benchley."

Thalberg was unapologetic about his system and the frustrating duplication of effort it entailed. Even though it led to confusion and ill will over who eventually got screen credit—and screen credit was key to employment and salary—he felt the needs of the studio had to come ahead of all else. Though all writers grumbled about it (they were writers, after all), some of them, like Lenore Coffee, understood his reasoning, which she characterized as "extremely astute. He had half a dozen stars who were enormously popular with audiences and he always had four or five scripts in preparation for each one, so he could never be caught without a picture. . . . There never was that hysteria of 'What are we going to do, we haven't got a story for Garbo! We haven't got a story for Clark Gable! We haven't got a story for Norma Shearer!' "

Not all writers thrived under Thalberg's system, and some of the biggest names came up short. Future Nobel Prize winner William Faulkner was brought to Hollywood by MGM, where he confounded story editor Samuel Marx by announcing, "I want to write for Mickey Mouse." Faulkner had success in Hollywood, but with other studios, which was also the case with James M. Cain, who described Thalberg as "one of the most unpleasant guys. . . . I was ushered into the 'Presence.' This pale guy sat there; whether he was listening or not was hard to say." And Herman Mankiewicz, for his part, was undone, with MGM at least, by his passion for gambling.

A celebrated wit whose career began as a silent film title writer ("Paris, where half the women are working women . . . and half the women are working men" was one celebrated example), Mankiewicz wielded wordplay so devastating that it impressed even his witty friend Ben Hecht, who wrote, "Never have I known a man with so quick an eye and ear—and tongue—for the strut of fools." Once Mayer had offered a five-thousand-dollar bonus to anyone who could come up with a slogan that would increase audience attendance at MGM films. Mankiewicz had suggested, "Show the movies in the streets and drive them into the theaters." Though Mankiewicz's comments on the man were invariably harsh ("A compliment from Mayer is like having Nathan Leopold tell you that you're lovable"), Mayer, in fatherly mode, would forgive the writer's excesses, up to a point. The story goes that the day after Mayer gave Mankiewicz a salary advance to clear his debts if he promised to stop gambling, the executive spotted the writer in a commissary poker game and terminated him. (According to Welles biographer Frank Brady, that firing had a silver lining: it freed Mankiewicz to collaborate with Orson Welles, first on radio scripts, then on *Citizen Kane*, a film Mayer despised.)

One of the especially noteworthy failures, because of the press it garnered, was that of popular British novelist P. G. Wodehouse, whose work methods proved to be as idiosyncratic as his fiction. He was paid a considerable sum weekly for an entire year and for a variety of reasons produced almost nothing except a memorable exit interview with the *Los Angeles Times*. "The motion picture business dazes me," he told the reporter. "They paid me $2,000 a week—$104,000—and I cannot see what they engaged me for. . . . They were extremely nice to me—oh, extremely—but I feel as if I have cheated them. If it's only 'names' they want, it seems such an expensive way to get them." Not amused at all by this kind of notoriety, reported Samuel Marx, was Loew's top man Nicholas Schenck, who phoned Thalberg and said, "'You are silly boys out there! You throw away our money.' Exasperated, Thalberg said, 'Nick, if you know how to make pictures without writers, tell me how!'"

With so many writers on the payroll, it was inevitable that glitches would occur. Marx tells from personal experience of a writer who got an MGM assignment because of a mix-up stemming from his living on the same street as the writer Thalberg was really looking for. Even more outlandish—it sounds apocryphal, but it was told by more than one source—is the story of the thriving career of not a writer but a celebrated personality who turned out to be entirely imaginary. All agree that the instigator was Charles MacArthur, with Howard Dietz, who says he was present at the creation, relating that he'd convinced a random young man to make a fourth in tennis with himself, MacArthur and MacArthur's wife, the actress Helen Hayes. MacArthur was so taken with the impeccable manner of this well-spoken young man, who turned out to be a visiting British accountant, that he came up with the scheme of passing him off at MGM as the mythical but esteemed London-based theatrical figure I. C. Nelson. Apparently, the deception worked well enough that Nelson was offered $1,000 a week by Mayer to produce pictures for MGM. He took the job and kept it for months by turning down all projects by saying "It's not up my alley" or "It's not up my street."

It's telling that this joke on Mayer was perpetrated by MacArthur, a Thalberg stalwart who was one of the group of key writers who not only survived MGM's system but prospered under it. (In fact, Ben Hecht's version of the story places it in "the time of Charlie's disillusionment" after Thalberg's death.) Aside from MacArthur, who himself died young at sixty, these writers, who included Lenore Coffee, Anita Loos, Frances Marion, and Donald Ogden Stewart, lived long enough to write memoirs which burnished the Thalberg aura while revealing rifts in his relationship with Mayer and his doubts about the value and purpose of the nascent Writers Guild.

It was Hecht, who was MacArthur's cowriter on the celebrated *The Front Page* as well as an accomplished script doctor in his own right, who took it upon himself in *Charlie*, his book-length tribute to his friend, to explain Thalberg's appeal to MacArthur. "Irving Thalberg was a fine boss for MacArthur," Hecht wrote. "Irving's delight in the new Metro employee included a respect for his carefully created sentences. . . . There was a certainty in Thalberg to which Charlie responded . . . 'He's too good to last,' Charlie said in Irving's heyday. 'The lamb doesn't lie down with the lion for long.'"

Loos had a longer film career than MacArthur, and her praise was if anything more unstinting. It was Thalberg who brought her back to Hollywood from New York to work on *Red-Headed Woman*. The impression he left on her was physically unimpressive. "In spite of mounting prestige, Irving was still a rather pathetic figure," she wrote. "His natural pallor was intensified by long hours in offices and projection rooms, shut away from the California sunshine. I was enormously touched that the shoulders of Irving's jacket were too obviously padded, in order to make him seem more grown-up and robust."

But despite his unpromising mien, Loos came to feel, "When I joined Irving Thalberg in 1931, he had turned all the inanity into excitement. He was like no other character in the entire film capital. When everybody else was bent on plugging his own personality, Irving remained aristocratically aloof. . . . Irving worked for the pure love of creating. . . . Collaborations with him were, to me, almost like love affairs. They had many of the thrills, none of the drawbacks, and were certainly due to last longer."

In print a year earlier than Loos's memoir *Kiss Hollywood Good-By*," Coffee's *Storyline* was published only in Britain, and her assessment of Thalberg is somewhat more acerbic. She credits him with "great creative sense" and admires the impression he gave that "our sole aim in life was to find out why some films could 'tune into' an audience and why others could not." But Coffee had several run-ins with Thalberg over salary and working conditions that rankled, as did an exchange when he said, "'What's this business of being a writer? Just putting one word after another.' My reply was, 'Pardon me, Mr. Thalberg—putting the right word after another.'"

Both Frances Marion and Donald Ogden Stewart had similar, initially passionate, trajectories. As much as anyone, Marion bought into Thalberg's "no 'I' in team" philosophy. "Mildly patronizing at times, his respect for human dignity set him apart from the undignified in the studio," she wrote. "Firm in his belief that we must all work in close harmony if the pictures were to succeed, he gave us the feeling that we were one mind concentrating on a gigantic project. Whenever a picture was successful Irving said, 'We have done a good job!' Always 'we' and never 'I,' yet he knew that he was the axis upon which the wheels of the studio turned."

Stewart, who was to win an Oscar for adapting Philip Barry's *The Philadelphia Story*, was similarly impressed, albeit from a different vantage point. Eventually to become what memoirist Salka Viertel characterized as Thalberg's "favorite writer and one of the most talented and expensive on the lot," Stewart came to MGM with a playwrighting reputation and was "still full of the happy illusion that I, as a more or less proven humorist, would be asked to create original comedies. But Irving had other ideas and Irving, as I soon discovered, was the Undoubted Boss. . . . We battled it out, and little by little I began to see that Irving knew quite a lot about pictures. It was the beginning of a great deal of wisdom about screen writing which I was to absorb gratefully from him during the next few years. . . . I became slowly, under Irving's severe, uncompromising surveillance, a devoted and loyal member of The Team. . . . It was the most fortunate experience that a writer could have in the film world, for Irving was the unrivaled Top." Yet, as shall be seen, both Stewart and Marion became, to different degrees, disillusioned with aspects of Thalberg that had yet to emerge in these early stages of Hollywood production.

One of reasons those who did thrive put up with Thalberg's system was the exhilaration, known to writers of any kind, of working with someone who was in essence a superb editor. Other studio personnel admired Thalberg—editor Margaret Booth, for instance, said, "He had a mind like an electric buzz-saw"— but writers had a special, more specific understanding of his gifts. These were often playwrights, naturally keyed into what screenwriting historian Tom Stempel describes as MGM's emphasis on individual episodes as opposed to narrative through line: "What Thalberg's approach does give are scenes for the stars to play. What we tend to remember are the great scenes from the MGM films," scenes which Thalberg himself characterized as "the most successful portions of a picture."

The executive's skill began with what Donald Ogden Stewart characterized as an encyclopedic, instantly accessible knowledge of film: "He could remember every scene he'd ever seen in pictures, and with that memory he would make suggestions for your own scenes or he would be able to judge them. He was the only producer that I worked for that I could say was also a creative person." Not one to throw around compliments, fellow writer George S. Kaufman said that after a meeting with Thalberg, "I feel like an idiot. That man has never written a word, and yet he can tell me exactly what to do with a story."

Perhaps the greatest indication of the sophistication of Thalberg's relationship with writers was the fact that he came to question aspects of it himself. Gilbert Seldes, one of the era's most thoughtful critics of film and popular culture, wrote, "About a year before his death Thalberg acknowledged (in a private conversation) the faults of his system. . . . *I've got a schedule to meet.* . . . I know they [writers] don't like it, and I don't like it myself. What can I do?' There was an almost morose intensity in Thalberg's approach to all the problems of making pictures. . . . He died young, and while Hollywood has possibly turned up equal talents, I doubt whether any of his contemporaries is so likely to worry over the dilemmas of production or is so anxious to find the right solution for its problems."

"A television director thinks at the most of 200 films per year. Irving Thalberg was the only one who every day thought of 52 films."

These admiring, astonished words, repeated as voice-over in French some half a dozen times, come from an unlikely source: antiauthoritarian Jean-Luc Godard, who chose Thalberg to be the first person mentioned by name in the director's dazzling eight part, years-in-the-making documentary series *Histoire(s) du Cinema*. Godard was not the only one impressed by Thalberg's ability to oversee a staggering amount of film. Ben Hecht, using a slightly smaller number, said, "Thalberg worked on the plots of some forty movies a year, cast them, edited them and guided them, scene by scene to the cameras."

That level of productivity was mandated by MGM's parent company, Loew's, which needed a constant supply of new product for its chain of theaters. And Thalberg truly did oversee, more than executives at competing studios, the day-to-day making of all his films, more than four hundred during his short career, an activity that fell to him, not Mayer, and demanded most of his waking hours. His affinity for the medium and capacity for work were critical to making it possible, but so was the system Thalberg set up, his creation of a small, intensely loyal group of what he called supervisors, men who worked directly for him and in effect produced without screen credit the films assigned to them.

These men—and they were all men—were extensions of Thalberg more than independent operatives. As historian Thomas Schatz summarizes, Thalberg had "developed a management style that was efficient without being inflexible, disciplined without being inhumane, extravagant without being wasteful," and it was the job of these individuals to see to it that his intentions were carried out, to handle low wattage crises and do things—

such as screening dailies—that his schedule did not allow for. These men's backgrounds and tastes were diverse, and they often learned on the job, leaving *Fortune* magazine to crack in 1932 that "without being able in most cases to act, write or direct, they are supposed to know more about writing than either the director or the star, more about directing than the star or the writer."

The first of these people, helping to share the load from day one, was Harry Rapf, who oversaw MGM's less prestigious bread-and-butter pictures. The group soon grew to five (eventually even more were added, including Thalberg's brother-in-law Lawrence Weingarten), but this initial five, essential though they were, stubbornly remain quasi-anonymous, thought of in the collective way Ad Schulberg described them to her son Budd: "first-rate minds like Paul Bern and the other bright young people Irving has around him."

Bern was often considered as first among equals not only because of his acknowledged closeness to Thalberg but also because of his championing of actresses who had been disconcerted by the system, Joan Crawford and Jean Harlow being the most prominent. Thalberg valued Bern's cultural sophistication as well as his degree from the American Academy of Dramatic Arts. Samuel Marx described Bern noncommittally as "an intellectual, and soft-spoken, with a slight Teutonic accent and gentle Continental manners," but others tended to take sides. To Lenore Coffee he was "kind but weak as water. That's why he clung so to Thalberg; he needed his strength." To Joan Crawford, whom he expertly mentored, Bern was "a kindly soul who somehow managed to carry another full-time load—the problems of those who were miserable." And Irene Mayer Selznick was even more effusive, calling him "the only person I ever knew who cherished people he loved as much for their frailties as for their virtues. . . . He always looked at those he cared for with such tenderness and mercy that one almost believed one partook of the qualities he attributed."

To the extent that they were creatures of Thalberg's system without noticeable independent power, it was perhaps inevitable that Rapf, Bern, and their three colleagues—Bernard Hyman, Albert Lewin, and Hunt Stromberg—also did their work without a great deal of admiration. David Lewis said Mayer told him Thalberg was the only producer he respected, adding, "The rest of them are all dummies." The screenwriters the supervisors dealt with also tended to take their frustrations with the system out on them. Hyman, a bright New York kid who'd known Thalberg since his Universal days, was dismissed by Ben Hecht as having "a puppy's eagerness for life." Lewin, the rare Hollywood college man who had graduated Phi Beta Kappa from NYU and had a master's in English literature from Harvard, was similarly described as "an eager little Mickey Mouse of a man" by Anita Loos, while S. N. Behrman quotes another writer saying Lewin "was like a glass of water without the glass." F. Scott Fitzgerald, for his part, names Lewin as one of the men surrounding Thalberg "who were very far below him."

Fitzgerald also had faint praise for Stromberg, calling the former journalist and publicity man "a sort of one-finger Thalberg, without Thalberg's scope, but with his intense power of work and his absorption in his job." Donald Ogden Stewart was much harder, mocking the man for the "touchstone" he applied to all scenes. "'Son,' he would say, 'I like it [spit]. I think it's a fine scene [spit]. But how about that dumb Scranton miner? Would *he* understand it?' Hunt had never been in Scranton and I don't think he had ever seen a miner, but every bit I wrote had to get the commendation of that mythical creature sitting in a Scranton movie house. Charlie MacArthur and I once tried to get a friend in Scranton to send us out a real miner, but he claimed he couldn't find one dumb enough."

Yet despite all this behind-the-scenes mockery, or maybe because of it, Thalberg's supervisors had considerable in-group cohesion. Thalberg and his team had regularly scheduled lunches together in a private dining room, and Albert Lewin, for one, remembered an inspiring unity. "Under Thalberg, everybody helped everybody else. Thalberg was the team captain and the team was small. Only about half a dozen of us made the entire product. . . . The fact that it was anonymous made everybody ready and happy to win glory for the team. It wasn't a jealous, political affair, as it became later on."

Still, convivial lunches or not, working for Thalberg could not have been easy. Unlike more laissez-faire types, Thalberg was a legendary perfectionist with an uncanny ability to spot errors in a situation. Douglas Shearer reported that Thalberg went on the *Mutiny on the Bounty* set and "instantly commented, 'Those sails on the Bounty are too gray for a bright sunny day,'" and Mervyn LeRoy remembered a conversation after a preview of *Tugboat Annie* about a comic scene with Wallace Beery where Thalberg asked him, "Don't you think it would be better if his shoes squeaked when he walked? Wouldn't that help the picture?" The director answered that a reshoot would be complicated and expensive, at which point

> Thalberg fixed me with his eyes. He could look stern when he felt like it.
> "Mervyn, I didn't ask you how much it would cost. I asked you whether it would help the picture."
> "Sure it would help."
> "All right, shoot it."

As the *Tugboat Annie* anecdote illustrates, what was most characteristic of Thalberg's filmmaking system, the place where his instincts for story and his unapologetic meticulousness came together, was in his exacting system of previews coupled with extensive reshoots to correct what had been discovered from public reaction. Thalberg was far from the first to make use of previews, with silent comics Fatty Arbuckle, Chaplin, Keaton, and then Harold Lloyd, "the first person to attempt to make the screening process 'scientific,'" preceding him. But Thalberg's ability to read audiences and his willingness to go for broke with changes set what he did apart from the way everyone else operated. As late as 1995 director Sidney Lumet wrote of films where "If I am wrong, I need the Irving Thalberg set-up to fix it: sets, costumes, actors, everything I'll need to reshoot anywhere from 5 to 50 per cent of the movie."

MGM previewed films in then outlying areas of Los Angeles like Glendale, Huntington Park, Pomona, Riverside, San Bernardino, and Santa Ana, places that were reachable by the once omnipresent and legendary Red Cars of the Pacific Electric Railway System. Previews were held with such frequency that a spur was built that connected the studio to the Culver City branch of the line and a chartered private trolley car would, at a cost of $400 per night, convey the group to whatever distant location was being used. That saved driving time and allowed Thalberg and his team, plus Mayer if he was attending, to dine and relax en route to the theater (the executives were avid cardplayers and Thalberg was a devotee of bridge) and discuss the film coming back. "He was like a surgeon," remembered an impressed David Lewis, "exploring, examining and ultimately healing."

Though his intense observation of the audience from different vantage points in theaters meant he sometimes didn't need anything else, Thalberg was a big believer in the response cards audience members filled out, which sometimes rubbed artists the wrong way. When MGM previewed 1931's highbrow Alfred Lunt/Lynn Fontanne *The Guardsman*, the cards were scathing, and when Thalberg began to read them aloud, Fontanne snapped. "Don't read any more of those things if they're all as moronic as the ones you've read," she said. "You will find an audience for it, but it won't be made up of people like the ones who wrote those nasty vulgar cards." Taking the reverse tack, Marion Davies reported, was her own mother, who anonymously filled out stacks of pro-Davies cards at the preview of 1927's *The Red Mill*. The actress was so chagrined that after Thalberg read them she contrived to get hold of the incriminating evidence and destroy it before he figured out the ruse.

While not everyone in Hollywood thought all the work involved in this preview and retake process was a great idea— screenwriter Frederica Sagor Maas called Thalberg "the worst perpetrator of waste in the business"—the executive who said, "always remember, there's nothing too good for the audience" considered it a dereliction of duty not to improve a movie if you could, and his colleagues at MGM agreed. "Up until Thalberg, you had a schedule, you finished the picture, and that was the end of it," said actor Conrad Nagel. "Thalberg conceived the idea that a picture could be redone." And not necessarily the really bad ones. "Why spend cash and time transforming a lemon into a lime?" he once asked, ever the realist. On the other hand, he felt "the difference between something good and something bad is great, but the difference between something good and something superior is often very small."

So, as Albert Lewin explained,

> If we had an extremely successful preview, as we often did in those days, most people would pat themselves on the back and be awfully satisfied. He would tear the picture apart and improve it. He would push and push to get the very last bit of excellence into a production. . . .
>
> Sometimes three or four days of retakes will improve a picture enormously, and Irving never hesitated to spend the extra money.

He did this so often—telling directors, Howard Hawks remembered, "Now, I think you could do a little bit better with this"— that the studio acquired the "Retake Valley" nickname, echoing the comment of Thalberg (who preferred calling the new material "added scenes") that "movies aren't made; they're remade."

Thalberg's most famous makeovers, as we have seen, included *The Big House*, *The Champ*, and *Red-Headed Woman*, but for the executive's most celebrated rescue you have to turn to a 1931 film, *The Sin of Madelon Claudet*, so emblematic of the legerdemain at his command that versions of the story can be found in more than a dozen books, and Thalberg himself wrote about it two years later in a November 4, 1933, bylined article for the *Saturday Evening Post* headlined "Why Motion Pictures Cost So Much." "We produced not long ago a beautifully pathetic story which brought tears to the eyes of every man and woman in the studio," he wrote, identifying *Claudet* by name. "But when we took a sample print out to a little theater just outside of Los Angeles and tried it on a typical motion-picture audience, there wasn't a wet eye in the house. . . . What we had thought was pathos was only bathos. If we had let that picture go to the public without spending any more money on it, however small, we would not only have sacrificed an outstanding artistic success but we would probably have ruined, almost at its inception, the career of one of the screen's most remarkable personalities." All of which is true as far as it goes, but it's the details Thalberg leaves out that make the story significant.

The unnamed actress is Helen Hayes, even then a force in American theater. The main reason she was making films at all was that she was married to Charles MacArthur, one of Thalberg's favorite writers. To make it easier for the couple to be together in Los Angeles, a project entitled "Lullaby" and loosely taken from a dated 1924 play of the same name was proposed for her. There were doubts from the beginning, with MacArthur considering the first draft script "so bad it would sink Garbo," so when Thalberg countersuggested he do the rewrite, MacArthur knew he had to agree.

Even at these early stages, what became *Madelon Claudet* was a purposeful tearjerker whose plot of a woman pretending to be dead so she can use her prostitution earnings to send her illegitimate son to medical school certainly pulled out all the stops. But as Thalberg had recounted, the initial preview had been a fiasco. Hayes herself reported, "It's hard to say who liked the picture least—the audience that hissed at the end or the trade paper critics who ripped it apart. Or me." Screenwriter/husband MacArthur was equally distraught. "Helen has been a star for 25 years," he worried, "and I've ruined her in an hour and a half."

What Thalberg's account doesn't reveal is that he was not at that initial preview. Rather, along with Norma Shearer, he was on one of his regular visits to the spa at Bad Nauheim, Germany, to get treatments for his heart. "When Irving returned," Hayes continued, "he asked about my picture and was told it was shelved permanently. He had it screened and decided it was only half-bad. Rewriting and reshooting could salvage it." With MacArthur doing the actual writing, Thalberg came up with key suggestions, first detailed by MGM chronicler Bosley Crowther, that deftly reconfigure the story, adding beats that seem obvious in retrospect but that no one else had thought of.

A scene was added midfilm showing Madelon's initial rejection of her infant son changing before our eyes to intense love. Another scene was added at the end, having her successful doctor son (one of Robert Young's first roles) examining her without knowing who she was. And the whole thing was framed by a prologue and epilogue underlining the theme of maternal sacrifice. Hayes, who was working days shooting *Arrowsmith* for Samuel Goldwyn, clandestinely worked nights shooting the new material so as not to upset the rival mogul. With a title change from the tepid "Lullaby" to the racier *The Sin of Madelon Claudet*, the picture that had been permanently shelved ended up winning Helen Hayes her first Academy Award.

Despite heroic rescue jobs like this, Thalberg made it a policy, perhaps his best-known one, not to put his name on screen for any of the films he supervised. "Credit you give yourself," he said more than once, "is not worth having." But on closer examination, the issue of Thalberg and credit is a perplexing, tangled one. Yes, he did not put his name on his films, and his belief in that dictum was sincere, an action that impressed even professional cynics like Ben Hecht, who extolled Thalberg's "modesty," calling it "as incredible in Hollywood as feathers on an eel. . . . To his death this leading Hollywood creator of movies remained to the public the little man who wasn't there."

But none of that means, especially in his later years when he was considering establishing his own production company, that Thalberg was averse to being known. He gave on-the-record interviews, wrote that bylined piece for the *Saturday Evening Post*, and, as the husband of a major star, was interviewed for fan magazine cover stories with headlines like "The Norma Shearer Irving Thalberg Loves," in which "the famous producer, lowering his guard of reticence, grants a rare interview." A mass-circulation magazine ad for his *Mutiny on the Bounty* (headlined "A Thousand Hours of Hell for One Moment of Love!") boasted that "Irving Thalberg, master-maker of motion pictures, has given all of us a chance to re-live a story that will never die." And *Ink-Stained Hollywood*, a study of the trade press, posits a tacit quid pro quo between Thalberg and *Hollywood Reporter* publisher W. R. Wilkerson: "In a private letter, Wilkerson thanked the producer for 'the font of information you furnish me on each and every visit we have.' For his part, Wilkerson made sure that Thalberg stayed in the news and his columns in a manner that Thalberg approved."

Following their boss's lead, the supervisors under Thalberg also did not take the kind of on-screen credit they would have been entitled to at other studios. Samuel Marx reported that during a bon voyage lunch before that 1931 trip to Bad Nauheim, Thalberg "thanked his associates for their accomplishments. He concluded, 'Supervisor is an old-fashioned word, you fellows are rightly producers.' He offered to credit them with that title on their productions for the first time. But he would not do it himself. They decided then not to put their names on screen either. It was an impressive display of 'follow the leader.' " It may have been caused by an unwillingness to displease Thalberg, but it is also possible that no one wanted to put any measurable distance between himself and his revered boss.

Speaking to this point in the most poignant way is an anecdote involving East Coast executive Bertram Bloch, who was visiting the studio and lunching with the supervisors when Thalberg called from New York just before boarding his boat to Europe. Bloch noticed,

> Nobody brought up business with Thalberg. They were all concerned with his health and wanted to know if he had taken along heavy underwear, and did he have a raincoat, rubbers and an umbrella?
>
> "Why was that?" Bloch asked, when the conversations ended.
>
> "Because," said [Bernard] Hyman, "as long as Irving lives, we're all great men!"

In addition to its other qualities, the MGM system inevitably marginalized directors, individuals who'd been untouchable kings of the hill until, as will be remembered, Thalberg fired Erich von Stroheim from Universal's 1923 production of *Merry-Go-Round*. Thalberg built on that leveling effect when he changed studios, even rejecting Samuel Marx's suggestion that he hire the destitute legend D. W. Griffith with a curt "I could never work with Griffith, nor he with me." Thalberg even had a set speech, Marx reported, that he gave to incoming directors: "I consider the director is on the set to communicate what I expect of my actors. It's my experience that many directors only realize seventy-five percent of our scenarios, and while audiences never know how much they missed, I do. . . . If you can't conform to my system, it would be wiser not to start your film at all." Individualistic director Frank Capra did work on the lot briefly, and the experience still rankled him decades later when he wrote about it in his autobiography. "They were 'organization' men," he said bitingly of his MGM colleagues, "as anonymous as vice presidents of General Motors." Though there were exceptions like George Cukor, for the most part MGM directors were expert craftsmen more than visionary artists, role players of whom Cukor himself said, "They cast directors, you know, like actors." One result, calculated writer Aljean Harmetz, who did the math, was that though "MGM pictures and actors won the lion's share of early Academy Awards . . . of the first thirty Academy Awards given for Best Director, MGM films won only two." As Anita Loos smartly (if a bit self-servingly) summed up, "The directors were dunces you know. That they ever made anything good was due to Irving Thalberg. He handed them scripts that were practically foolproof."

If there was a filmmaker who prospered under the MGM system, it would have to be W. S. "Woody" Van Dyke, who began at the studio in 1926 with a series of Col. Tim McCoy Westerns and went on to make dozens more films, including *Tarzan the Ape Man* and the Clark Gable/Spencer Tracy *San Francisco*, before his premature death in 1943. Celebrated as a no-nonsense fast worker, a quality both Mayer and Thalberg valued, Van Dyke in 1936, his most prolific year, directed six films, including *After the Thin Man*, the first sequel to the 1934 original, which he had also directed.

Most stories about Van Dyke reflect astonishment at the man's sheer audacity. McCoy, a former cavalry officer, remembers him as "annoyingly arrogant, maddeningly self-opinionated, dammed sure of himself and utterly ruthless" but greatly admired his skill. Though he gave up and classified Van Dyke under "Miscellany" in his authoritative *American Cinema*, critic Andrew Sarris also couldn't resist the work: "Woody Van Dyke made more good movies than his reputation for carelessness and haste would indicate. Perhaps carelessness and haste are precisely the qualities responsible for the breezy charm" of his best pictures. Van Dyke was a hard drinker as well as a hard worker who warned his actors, "If you can't get up with me in the morning, don't go out with me at night." The closest he came to formulating a philosophy was when he told a magazine reporter, "The trouble with most movie people is that they take the whole thing too seriously."

Before Van Dyke or one of the other studio directors got their hands on a finished script, before a first draft to be fussed over by Thalberg's teams of screenwriters even existed, attention was focused on the studio's foundation stone, the story department, the place from whence all ideas came. That it became one of MGM's great strengths stemmed not only from its breadth and depth but also from the ways its key personnel were linked to Thalberg and, in a particularly quixotic way, to Louis B. Mayer as well.

The studio devoted considerable resources to the department because Thalberg believed it was important to be on top of intellectual property no matter where it came from, and MGM had the wherewithal to make that happen. The enterprise was so vast that people writing about it both then and now have difficulty agreeing on its actual size. The figure dating from closest to the studio's heyday was Philip K. Scheuer's 1934 estimate in the *Los Angeles Times* that MGM had 500,000 synopses that were added to "at the rate of about 14,000 yearly." These weren't just filed away; there also existed "an elaborate cross index listing the plot structure, the dramatic possibilities, and the characteristic comic or tragic elements of the story," as well as "their relation to the available stars and featured players."

Thalberg, who prepared for his staff an elaborate "The Ten Commandments for Studio Readers" ("Your most important duty is to find great ideas"), could also make decisions on a moment's notice. Samuel Marx relates that "in his office, late one evening,

I casually mentioned that an interesting play had appeared in New York the previous night" and gave a brief synopsis.

> Thalberg was ready to leave his office but he stopped, picked up the phone and called an M-G-M executive in his New York home.
>
> "They're asking fifty thousand for the film rights," said the executive.
>
> "Buy it," said Thalberg, and went home.
>
> The play, *As You Desire Me* by Luigi Pirandello, proved one of Garbo's biggest hits.

Though Marx was MGM's story editor from 1930 until Thalberg's death, another story employee, officially only Marx's subordinate, had a kind of influence even he did not: Kate Corbaley, known unofficially throughout the studio as "Mayer's Scheherazade."

Corbaley, a Phi Beta Kappa from Stanford, predated Marx at the studio, arriving in 1926, and probably could have had his job except that it demanded travel and she was a single parent devoted to raising four daughters. She had, like Thalberg, an encyclopedic knowledge of stories ("although her mind was filled with their plots," said Marx, "she remembered every one, conjuring up their details at the mere hint of a title"), but that is not why Mayer valued her. Rather, in a manner several observers said reminded him of his beloved mother, Corbaley was a wondrous storyteller. For Mayer wouldn't read scripts; instead, he had them, or their source material, read to him aloud in summary or word-for-word form. More than one person belonged to a group screenwriter George Oppenheimer called "the lady story-tellers, the Metro troubadours," and they were so effective before the fact that prudent writers like Donald Ogden Stewart "saw the light and whenever assigned to a script, made a deal with the girl to let me know the gospel according to her before attempting any of my own interpretations."

But Corbaley had a special gift, able among other things to make Mayer cry, which he did no fewer than three times during her reading of a draft of William Saroyan's *The Human Comedy*. Marx, who heard her frequently, has left the only record of the "special finesse" of her technique: "She never forgot a detail, never needed to retrace her steps," he recalled. "She injected color, clarity and characterizations that might well have won the envy of the original author. Because she literally thought in pictures, she could embroider a plot into a movie with elements its creator might have overlooked." When Corbaley died in 1938 at age sixty, Marx was a pallbearer and at the service was witness to quite a moment. "Louis B. Mayer and I sat side by side on a church bench. During the eulogy, he leaned close and said, 'I would rather have lost any star than this woman.'"

15

Fissures

MEDIA ENTREPRENEUR Henry Luce, cofounder of *Time* magazine, promised potential advertisers many things when he sent out a 1929 prospectus for his new high-end journalistic venture, *Fortune*, including issues "so richly illustrated and so distinguished in appearance that it will be instinctive to turn the pages." One thing he did not promise, however, was distinguished bylines. Henry Luce did not believe in bylines, distinguished or otherwise. That's why the names of the writer or writers who wrote the December 1932 *Fortune* story on MGM are lost to history.

Which is a shame for several reasons. The MGM spread covered an impressive fifteen heavily illustrated pages in the sumptuous eleven-by-thirteen-inch issue, not counting a full-color four-page insert showcasing what the magazine called a "*pastiche* of M-G-M promotion." But more than that, more than the veiled antisemitism of some of its text, the magazine's de-

199

scription of the studio and how it worked noticeably increased the distance between MGM's pair of leaders, a tension that only worsened over time.

Certainly, at the outset 1932 had not seemed like a year that was going to be trouble. Fiscally, as the *Fortune* piece indicated, the outlook was excellent. MGM had amassed $15 million in profit in 1930, $12 million in 1931, and in 1932 its $8 million net would make it the only studio in the black in that heart-of-the-Depression year. Some of the money came from an unexpected source, a film that created new stars rather than profiting from established ones, as had become Mayer and Thalberg's pattern: *Tarzan the Ape Man.*

Created in 1912 by Edgar Rice Burroughs, Tarzan and his adventures as an infant British lord raised by great apes to athletic manhood in the jungles of Africa was not a newcomer to film, not even close. The first movie version, *Tarzan of the Apes,* starring Elmo Lincoln, appeared in 1918 and numerous others appeared in the 1920s. But none of this previous work fazed Mayer and Thalberg, who focused on the Tarzan stories after the success of the Africa-set *Trader Horn* encouraged them to look around for similarly exotic material. On the same page about this, the two were confident, correctly as it turned out, that adding the MGM gloss to even familiar material would make audiences disregard the past.

MGM did not want any specific Tarzan stories, it wanted use of the character, and Thalberg sent Samuel Marx to negotiate with the business-minded Burroughs, who lived on a property he had bought from *Los Angeles Times* publisher Harrison Grey Otis in what is present-day Tarzana. The author asked for $100,000, Marx offered $15,000, the agreement was made at $40,000. "When we closed the deal, he admitted he had always wanted the picture made at MGM and if I had held out, he would have let it go for nothing. 'If you had held out,' I told him in return, 'you would have got your hundred thousand.' It was true; Thalberg had said, 'Don't lose it.'"

Woody Van Dyke was chosen to direct—fittingly, because chunks of the Africa footage he shot for the earlier *Trader Horn* appeared in the new film. The script did away entirely with Tarzan's backstory, jumping directly into a plot about comely young Englishwoman Jane Parker joining her father on a quest for a legendary elephant graveyard where a million pounds of ivory was said to be lying around for the taking. Spoiler alert: Tarzan lives in the neighborhood and has his own thoughts on the matter.

J.J. Cohn, MGM's executive head of production, turned out to be one of the first executives to sense the film's potential. "If there was any argument about budget, Mayer was the arbitrator," he told Mayer biographer Gary Carey. "On the first *Tarzan* film, I went to Thalberg and showed him a budget he thought was too high—*Tarzan the Ape Man* was originally intended as a programmer. I argued that some special effects might help the film, though they would add maybe $100,000 to the budget. Thalberg sent me to Mayer. He said, 'Do what you can,' which meant, I deciphered, 'Do it right *but* do it as cheaply as possible.' The picture cost about $450,000, a considerable amount for that time, but it grossed about $2 million, and I doubt that it would ever have made that much had it been produced on the cheap."

The key to that success was the freshness and charm of the pairing of Johnny Weissmuller as Tarzan and Maureen O'Sullivan as Jane. It began when screenwriter Cyril Hume, who was staying at the Hollywood Athletic Club, saw Weissmuller at the club's pool. This was no surprise, for the 6-foot-3, 190-pound athlete was a celebrated swimmer, having won a total of five gold medals at the 1924 Paris and 1928 Amsterdam Olympics. Never having acted before, Weissmuller passed muster with director Van Dyke and supervisor Bernard Hyman in large part because his previous life had both toned his body and made him at ease when performing with few clothes on. Maureen O'Sullivan had had her Fox option dropped just two weeks before her MGM test, and she signed her contract the day before shooting began. As many had before, she had trouble adjusting to Van Dyke's speed: "'Can I do it again?' 'No, you should have thought about it the first time.'"

When *Tarzan* became a hit, the studio immediately began planning for a sequel. Given that the complexity of Burroughs's legal arrangements allowed other Tarzan films to enter the marketplace, Mayer and Thalberg wisely chose not to rush the sequel but to put some work in it and schedule the next appearance of "the best known, the most loved character ever conceived in the mind of man" far enough in the future that they could accurately advertise *Tarzan and His Mate* as "Two Years in the Making."

MGM ended up doing six Tarzan movies with Weissmuller and O'Sullivan between 1932 and 1942, with trailers making sure to emphasize each as "All New! All Different!" Weissmuller loved the part, going on to do six more Tarzan movies for RKO, but to O'Sullivan, who soon tired of the jungle, it seemed the studio "turned them out perpetually, one after another, it was just an endless stream." People could not get enough of Tarzan, and this included prestigious director William Wellman, who told critic/historian Richard Schickel he had done some last-minute substitute directing on *Tarzan Escapes*, the third film, and "loved it. I went in to Mayer and I said, 'I want to do the next Tarzan.' He said, 'What are you talking about? It's beneath your dignity.' I said, 'To hell with it. I haven't got any dignity.' And I begged him to let me do another Tarzan and he wouldn't let me do it. I never had so much fun making a picture."

Aside from *Tarzan the Ape Man* the other major success for Thalberg and Mayer in 1932 was of course *Grand Hotel*, and the April 16 premier provided an unexpected moment of what seemed like more good news. Paul Bern, the MGM supervisor known both for his closeness to Thalberg and his willingness to provide friendship and support to young women enmeshed in the studio system, showed up with a surprise date: the studio's rising platinum blonde star Jean Harlow, whom he'd championed for the title role in *Red-Headed Woman*. It was their first major public appearance, and it was noticed. But more was yet to come: on July 2, Bern and Harlow were married at a small private ceremony in Beverly Hills, with the first slices of wedding cake going to Thalberg and Shearer. He was forty-two, a resident of hotels for much of his adult life; she was twenty-one, up to now under the domineering thumb of a mother who insisted on always calling her "The Baby." Though Hollywood cynics scoffed at the union, both had good reasons, being in love aside, for wanting a life of their own.

Then came tragedy. On Labor Day morning, September 5, an employee discovered Bern's naked body in the dressing room of his Benedict Canyon home, a .38 caliber revolver nearby, death caused by a bullet to the head. A note, intended for Harlow (who had spent the night at her mother's house) was found. Addressed to "Dearest Dear," it read, "Unfortunately this is the only way to make good the frightful wrong I have done you and to wipe away my abject humiliation. I love you." Added after the signature was "You understand that last night was only a comedy." Because this was Hollywood, Mayer was called before the police, and soon Mayer, Thalberg, and publicity director Howard Strickling were at the death house. Also because this was Hollywood, nothing else about the case has been universally agreed upon.

Was the note genuine, a forgery, or something written earlier that had been cannily repurposed? Was it on a piece of paper small enough for Mayer to pocket it before Strickling persuaded him to give it to the police, or was it part of a larger guest book?

Was Bern's death suicide (as a coroner's jury was eventually to rule), or could there have been foul play? If it was suicide, was Bern sexually impotent, and if so was that a factor in his action? Did Mayer call in favors from district attorney Buron Fitts to protect Harlow's career? Who was Dorothy Millette, and did she have a part in what transpired? Advocates can be found on all sides of each of these complicated positions, including Samuel Marx, part of the MGM group at the house, who at age eighty-eight coauthored a book called *Deadly Illusions: Jean Harlow and the Murder of Paul Bern*, which explored the Dorothy Millette connection.

Millette, as it turned out, was a woman who had lived with Bern in New York long enough to be considered his common-law wife, calling into question the legality of his marriage to Harlow. Did Millette visit Bern the night of his death? Did she murder him, or if his death was a suicide, was she the cause? Millette herself would never answer these questions: the day after Bern's body was found she boarded the *Delta King*, a stern-wheel riverboat ferry headed upriver from San Francisco to Sacramento, and a week later her body was found in the water, her death ruled a suicide. But whatever caused it, the effect of Bern's death on Thalberg was profound and unmistakable.

Bern's service was attended by MGM's top echelon, with Samuel Marx reporting that while "Mayer sat stiffly between Mannix and Strickling," his bearing was "in stern contrast to Thalberg, shoulders hunched, weeping bitterly." Albert Lewin, seated directly behind the customarily reserved Thalberg, concurred that "Irving loved Paul. He sobbed through the entire ceremony." Not only did Thalberg lose his entrée to areas of cultural sophistication that were relatively new to him, he lost a colleague and confidant as well. And Bern's death was more than a *memento mori*, an unwelcome and unneeded reminder of the projected shortness of his own life, but also a distinct shock. Given his own ever-looming mortality, Thalberg probably had

Thalberg at his most distraught, testifying in September 1932 at the
inquest following the controversial death of his close friend Paul Bern.
(CSU Archives/Everett Collection/Bridgeman Images)

instinctively assumed that he would be the first of his contemporaries to die, and with Bern's death following Chaney's, that
had proved not to be the case.

Given his temperament, it's not surprising that Thalberg
sought solace in work, as did Harlow, who was in the midst of
shooting *Red Dust*, the first of her five successful costarring
ventures with Clark Gable, when Bern died. But work for Thalberg proved to be insufficient. As biographer Bob Thomas reported, Thalberg "suffered moods of depression in the weeks
following Paul Bern's death. It was a rare and dangerous mood,

. . . 'What's it all for?' he muttered to one of his closest associates. 'Why the hell am I killing myself so Mayer and Schenck can get rich and fat.'" It was not only Bern's death that weighed on him; he was also upset that Mayer, his mind as ever focused on the studio's well-being, had orchestrated media coverage of the sordid details of his friend's death to focus on Bern's supposed impotence and thereby keep a valuable asset like Harlow scandal free.

Mayer's irritation with Thalberg over what he saw as the younger man's continued unreasonable demands for money, was aggravated by Thalberg's displays of dissatisfaction after Bern's death. Compensation had been an issue for Thalberg as recently as April of 1932, when he had successfully fought for a richer deal before signing a new five-year contract. Now, just a few months later, it came up again after Bern's death, but with a different twist. Clearly distraught, the man who had all but lived for his work said he wanted out, announcing to Mayer in late September that he was ill and did not want to be MGM's head of production any longer, contract or no contract. Nicholas Schenck was notified in New York, and the head of Loew's took a train to Los Angeles for face-to-face meetings to straighten things out.

Schenck met with Mayer first, and biographer Bosley Crowther reports that the studio head told him, "I believe the boy is getting spoiled. People are telling him how good he is. I believe it is turning his head a little. There are all kinds of offers." The offers part was certainly true, as Thalberg's gifts were well known, with Samuel Marx, for instance, relaying an anecdote about a Paramount sales conference. "An executive of that company announced that MGM would lend them their great stars. A voice from the rear called out, 'But will they lend us Thalberg?'"

A series of meetings involving Schenck, Thalberg, Mayer, and attorney J. Robert Rubin took place in Schenck's hotel suite, where Thalberg's demand changed to a year's leave of absence to rest and reset. The tension between Schenck and Thalberg was so intense that Mayer and Rubin, no strangers to verbal combat, could not stand to be present. "I was watching Schenck," Mayer remembered. "His fingernails were purple as he held onto the side of his chair. Irving was riding him terribly hard. . . . He told Schenck he didn't give a damn; that he was cold as ice, that he wasn't even human just as long as we made lots of money for the company. Oh, it was just fierce! And Schenck kept yelling back, 'Damn it, I've been decent and right with you!' . . . Oh it was hell! We got out of the room."

Though money was not on the table when Thalberg's existential crisis began, finally, as was often the case, money was what it all came down to. The complexity of MGM's financial situation made another pay raise impossible, so Schenck came up with the idea of offering Thalberg the opportunity to purchase shares of Loew's stock well below market value. Thalberg was offered 100,000 shares on this basis, and, in an attempt to make everyone a little happier, Mayer was offered 80,000 shares and Rubin 50,000. Agreement was reached on those numbers, but that does not mean everyone was happy. Mayer, in particular, saw himself demeaned by his lower number. He felt more strongly than ever that Thalberg cared more about himself and his financial situation than he did about the studio that bore the Mayer name. As for Schenck, always looking to divide and conquer where his West Coast executives were concerned, he took note of this split and filed it away for future use.

It was into this already superheated atmosphere that the *Fortune* story on the studio, dated December but available a month earlier, was published. Mayer is referred to in the first paragraph (without yet being named) as "a Polish immigrant who sometimes makes $500,000 a year and once spent the week-end with the Hoovers at the White House," but most of the skillfully written article that follows spends its time lauding Thalberg and his methods as "what Hollywood means by MGM . . . the reason for MGM's producing success." More than that, "he is now called a genius more often than anyone else in Hollywood, which means that the word is practically his nickname."

The piece does eventually get to Mayer, but first come a string of questionable ethnic descriptions: Samuel Marx is "an intelligent Hebrew with a Neanderthal forehead," Thalberg is "a small, finely-made Jew," his supervisors a group of "somber, sagacious Jews." When Mayer is talked about, much more concisely than Thalberg, it is as "the diplomat, the man of connections" someone who "probably does not spend more than half his time on matters closely pertaining to MGM." His relationship to talent, Mayer's greatest source of pride, is dismissed, and he is depicted as merely "a commercial diplomat. Contacts and contracts are his specialty."

Even more telling is the treatment of the two men in the more than two dozen black-and-white photographs reproduced to advantage on the magazine's thick stock. Not only is there a full-length portrait of Thalberg and Shearer, but there's also a George Hurrell glamour shot of Shearer, a photo of Thalberg's screenwriter sister Sylvia, a group shot of the Thalberg/Shearer wedding party ("The (Production) Brains & Wife & Relatives"), a glimpse of the exterior "*Chez* Thalberg," their Santa Monica home, even a shot of Thalberg's empty desk. Mayer, by contrast, gets no stand-alone portrait, appearing only in two group shots, one as part of that Thalberg wedding party, the other as a studio diplomat introducing Lionel Barrymore to a quartet of visiting U.S. senators.

Perhaps most wounding of all, Mayer is pointedly described as MGM's last remaining link to "the old regime of fur peddlers, secondhand jewelers, and nickelodeon proprietors who started all the major cinema companies." Having worked so hard and so long to transcend his immigrant status and become an American like Thalberg, even going to the extreme of declaring his birthday to be July 4 and perhaps taking diction lessons from actor Conrad Nagle, to be relegated to steerage one more time must have been especially galling. If Thalberg could never get enough money, Mayer could never get enough respect, and the *Fortune* piece put his insecurities into overdrive. And when anxiety took over, Frances Marion reported from experience, Mayer became an "injured lion lashing out blindly and furiously."

One of the first things Mayer did in the aftermath of the grueling battle over Thalberg's status was reach out to his son-in-law David O. Selznick. Selznick, who had married Mayer's daughter Irene in 1930, was currently doing quite well as executive vice president in charge of production at RKO. Searching for ways to be less dependent on Thalberg, Mayer invited Selznick to join MGM as head of a producing unit. Soon to become celebrated for the length and specificity of his memos and letters, Selznick wrote a detailed "Dear Dad" communication to Mayer on November 12, starting with the unambiguous declaration, "I have decided that under no circumstances would it be right for me to go with MGM." His reasons were many but perhaps most important, "I have the most enormous respect for Irving Thalberg. I regard him as the greatest producer the industry has yet developed. . . . I could not help but be subordinate to Irving—and much as I respect him, I do not want, in my own field, to be subordinate to anyone."

Six weeks after that letter, in a way that might have been scripted by MGM's stable of writers, an often feared but still unnerving crisis upended all previous calculations. The force of preexisting stresses—Paul Bern's calamitous death, the worsening of the relationship with Mayer, the battle over what he felt he was due from his bosses—was compounded for Thalberg by his celebrating with more gusto than usual at the raucous MGM Christmas party. The result was inevitable: the man who had worried his whole life about his heart had another attack, his first since 1924. The studio initially tried to pass it off publicly as influenza, but, as Salka Viertel remembered, "there were rumors he had suffered a heart attack," which MGM soon confirmed.

Shearer, whose strength of will was fully Thalberg's equal, took charge of her husband's convalescence. Told by his doctor that he could receive no visitors, she initially turned away not only Mayer and Schenck, who made the trip from New York expressly to see him, but his mother Henrietta as well. The couple's annual spa trip to Europe was planned for February and was to be extended for a greater time than usual. But while Thalberg rested, maneuvers were taking place in the wake of his illness. Mayer and Schenck, still smarting from the harshness of their verbal jousting with Thalberg, found common ground (under the guise of doing what was best for the studio and their colleague's health) in planning to make themselves less dependent on Thalberg for the quality pictures that were MGM's signature product.

David O. Selznick, as it turned out, had had a change of heart. His negotiations with RKO were at an impasse and his beloved father Lewis had died on January 24, 1933, his last words to David being "Blood is thicker than water." "Louis B. Mayer wasn't Mr. MGM, he was family," Irene Mayer Selznick, who was fiercely against the move, explained, "and David was Little Boy Lost." Even though Thalberg was still head of production, it was announced in February that Selznick was to have his own independent unit, an MGM first, at a magisterial salary of $4,000 a week. As his unhappy wife reported, "The press came up with good old nepotism: 'The Son-in-Law Also Rises.' Unfair or not, that line dogged him for many a year. For a man who boasted of his reputation as a free spirit, it was devastating." Frances Marion reported Mayer was telling people, "I'm doing this to spare Irving, who is so dear to me . . . just like a brother," to which Marion couldn't help adding *sotto voce*, "Yes, just like Cain who killed Abel."

Thalberg was still recuperating and anticipating his European trip, but Mayer did manage to deliver the news about Selznick in person, which led to a tremendous row, both men falling into what Bosley Crowther characterized as a "furious, abusive fight," with Mayer defensive and Thalberg angry that something so significant had been done behind his back. Once again, like a father bedeviled by a lack of comprehension between himself and the son he loved (roles that he and Thalberg invariably fell into), Mayer did something Crowther characterized as "extraordinary—probably unique." He took on "the most humble act that Mayer ever performed—at least in his business dealings," composing a letter of apology to Thalberg.

Mayer's letter, dated February 23, feels unmistakably sincere. Mayer was, not surprisingly, a gifted compartmentalizer, able to separate his ruthless business side from the emotions of his personal feelings. He gets right to the point, saying, "I cannot permit you to go away to Europe without expressing to you my regret that our last conference had to end in a loss of temper, particularly on my part." Bemoaning nameless colleagues who would be "only too glad to create ill feeling" between them, he insists he never would "cease to love you or entertain anything but a feeling of real sincerity and friendship for you." Mayer seems genuinely hurt by the "air of suspicion on your part towards me," by the way Thalberg "chose to bitingly and sarcastically accuse me of many things, by innuendo, which I am supposed to have done to you." Still, Mayer never strays from the job at hand. "I am big enough to apologize to you. . . . Believe me to be your real friend, and to know that when I tell you I have the greatest possible affection and sincere friendship for you, I am telling the truth. . . . I assure you I will go on loving you to the end."

Thalberg tried to respond in kind in his February 25 reply, but his sense of injury and his habit of distance precluded that. His initial apology—"For any words that I may have used that aroused bitterness in you, I am truly sorry and I apologize"— feels pro forma, in part because it is followed by Thalberg defiantly sticking to his guns: "There are, however, loyalties that are greater than loyalties of friendship. There are the loyalties to ideals, the loyalties to principles without which friendship loses character and real meaning." Thalberg did, however, end with an olive branch, asking Mayer to visit again before the European trip, "as nothing would make me happier than to feel we had parted at least as good personal friends, if not better, than ever before."

There was another letter, however, that Thalberg was working on at the same time, multiple drafts of which, including one handwritten on stationary from Lake Tahoe's Squaw Valley resort, are in the Academy's Margaret Herrick Library. It was a long and through letter to Nicholas Schenck, filled with detail about specific actors ("Beery and Dressler must be handled with supreme care or there will be very little left to their value as stars") in which Thalberg gave his emotions free rein. Speaking frankly of his new colleague in an early draft, he writes, "I think it was very wrong of you to force me to consent to a contract with David Selznick, permitting him to produce as he sees fit and paying him a salary of $4,000 a week. . . . I believe the type of contract and the money paid him will destroy the harmony and loyalty that has existed on our lot." Thalberg also doesn't hesitate to speak up for himself: "For nine years I have guided the production policy of this company with ever increasing success. . . . I have brought together, developed and maintained a great array of stars and other talent . . . until today we possess more box-office stars than the balance of the industry combined." And he underlines his belief in the system he created and ran, his "firm conviction that without the supervision of one chief executive with the experience, wisdom and skill sufficient to enable him to maintain certain policies, no company can be assured of success."

Troubled though he was at what he viewed as an insulting, short-sighted disregard for what he had achieved, Thalberg felt the differences of opinion between himself, Schenck, and Mayer were still open for debate. "Upon my return from my trip," he wrote in a brief note to Schenck, "I shall again discuss this matter with you at great length." He had no idea the MGM he would return to would not be the MGM he left.

16

◆｜◆｜◆

Alone Together

HELEN HAYES WAS a vivid storyteller as well as a great actress, and to hear her recount the exact moment when Irving Thalberg found out the roof had fallen in on him is riveting. She and husband Charles MacArthur had accompanied Thalberg and Norma Shearer on their extended European sabbatical. The couples were staying at the French Riviera's luxurious Hôtel du Cap, when, as Hayes recounted in the documentary series *MGM: When the Lion Roars,* "there was a knock on the hotel door. It was Norma. 'Charlie, Charlie, come help,' she said. 'Irving has had an attack.' Irving was lying on the bed, his beautiful face ivory white, his eyes closed. All he said was, 'They knifed me, Charlie. They knifed me.'"

What a cable from Mayer had just informed Thalberg was that his position as vice president in charge of production had been abolished. When he returned to Culver City, he would not oversee the studio's half a hundred films but only those made

214

by his own unit, just like David O. Selznick. Though Thalberg, given the arrival of Selznick, had likely entertained worst-case-scenario fears of something like this happening, having a nightmare suddenly materialize must have been shattering. And Mayer including the words "AM DOING THIS FOR YOU" did not help.

Thalberg eventually learned the specifics of the studio restructuring. As Bob Thomas described the scenario, Schenck came out in person to talk to Thalberg's group of supervisors on behalf of himself and Mayer, starting with the statement "We don't know when or if Irving is coming back." Stressing that concern for Thalberg's health was foremost on their minds, "we are breaking the studio up into autonomous units, and we're asking you men to head the units. You will be full-fledged producers, and you will get screen credit for the films you produce. When Irving comes back, he will have his own unit, too." Everyone but the ever-loyal Albert Lewin said yes, and the deed was done.

Mayer, especially, was at great pains to inform all and sundry about his concern for Thalberg's health, telling Helen Hayes, "I'm doing it for the little fella's good. He was killing himself." Irene Mayer Selznick, perhaps not surprisingly, was the rare observer who agreed with him. "Much has been made of my father taking over the studio completely at this time, as though he had been in a tug-of-war with Irving," she wrote. "The truth of the matter is that the crisis of Irving's health had created a vacuum." Mayer's concern for Thalberg was genuine as far as it went, but it fit a little too conveniently into his and Schenck's plans for increasing their control over production. No matter how Schenck and Mayer tried to spin it, the feeling on the lot was as writer Donald Ogden Stewart described it on returning to Culver City: "I found that there had been a rather disturbing palace revolution at M-G-M and that the new king was Louis B. Mayer's son-in-law David Selznick." A group of exhibitors even went as far as telegramming Thalberg their support, writing they were "incensed because Louis Mayer taking full credit for product and placing you same status as Selznick. Entire industry for you."

Another reason Thalberg did not take well to Mayer's move is that the two men had become reflexively suspicious of each other's actions no matter what the situation. When Thalberg got to New York from Los Angeles on the first leg of his European trip, for instance, he had not been pleased to learn that Mayer had done some fancy verbal footwork to persuade studio personnel to accept, in the wake of President Franklin D. Roosevelt's bank holiday, a Depression-related 50 percent pay cut, calling it a threat to "the morale and loyalty of my people." Which, creating as it did an impetus to the formation of both the Screen Actors Guild and the Screen Writers Guild, is what it turned out to be. "Oh that L. B. Mayer," writer Albert Hackett said. "He created more communists than Karl Marx."

The details of Mayer's performance on that March 1933 day are worth repeating. He entered the all-studio meeting, remembered skeptical participant Samuel Marx, twenty minutes late,

> his face stubbled and his eyes red, as if his nights had been as sleepless as his days were unshaven. He began with a soft utterance: "My friends . . ." Then he broke down. Stricken, he held out his hands, supplicating, bereft of words.
>
> Lionel Barrymore spoke up huskily. "We all know why we are here. Don't worry, L.B. We're with you."
>
> [Screenwriter] Ernest Vajda was not with him. "I read the company statements, Mr. Mayer," he said. "I know our films are doing well. Maybe these other companies must do this, but this company should not. Let us wait; there's no reason to cut our pay at this time."
>
> Then Barrymore, with his commanding, stage-trained voice, drawled, "Mr. Vajda is like a man on his way to the guillotine, wanting to stop for a manicure."

The assemblage laughed and applauded. . . . When Mayer called for a vote, the pay cut was approved.

The group dispersed, and I was a few steps ahead of Mayer and [talent executive Bennie] Thau as we crossed the iron bridge to the front office building. Oblivious to the fact that I could surely hear him, he asked the talent expert, "How did I do?"

Donald Ogden Stewart missed the meeting, so, as he wryly remembered, he received the same treatment from Mayer on a more personal level. "I was invited to his office, and after he had explained to me—calling me 'Don' for the first time—about the distressing financial condition of the industry, his eyes suddenly filled with tears. I accepted, voluntarily of course, his suggestion that I take a 50 per cent reduction and offered him my handkerchief. I'm no monster—especially when a nice fellow like 'L.B.' needs my help. It was about this time that the first Screen Writers Guild was formed for protection against any further unselfish volunteering."

The rationale for Thalberg and Shearer's trip to Europe was a return visit to the sanatorium at Bad Nauheim in Germany where the German-speaking Thalberg had previously benefited from Dr. Franz Groedel's heart treatments. But this time the experience was different. Though the Nazis were not yet fully in power, they were strong enough to make their presence felt, and because the doctor was part Jewish, his establishment had had swastikas scrawled on it. Years later Shearer remembered to actor Eddie Lawrence that she and Thalberg "witnessed an attack on a couple from their window. As the couple were being beaten in the street below, Norma said, Thalberg alerted the hotel reception to call the police, but no police came. After that the Thalbergs saw at least one march of brown-shirted Nazi storm troopers, and Thalberg was able to translate the racist chants for Norma." Part of the reason for this trip was a tonsillectomy for Thalberg, which Dr. Groedel now wanted to post-pone, saying, "If anything happened to you, I and my country will both be blamed. They will say a prominent American Jew has been deliberately killed." But Thalberg insisted, and the operation, which was supposed to help his heart, proceeded as scheduled.

Thalberg's experience in Germany couldn't help but have an impact on him, but reports differ on what that impact was. Frances Marion, his close screenwriter colleague, recalls him saying, "I'll never return to Germany. There is corrosive evil destroying its roots." And when anti-Nazi fundraising banquets began to take place, like one in 1936 for Prince Hubertus zu Löwenstein, a Catholic anti-Nazi exile, Thalberg could always be counted on to attend. And his in-person involvement in a 1936 Hollywood Bowl production that was to aid Jewish char-ities was consuming enough to be a factor in his death.

But on the other side, writer Kyle Crichton reported en-gaging Thalberg in a discussion at a dinner party about the need to take a stand against Adolf Hitler and having the executive coolly insist that though "a lot of Jews will lose their lives," the end result would be that "Hitler and Hitlerism will pass; the Jews will still be there." More than two decades later, Crichton wrote, "I look back on this as one of the most remarkable expe-riences of my life. Even at the height of the argument, when we were bombarding him furiously, I couldn't help admiring the patience with which he parried the assault. In a sense, I suppose history has borne out his thesis: Hitler is gone; the Jews still live. But I can't help thinking of the millions of Jews who per-ished before this came about."

On a deeper level, it's not a surprise that Thalberg was always negotiating his balance on his private tightrope of what it meant to be Jewish in America, always weighing how publicly involved he could afford to be. As an American-born German Jew, he did not share in the Yiddishkeit of Mayer and the other founding moguls. But though not noticeably observant, Thalberg had a strong sense of Jewish identity, much of it revolving around Rabbi Edgar Magnin and the Wilshire Boulevard Temple and its commitment to Americanized Judaism. Budd Schulberg, definitely not a fan, still conceded, "Magnin was the right rabbi in the right temple in the right city at the right moment in time." And when Magnin decided he needed a bigger stage, not only did the massive 1929 Temple, inspired by Rome's Pantheon, take shape, but Hollywood studio heads lined up to lend a hand. While the major moguls made appropriately substantial gifts—the three Warner brothers funded studio artist Hugo Balin's creation of the sanctuary's wraparound murals, Carl Laemmle paid for eight spice-box-inspired bronze chandeliers, and Mayer donated two massive stained-glass windows—Thalberg's contribution was made with his usual perspicacity. He chose to pay for the painting of the Sh'ma, Judaism's foundational prayer, in gigantic gold-leaf Hebrew lettering surrounding the oculus, the central opening in the sanctuary dome 110 feet off the ground. Visible but not overpowering, significant but not ostentatious, it was exactly right.

Particularly noteworthy in this context is how prevalent antisemitism was in mainstream American culture of the time and how often it targeted Thalberg in particular. It wasn't just that Hollywood's Jews had to create their own country club, Hillcrest, because no Los Angeles club would admit them, but also that unpleasant caricatures of the MGM executive were not hard to find.

In the 1920s, for instance, the *Saturday Evening Post*, the largest-circulation weekly in the country, published a series of short stories by George Randolph Chester about an aspiring young studio executive named Isidor "Izzy" Iskovitch, a character whose relationship to Thalberg was clear even before "The Boy Wonder" story was published in May of 1923. Driven by craven love of money and the desire to be "a future motion picture magnate before whom all others should pale," Iskovitch, "with the curly hair and dark brown eyes and olive skin of his race," spoke exclusively in the kind of semiliterate clichés ("I got a job like there ain't any on any other lot") that must have pained the polished Thalberg. And there was worse to come.

In 1930 the brothers Carroll and Garrett Graham published *Queer People*, an intentionally scandalous novel about a journalist making his way through the cesspools of the movie business that was later republished with the more accurate title *Fleshpots of Malibu*. Even Budd Schulberg, who praised the novel as a forerunner of his *What Makes Sammy Run?*, cited a liberal use of "kikes" and "yids" as evidence of an "anti-semitism [that] even in those pre-Nazi days was a burr under the saddle cloth of the sensitive." In this roman à clef Thalberg was unmistakable as the villainous Israel Hoffberger, the lecherous exploiter of young actresses who "kept famous writers waiting hours to see him, made or killed stars with a word, ruled thousands of employees by fear and broke those who stood up against him." There's no evidence Thalberg ever read this slanderous narrative, but if he did, he probably put it down, as he did the antisemitic fury of clergymen furious at immoral movies, as one of the costs of doing business in an American society whose paper-thin tolerance of Jewish Hollywood felt as if it could vanish in an instant.

When Thalberg and Shearer landed in New York on the S.S. *Majestic* in mid-July 1933 at the end of their European journey, he did not immediately board a train for Los Angeles to take stock of what had happened at the studio in his absence. Instead, he made his way to Long Island at the invitation of his ultimate boss Nicholas Schenck to talk about his future. Eager to have the executive back on the lot, Schenck emphasized the positives of Thalberg's having his own unit, of having the pick of studio talent while being responsible for only half a dozen quality pictures a year. "As far as the company is concerned,"

Schenck argued, "we will be better off because we will get more money out of that than we would when you spend a great deal of your time on things you don't really have to." Ever in divide-and-conquer mode, Schenck anticipated one of Thalberg's qualms and said he himself would approve future picture ideas, so reporting to Mayer would not be necessary.

Publicly, at least, Thalberg made the most of his new situation, telling the press at Grand Central Terminal as he boarded a cross-country train that his new pictures "will be of the quality and type that I have endeavored to make in the past fourteen years." When the train arrived in Pasadena, he made the same point: "Good pictures are thriving everywhere, and poor pictures are suffering more by comparison." The next day, in his new office, he said it one more time: "Quality pictures pay."

That new office, a bungalow previously the lair of Cecil B. DeMille now spiffily redesigned by Cedric Gibbons, turned out to be next door to David O. Selznick's similar setup, a Solomonic attempt by Mayer to indicate that everyone was equal in the new MGM. In truth, for different reasons neither man was happy at the studio, but their regard for each other's moviemaking gifts was stronger than anyone anticipated, and they never became enemies. Helping their relationship was the shared experience of being Mayer's surrogate sons, and even though Thalberg was the fantasy son the older man could never have and Selznick was the actual son-in-law who might have been a son, that parallel situation gave them a certain amount of emotional kinship.

This good relationship existed even though Selznick, whose relationship with MGM had often been difficult, had been fired by Thalberg in connection with *White Shadows in the South Seas*. Now back at MGM a few years later, Selznick's unhappiness this time around centered on studio personnel he felt were giving him the cold shoulder because of the perception that he was usurping Thalberg's position. Even his wife had difficulty telling how much of this was real and how much was David's per-

Despite his frailty, Thalberg enjoyed sports. Here, facing the camera, he plays beachside table tennis with his friend and colleague David O. Selznick. (Marc Wanamaker/Bison Archives)

ception, but she respected that it was "his truth and his pain." So much pain, in fact, that as early as June 1933, with Thalberg still in Europe, Selznick sent another of his long "Dear Dad" letters to Mayer, this one asking to be let out of his contract. "I want to get out of MGM, and the quicker the better," he wrote. "My grief started from the first hour I came here and has continued unabated up to this writing. . . . I have yet to ask you, since I have been married to Irene or before, a solitary favor. I ask now my first: please, please release me from my contract."

Even though Selznick signed it "Affectionately, sincerely,

and passionately yours," Mayer turned his son-in-law down. But distracted and unhappy though he was, Selznick at MGM was driven enough to come into his own as a formidable producer, someone who believed "Any picture worth making is worth being obsessed with." As he later explained to writer Art Buchwald, "The way I see it, my function is to be responsible for everything."

Selznick's first film at the studio was 1933's very profitable *Dinner at Eight*. Though it broke with Thalberg tradition by placing a "David O. Selznick's production of" line in the title credit, it was a writ-large example of the multistar pattern Thalberg had pioneered with *Grand Hotel*. No fewer than eight actors with coequal billing were featured in the advertising, including John and Lionel Barrymore, the irrepressible Marie Dressler, and Jean Harlow.

Dressler was the first cast at the insistence of Mayer, though director George Cukor, in the first of many films at MGM, initially thought she was wrong for the role of an aging theatrical femme fatale ("She looked like a cook and had never played this type of part"). But she handled things beautifully, combining with Harlow for the film's celebrated closing line, where Harlow in a knockout Adrian gown worries that "machinery is going to take the place of every profession." "Oh, my dear," a knowing Dressler responds, giving the young woman an appraising look, "that's something you never need worry about." Donald Ogden Stewart, who wrote the exchange, expressed pleasure decades later at having "ended that picture on a much-appreciated laugh."

It's a measure of Selznick's ability that he and Thalberg were the producers that Garbo preferred to work with. Always shrewd financially, Garbo was legitimately unhappy in Hollywood and, she told her friend Cecil Beaton, she used that feeling to get a 1932 contract that paid her an unprecedented $250,000 per film. "When I finished the [previous] contract I said to [Mayer]: 'This is the end. I don't want to continue: I want to get out of pictures.' He and his minions were all so worried. . . . 'You can't quit now. We won't let you. You're at the very peak of your career.'" The result of this maneuver, besides the new contract, was eight months' time off in Sweden and elsewhere and a next film (inevitably trumpeted as "Garbo Returns!") that was her own choice. That was *Queen Christina*, based on the real-life seventeenth-century Swedish monarch who wore pants, transgressed gender roles, and was publicized by the studio as "A Queen Whose Love Affairs Were as Modern as Tomorrow's Tabloids!" Because of the actress's stature, both Thalberg and Mayer involved themselves in the production.

Salka Viertel, one of Garbo's confidants, was the film's cowriter and an early proponent of the story. Even though Garbo considered Thalberg "the most capable producer to deal with," Viertel had problems with him and his insistence that the film include a love story, but this changed when the producer made one of his patented unexpected suggestions. He asked Viertel whether she'd seen the controversial German film *Mädchen im Uniform*, which "dealt with a lesbian relationship. Thalberg asked: 'Does not Christina's affection for her lady-in-waiting indicate something like that?' He wanted me to 'keep it in mind,' and perhaps if 'handled with taste it would give us very interesting scenes.' Pleasantly surprised by his broadmindedness, I began to like him very much."

The love story Thalberg mandated became the made-up romance between the Queen and Don Antonio, the dashing Spanish ambassador, a role that a young Laurence Olivier was seriously considered for. But Garbo found him unconvincing and put her not inconsiderable influence into the hiring of her old flame John Gilbert, who had never found his footing in sound pictures. This idea needed the approval of Mayer, whose long hatred of the actor had not abated.

"She knew Jack was having trouble finding work and that

his spirts were down," reported actress Colleen Moore. "So she simply marched into Louis B. Mayer's office and said it would be Gilbert or nobody. Mayer went through the roof of course. . . . Garbo, as always, said nothing until he was finished. Mayer knew it was useless to argue with her. You can't really argue with someone who's just as happy to go home if she doesn't get her way."

Though Gilbert does a lovely job, and his scenes with Garbo have the kind of poignance working with Olivier would not have produced, the situation was problematical. S. N. Behrman remembered that "Gilbert would disappear for a day or two—he drank. This stopped everything. The delays were tremendously costly. . . . I complained to Garbo: 'How could you have ever got mixed up with a fellow like that?' It was a rhetorical question; I expected no answer. But I got one. Garbo meditated; it was a considered reply, as if she were making an effort to explain it to herself. Very slowly, in her cello voice, she said: 'I was lonely—and I couldn't speak English.'"

Though the film's story of a queen who ends up abdicating her throne has passages that speak eloquently to Garbo's own career quandaries ("I'm tired of being a symbol, I long to be a human being"), as directed by Rouben Mamoulian it is best known for its unprecedented ending, a shot nearly half a minute long of Garbo standing on the prow of a ship and simply looking into the distance. The director reported that Mayer felt on paper the ending was too unhappy, but Mamoulian insisted it had to be seen on screen. "Nicholas Schenck came from New York, Thalberg was there, Mayer, everybody [came] to see how depressing it was going to be. And they all walked out on cloud nine."

It fell to Selznick to do *Anna Karenina*, Garbo's next major film, which turned out to be one of her most moving performances despite (or maybe because of) having played the role of the heartbroken Anna once before, in 1927's silent *Love*. MGM outdid even itself for this glamorous Clarence Brown–directed epic, but the actress kept to herself off-screen, with Fredric March saying, "Co-starring with Garbo hardly constituted an introduction," and fellow actors Freddie Bartholomew and Basil Rathbone both reporting that she point-blank refused their personal requests for autographed photos. But on the screen, she is impeccable, conveying heart-stopping emotion without visible effort and remaining timeless in a way no one else could quite manage.

By any measure but his own, Selznick was a major success as an MGM producer, with other hits like *David Copperfield, A Tale of Two Cities,* and *Viva Villa!* to his credit. But the yearning to be his own person, to be free from anyone's control, never went away. Selznick International came into being in 1935, and it is indicative of the actual closeness he had with his reputed rival that "Thalberg was my first investor in the new company. He said to me, 'Have you raised your money?' I said, 'Not a dollar.' He said 'Norma and I would feel very pleased if you would let us be your first stockholders,' and they put in $200,000." As Thalberg loyalist David Lewis noted, "Thalberg was not a man who gave a damn about rivalry. He had no jealousies of any sort."

As for Thalberg himself, the early months after his return to MGM were rocky for other reasons. The easy access to the studio's acting and writing talent that Schenck had promised did not materialize. "Thalberg was running into obstacles he had never known before," remembered Samuel Marx. "The other producers on the lot were also his competitors." Thalberg also objected to what he viewed as a studio trend toward doing assembly-line pictures that lacked originality and style, going so far as to coauthor that "Why Motion Pictures Cost So Much" *Saturday Evening Post* article in which he railed against "the present destructive system of rushing out pictures poorly made, of destroying stars by robbing them of their glamor and their ability to give distinguished performances."

Mayer for his part felt aggrieved that Thalberg did not appreciate how hard he'd worked to hold the studio together during that extended European trip and beyond. "Mayer did everything he could to accommodate Thalberg," said executive J. J. Cohn. "Schedules were rearranged, shooting dates were delayed or set ahead, all to give Thalberg whatever he wanted. But sometimes it just wasn't possible. After all, Mayer was running a studio, not a one-man Thalberg operation." Whether or not one agreed that this period was, in David Lewis's glum words, "the time of Thalberg's Valley Forge," it was clear, as publicity director Howard Strickling regretfully observed, that Mayer and Thalberg "were never to be as close as before."

The one aspect of MGM that Thalberg could focus on without fear of interference was the career of his wife, Norma Shearer, who was proving especially adroit at simultaneously looking after her thriving career and tending to her much-envied marriage. On the one hand, she could do things that would have surprised those who saw her only as an icon of sophisticated glamour. David Lewis, for instance, whose entry level job as Thalberg's assistant included driving him home after his inevitably long workdays, reports, "I never knew Norma, even when she was shooting, not to be there when he came home, even at two o'clock in the morning. He was usually a little hungry and wanted something. She would go into the kitchen, although they had an enormous staff of help, and make fried bread sandwiches—her specialty. Irving loved sandwiches prepared that way."

On the other hand, when Shearer saw a career opportunity that she felt Thalberg did not appreciate, she did not hesitate to take action on her own. She understood that she was an aspirational figure to her largely female audience, both for what she wore and for the "modern" nature of her characters, willing to push society's moral boundaries but still come out on the right side in the end. A key example of this, as well of Shearer's willingness to go with her instincts, took place in 1930 with *The Divorcee*.

Shearer wanted the role of Jerry, a woman willing and able to unapologetically play around, but Thalberg, whose decisions on casting were rarely questioned, felt she didn't have the right kind of screen presence to pull it off. Challenged more than daunted, Shearer, without telling her husband, arranged to pose for George Hurrell (whose photos of Ramon Novarro she'd admired), at that point a freelance photographer with a studio far from the lot. "Thalberg had doubted she could be sexy enough to bring off the part, and my pictures proved she could," Hurrell remembered, adding, "The idea was to get her looking real wicked and siren-like, which wasn't the image she had at the time, and so I suppose nobody thought she could get away with it." Those portraits, still steamy, convinced the reluctant Thalberg. Shearer not only got the role but also won her only best-actress Oscar and enabled Hurrell to become MGM's preeminent glamour photographer.

Shearer's consistent ability to work a situation to her advantage comes out as well in how she dealt with the question of children. All about her career, Shearer left to her own devices would quite possibly not have had any. However, Thalberg's strong interest in family made her willing, and she was able to use the first of two pregnancies to achieve something she'd long wanted: a house of her own, not one shared with and run by Thalberg's indominable mother Henrietta, as had been the case since the wedding. "When Norma became pregnant four years later," Irene Mayer Selznick reported, "she told Henrietta, 'Alas, we will be too many; I just can't live here any more. Isn't that a pity!' To us she said, 'It was the only way I could get out of there.'" The child, Irving Thalberg Jr., was born on August 25, 1930, coincidentally the day before Lon Chaney's death. According to Samuel Marx, the father's reaction was notably lighthearted: he told studio colleagues "The doctor says he has the intelligence of a three-week old!"

The house the new family moved into, on a triple lot at 707 Ocean Front, variously described as French Provincial and Tudor in style, still looks the same from the outside as when it was built in 1931 close to the home of Louis B. Mayer at the foot of the Santa Monica Palisades on today's Pacific Coast Highway. It was, as stipulated by Shearer and Henrietta, the rare house of the time to be completely air-conditioned, as sea air was thought to be bad for Thalberg's health. It also was sound-proofed and fitted with double-glazed windows, as Thalberg was a light sleeper and was disturbed by the sound of waves. "We were, I think," Shearer added in her memoir, "the first to have a real projection room in our home equipped for sound, including a permanent screen about 8 × 12 which would appear and disappear with the press of a button." When F. Scott Fitzgerald visited, he described the house as "built for great emotional moments. . . . There was an air of listening, as if the far silences of its vistas hid an audience."

The couple's second child, Katharine, was born on June 14, 1935, and caused another confluence of the personal and the professional for Shearer. According to Helen Hayes, a newly pregnant Shearer worried, "Irving is going to be furious with me, because he's got my new picture all lined up, and I'll never be able to finish it if I start now." More than that, Shearer said, "I know I'll have to tell him. But first I must tell Louella Parsons. I promised to let her know the minute I got pregnant—that she would be the first to know." Even Hayes, the consummate professional though she was, confessed, "I didn't know what to say."

Time off taken for maternity leave plus the months spent in Europe with Thalberg meant Shearer was not only losing roles she'd wanted (like 1930's *Paid*, which went to the always striving Joan Crawford) but appearing in far fewer films than was usual for stars of the period. That absence turned out to coincide with the strengthening of the Production Code, which meant that by the time she returned to the screen the kinds of genteelly racy stories she specialized in were going away. Shearer had always valued Thalberg's career advice; their professional collaboration was one of the pillars of their marriage, and after the shaky box office of 1934's modern drama *Riptide*, her first film after an eighteen-month screen absence, an eternity in the 1930s, he decided there needed to be a change. *Riptide* was to be Shearer's last modern-dress film for five years, as Thalberg while he lived put her exclusively into highbrow period romances, prestige projects heavy on the costumes, that had either theatrical or literary antecedents.

The first of these, in 1934, had both. *The Barretts of Wimpole Street* was based on a successful play about the real-life love story of poets Elizabeth Barrett and Robert Browning. It was such an attractive property, as it turned out, that Thalberg (who had turned the play down and then changed his mind after seeing Katharine Cornell star on stage) had competition. If he wanted it for Shearer, Hearst had similar designs on the material for Marion Davies, and even went so far as having her shoot test footage. Ironically, neither actress was eager to play the part of the invalid, initially all-but-immobile Barrett, with Davies going so far as remembering, "I didn't want a part where I was just going to sit on my tail and recite poetry." More than wanting the part for Shearer, Thalberg felt that Davies, whose best instincts were comedic, was wrong for the role, a sentiment many critics seconded when word of her possibly starring in the huge stage hit leaked out. "Miss Davies has as much ability and fitness for that role," W. E. J. Martin wrote in a *Buffalo Courier-Express* column reprinted in *Cinema Digest*, "as Jimmy Durante, usually working for the same company, has for the part of Robert Browning."

MGM had managed to acquire the property by this point, and because of the delicacy of the situation the casting decision fell to Mayer alone. Given the fraught state of his relationship with Thalberg, Mayer could have seized an opportunity to be vindictive and gone with Hearst and Davies. That he chose the more suitable Shearer, just as he had allowed Garbo to have the hated Jack Gilbert as her costar in *Queen Christina*, is indicative of his fealty above all else to Metro-Goldwyn-Mayer. If it was good for the studio, it was good for him, end of story. Hearst, less magnanimously, initially responded by telling his papers not to publicize the film, but more serious repercussions were to come.

Fredric March was cast opposite Shearer as the "handsomest poet in England" whose industrial strength joie de vivre eventually wins Elizabeth's heart and changes her life, but the film belongs to Charles Laughton. The British actor, coming off an Oscar for playing Henry VIII, lost fifty pounds to become the humorless, unbending Edward Moulton-Barrett, Elizabeth's father, a domestic tyrant without peer. The play's success as a theater piece was partially due to its daring suggestion that incestual thoughts were a driving force for the father's behavior, and it is no surprise that when the film project became public, a Production Code functionary wrote Thalberg that the suggestion that the father "has an interest in his daughter which is more than parental . . . would of course not be permissible under the Code."

A believer that the best defense is a good offense, Thalberg took the initiative, with PCA head Joseph Breen later reporting that after he and his people had objected to what was on the screen, Thalberg "gave us to understand that he thought our estimate of the 'BARRETTS' was not only definitely wrong, but incredibly stupid." Numerous back-and-forths later, Thalberg agreed to a few lines being rewritten, plus some brief additions, and the film was then passed as "a first-class piece of screen entertainment [that] should prove a great credit to the industry." To no one at MGM's surprise, those hints of incest remain because, as Laughton told Thalberg, "they can't censor the gleam in my eye." Gleam or not, the result was a success, winning *Photoplay* magazine's Medal of Honor as the film of the year and getting a best-picture nomination.

By this point in time, MGM was such a high-efficiency film factory that productions could become hits without significant input from either Mayer or Thalberg. Sometimes, as with 1934's *The Thin Man*, the film's success came not because of Mayer's good instincts but in spite of his misguided ones. The studio had purchased Dashiell Hammett's snappy 1933 novel, and hard-working director Woody Van Dyke immediately envisioned William Powell and Myrna Loy (he'd just directed both in *Manhattan Melodrama*) as Nick and Nora Charles, the husband-and-wife team who wise-crack their way to solving a crime while their short-haired terrier Asta mugs for the camera.

Far from being enthusiastic about what was to become a successful long-running team to rival Tarzan and Jane, Mayer had his doubts about both elements. Powell had been a detective before (S. S. Van Dyne's Philo Vance for Paramount) to indifferent effect, and the Montana-born Loy had somehow ended up typecast as an exotic vamp. "There was no precedent for casting me," Loy remembered. "Oh they had a terrible battle! 'She's all right,' Woody insisted. 'I've pushed her in my pool.' Which he had—that was his test and apparently I'd passed. When Woody threatened to walk out, Mayer relented." Though it was made like a programmer ($200,000 budget, eighteen-day shooting schedule, including two days of reshoots) it proved a tremendous hit and the first of five sequels, 1936's *After The Thin Man*, became MGM's top grosser of the year after taking in twice as much as its progenitor.

Even when they weren't directly involved, Mayer and Thalberg had such an aura of inevitable success around them in the mid-1930s that it's worth taking a moment to look at a few misfires, situations where, both jointly and singly, mistakes were made. One of the biggest personnel backfires in the studio's history came in 1934, when an attempt to punish an actor ended up enhancing his career.

That would be Clark Gable. As an MGM contract player, he could be loaned out without his consent, a move which both made money for MGM and, if the loan was to a less prestigious studio, was intended as a disciplinary measure to chastise headstrong players. Whether Mayer's loan of Gable to Columbia, known in Hollywood as a Poverty Row establishment, was disciplinary or not (one biographer says it was purely economic), there is little doubt that Gable, who'd already made a name for himself (and wanted more money for) costarring with Crawford, Harlow, Shearer, and Garbo at MGM, took it as an affront.

Before Gable got involved, however, there had been a plan for Columbia to loan their top director, Frank Capra, to MGM for *Soviet*, a film that Irving Thalberg wanted to make about the noble struggles of ordinary Russians. But while Thalberg was in Europe recuperating from his heart attack, Mayer seized the chance to cancel a project he'd never liked, and Capra went back to Columbia. There studio head Harry Cohn told him that a film he'd given up on, provisionally titled *Night Bus*, was back on. As Capra explained to Richard Schickel, "Cohn says, 'No, no, we have to make it, Louis B. Mayer wants to punish an actor and he's told me I could have Clark Gable.' That was an order from Louis Mayer. Every time Mayer got a cold, Cohn did the sneezing. And so we had to make the picture because Louis Mayer had to punish Clark Gable. This is not a pretty way to start a film."

Unpromising or not, the story of the unlikely romance between Gable's newspaper reporter and Claudette Colbert's runaway heiress who meet on a bus (this was the 1930s after all) was a treat. Written by Robert Riskin and retitled *It Happened One Night*, it took all five major Oscars: best picture, director, actor ("I honestly never expected to win one of these" Gable said), actress, and adapted screenplay. So much for teaching an actor a lesson.

The mistakes surrounding another film, *Rasputin and the Empress*, were of a different order entirely, with consequences that were both more serious and slower to play out. Remembered today as the only screen appearance of all three Barrymore siblings, John, Ethel, and Lionel, it was released in 1932, but the extent of the damage unthinkingly done on its behalf was not visible until two years later.

A story of Russia before the revolution, of the pernicious hold the charismatic, lustful, self-appointed man of God Grigori Rasputin (the film's British title was *Rasputin the Mad Monk*) had on the ruling Romanov family, was troubled almost from the beginning. Yes, as John had said, "the three Barrymores would have some box-office value, like a circus with three white whales," but Ethel Barrymore, more tied to the stage than her brothers, had a limited window she was willing to devote to Hollywood, which meant the film started shooting without anything like a completed scenario. The siblings only intermittently got along ("Disputin'" became the production's gag title), and attempts made to give the film more punch had unforeseen effects.

Ethel played the Czarina, devoted to Rasputin (Lionel, with a beard that would do credit to Hammurabi) because of his seeming healing powers over her hemophiliac son. John played Prince Chegodieff, who saw past the beard to Rasputin's flagrant immorality and murdered him for the good of Mother Russia. Despite the name change, the Prince was obviously based on the exiled Prince Youssoupoff, who had written a book detailing the pains he'd taken to bring about the death of the bogus holy man. Dramatic as this may sound, it was apparently not enough for MGM. According to Bosley Crowther, Bernard Hyman, the film's supervisor, was a believer in something called "shock progression," so he asked screenwriter Charles MacArthur for a completely fictional scene in which Rasputin would rape Princess Natasha, the fiancée of the prince. Others say the idea originated from Thalberg himself. Whoever it came from, remembered Helen Hayes, married to MacArthur, the result was that "Charlie was furious."

"But their paths never crossed," he said.

"Doesn't matter," they said. "We need a motive the audience can understand." . . .

Charlie continued to object—he couldn't bear to deviate from the truth like that—but it was no use. The picture opened.

But not before Hyman decided to write what turned out to be an ill-advised opening title: "This concerns the destruction of an empire brought about by the mad ambition of one man. A few of the principal characters are still alive—the rest met death by violence."

At this point attorney Fanny Holtzmann enters the picture, so to speak. An experienced litigator, she was the longtime friend of Mayer's who'd served as a beard for Thalberg during the early days of his courtship of Norma Shearer. Socially acquainted with Prince Youssoupoff and his wife Princess Irina, now living in England, the attorney saw immediately that Hyman's opening title gave the couple grounds to sue for libel. Despite the name change, the Youssoupoffs are clearly recognizable as "principal characters still alive." Since the prince admitted (some say exaggerated) his role in Rasputin's death, he could not litigate that detail, but since his wife had never so much as met Rasputin, suit was brought that the rape scenario defamed her good name.

The resulting trial was a sensation in 1934 London and even led to a detailed book, *Rasputin in Hollywood*, half a century later. Modern observers feel that a guilty verdict was inevitable given Britain's "strong royalist sentiment" and the fact that "the British court had the distinct pleasure of slapping a hefty financial penalty on a major U.S. company." But the size of that penalty was a shock. The jury awarded the Youssoupoffs £25,000, roughly $125,000, reputed to be the country's biggest libel judgment since 1684. Persuading the Youssoupoffs not to sue in the multiple other jurisdictions where the film had shown cost the studio more money, a lot more, with contemporary estimates ranging from $700,000 to $900,000. "That settlement," said Holtzmann, who tried in vain to use her friendship to get Mayer to settle out of court, "was for a lot more money than they'll admit at Metro-Goldwyn-Mayer." More than that, the Rasputin affair had yet another repercussion. It led directly to the omnipresent movie disclaimer noting that "This is a work of fiction. Any similarity to actual persons, living or dead, or actual events, is purely coincidental." Even today, this holdover from a Mayer/Thalberg misjudgment still looms large.

17

———◆◆◆———

Endgame

No one knew it, and it was not inevitable, but the twenty-plus months that began with January 1935 turned out to be the literal end of days for the Mayer-Thalberg partnership that had both made the studio the success it was and changed Hollywood in the process. Thalberg, with health concerns always running like a muted soundtrack in the back of his mind, was nevertheless gradually considering the possibility of a major change, while Mayer was looking to ensure that his recently acquired upper hand was undisturbed. And, because it was second nature to both, they continued to oversee actors and pictures, in certain situations working in collaboration to overcome difficulties with a performer who needed special handling or who had strong connections with each of them. Such was the case with Jeanette MacDonald, named "the best soprano voice in films" by *Vanity Fair*; her gift for adroit studio career management rivaled only by Garbo's.

After moving from Broadway to Hollywood in the first rush of studio excitement over sound, MacDonald had been called everything from "the Lingerie Queen of the Talkies" (for her abbreviated pre-Code costumes) to "The Iron Butterfly," a tribute to her determination to make the best musicals possible, a drive that inevitably led to MGM.

Before any specific conversations about working in Culver City, however, MacDonald had met Thalberg and Shearer socially during the same 1933 Hôtel du Cap stay when Thalberg had received the fateful Mayer cable. MacDonald and Shearer had become close in the south of France, with the former even lending the latter her personal hairdresser. Though this meeting is usually presented as pure coincidence, MacDonald biographer Edward Baron Turk says it was planned, part of a strategy concocted by the actress and her manager Bob Ritchie to establish a personal connection before any business was transacted. And though the two couples became great friends, Mayer's ascendent status at the studio and his enthusiasm for an actress characterized by biographer Turk as "his Jewish fantasy of the clean-cut American shiksa" meant that letting Mayer and not Thalberg reap the credit for signing the actress seemed the wisest play.

MacDonald, however, soon returned to Thalberg's orbit, as her first significant film at MGM turned out to be one of his unit's prestige productions, 1934's *The Merry Widow*. While based on the same 1905 Franz Lehar operetta that inspired the 1925 MGM silent, it was as different in tone from that brooding earlier film, characterized by one critic as a work of "insinuated depravity," as director Erich von Stroheim was from new man Ernst Lubitsch, the embodiment of genial, tasteful sophistication.

But even though *The Merry Widow* is considered one of MacDonald's best MGM performances, despite all her maneuvering it was a role she almost didn't get. Thalberg, who had long had the idea of doing a sound version of the story, had already hired Maurice Chevalier, another actor he'd had a complex history with, for the role of the suavely seductive male lead, Count Danilo. In Paris with Shearer in 1928, Thalberg had taken the suggestion of Douglas Fairbanks and gone to see Chevalier's cabaret act. He was impressed enough to go backstage, but the actor's response was not what he expected.

"Though I had no idea who they were, [I] agreed to having them shown in," Chevalier relates in his memoir, *With Love*. "But as I rose to shake hands with the thin, somber-eyed man I was thinking he was much too young and almost shy in his manner to be anyone very important." So, when Thalberg offered him a screen test and a possible contract, "it came out so flatly it sounded as if he were proposing a lunch date he didn't care too much about keeping, and I regarded him doubtfully. . . . Surely those in a position to offer such a chance, I was thinking, would have more force and authority than this young stranger." Thinking he was being pranked, Chevalier turned the offer down, only to discover the truth moments later and having to send his secretary running after Thalberg. Chevalier agreed to the test, but contract terms proved difficult to settle on, and he ended up signing with Paramount.

When that contract ended, Thalberg renewed his quest for Chevalier's services and signed him for MGM. The first film he proposed was *The Merry Widow*, with Lubitsch tabbed to direct. A clash developed, however, over who was to play Chevalier's titular costar, the wealthy widow (played by Mae Murray in the silent version) who owns so much of a mythical kingdom that a prince is sent to Paris to convince her to marry him and keep her fortune in the country. Chevalier wanted Grace Moore, the Metropolitan Opera star, and he was set against MacDonald, with whom he had successfully collaborated at Paramount despite an icy personal relationship. "We had already done three pictures together," Chevalier reasoned. "Wasn't it time for each of us to have a new partner?"

But Thalberg, whom Chevalier archly called "the great manitou of Metro-Goldwyn-Mayer," was not so easily swayed. He declared Grace Moore "unphotographable" and told Chevalier, "We've got to find a girl to play the widow who's extraordinary and beautiful and dynamic and unknown!" Thalberg even sent the actor a private note assuring him that MacDonald would not be cast. When MacDonald was in fact selected (after diplomatically agreeing to Thalberg's plea that she take second billing), it did not improve Chevalier's feelings for the executive. Though *The Merry Widow* lost money, Thalberg wanted to use Chevalier again. This was to be a film to surprisingly costar Grace Moore (who in the interim had had a major success for Columbia in *One Night of Love*), but the actor would have none of it. Refusing to take second billing to the singer, he got out of his contract and didn't return to MGM until he did *Gigi* in 1958, decades after Thalberg's death.

If operetta duets with Nelson Eddy (like "Indian Love Call" from 1936's *Rose Marie*) were the mainstay of MacDonald's MGM career, this was not all she could do. The actress demonstrated that when she costarred, also in 1936, in *San Francisco*, aka "the first disaster musical," holding her own with two of MGM's biggest male stars, king of the hill Clark Gable and the up-and-coming Spencer Tracy in the first of his nine Oscar-nominated roles. Though putting these three actors together may seem like the Mayer/Thalberg machine at its most mechanically efficient, how this film came about, and MacDonald's place in it, exemplify the role of quirkiness, happenstance, and sheer determination in studio affairs.

Certainly no one was more eccentric among the writers on the MGM staff, or had a more ephemeral specialty, than Robert "Hoppy" Hopkins. As Anita Loos, credited for the *San Francisco* screenplay from Hopkins's story, described it, "Hoppy's position in the scenario department was unique. It had nothing to do with writing. He had been hired by our studio boss, Irving Thalberg, to inject jokes, ad lib, into any script that tended to be dull. Hoppy was the studio's only 'gag man.'" Hoppy's concise idea ("San Francisco—earthquake—atheist turns religious") became a blockbuster about a gambling hall proprietor (Gable), a singer who yearns for better things (MacDonald), and a childhood friend of the gambler (Tracy) who's now a priest who still packs a mean punch in the boxing ring.

In fact, one of the best stories involving the making of *San Francisco* involves boxing. Loos had written a scene where the gambler tires of the priest's sermonizing and wallops him. Joseph Breen, the Production Code Administration enforcer, sent for Loos and Hopkins and probably Thalberg as well and told them, "Look here, folks, we can't allow that so-called hero of yours to humiliate a Catholic priest." Rather than cut the scene, Loos added a new one where "we establish that the husky young priest could easily outbox, outslug, and outsmart our anti-hero." So later in the film, "when Clark Gable strikes Tracy, we know Tracy could kill him but he won't do it." The new scene, as it turns out, plays better than the one it saved.

Understanding the rarity of such a dramatic singing role, as well as the value of costarring with Gable, MacDonald was all for this project, but as for Gable, not so much. According to the singer, the actor complained to executive Eddie Mannix, "Hell, when she starts to sing nobody gets a chance. I'm not going to be a stooge for her while she sings in a big, beautiful close-up and the camera shoots the back of my neck!" Hardly the type to fade under pressure, MacDonald took the risky step of sidestepping Mayer and Thalberg and writing directly to Felix Feist, the New York–based sales and distribution executive who normally heard only from Mayer, enthusiastically banging the drum for Gable's participation: "The entire outlook was so perfect, the whole setup so 100% box-office, with a brand new team from the public's point of view, also Metro's, that I am heartbroken and at the same time furious that such an opportunity is going to be missed."

Because MacDonald's contract allowed her to work on a film-by-film basis, and because she was willing to postpone other projects (and not get paid) to sync her schedule with the busy Gable's, he was leaned on by Mayer to get on board, and he reluctantly did. Things were different for third-billed Spencer Tracy, who became MacDonald's on-set confidant. Tracy was new to the lot, having made nineteen films for Fox in five years. Thalberg, who had a knack for seeing potential in actors that others did not, felt his particular brand of masculinity would help the studio. "Spencer Tracy," he presciently told columnist Louella Parsons, "will become one of M-G-M's most valuable stars." Indeed, this became his breakthrough performance.

San Francisco not only made money, it became the most profitable film in the studio's history up to that point. What thrilled audiences were the state-of-the-art special effects used to re-create the famous 1906 San Francisco earthquake, including an especially vivid shot of sidewalks separating. The impressed *New York Times* critic Frank Nugent (later to become a successful screenwriter) called the quake "one of the truly great cinematic illusions; a monstrous, hideous, thrilling debacle." According to Samuel Marx, Louis B. Mayer had a more succinct summation after he saw the film for the first time: "That's my idea of a prestige picture."

Perhaps one reason Gable was difficult on *San Francisco* was that he'd recently finished another film that found him out of his comfort zone, albeit one that also had a successful conclusion. *Mutiny on the Bounty* ended up with eight Oscar nominations for 1935, including one for the man himself for best actor. It won only one, but that was for best picture, and Thalberg can be seen in a Hearst Movietone newsreel modestly telling presenter Frank Capra, "It is obvious but nevertheless true for me to say I am happy that *Mutiny on the Bounty* won this award."

Since his return from Europe to a diminished role at the studio, Thalberg had used his production unit to make high-profile prestige films. *The Barretts of Wimpole Street* had been his first foray in that direction, and *Mutiny on the Bounty* turned out to be one of his most successful. It happened despite objections from Mayer, who was not surprisingly offended by the idea of making heroes out of mutineers and worried about the lack of a strong romantic element. Thalberg, however, argued, "People are fascinated with cruelty, and that's why *Mutiny* will have appeal."

As was often the case with Thalberg, the idea came from a previously successful literary property, in this case a novel by Charles Nordoff and James Norman Hall (the father of future cinematographer Conrad Hall), a book that MGM claimed had had twenty-five million readers. Frank Lloyd, a journeyman director with an interest in things nautical ("He had better luck with ships than people," said actress and singer Geraldine Farrar), had purchased the property early and was happy to sell it to MGM on condition that he be allowed to direct.

Beginning in 1789, *Bounty* largely takes place on the British Navy frigate of the same name. Its focus is on the bitter hostility that develops on a long voyage and a layover in Tahiti between the ship's terrifying captain, William Bligh, and his second in command, Fletcher Christian, over Bligh's savage treatment of the crew, an enmity that led to the most famous mutiny in English naval history.

Casting these two men correctly was essential to the film's success, and Thalberg's vision of having Charles Laughton's captain face off against Clark Gable's Mr. Christian, though undeniably risky, worked out exceptionally well. Laughton was the easier choice, given that he was British and had enjoyed working with Thalberg on *Barretts*.

For Gable, however, the choice was nowhere near as easy. He worried about whether he'd look foolish in the traditional knee breeches and pigtail, he absolutely hated to lose his signature mustache (they were forbidden in the British Navy at the time), and he worried that his American accent would sound out of place. Press gangs of MGM executives, including Eddie Mannix and Kate Corbaley, were employed to bolster his confidence, with Thalberg the most persistent. "Do this one for me," he pleaded, as he had with John Gilbert. "If it isn't one of your greatest successes, I'll never ask you again to play a part you don't want to do." As it turned out, Gable had only to be himself, to exude what Laughton biographer Simon Callow calls "the rare quality of relaxed masculinity," to provide the perfect foil to Laughton's sneering, malevolent martinet.

Not only was Thalberg involved in the casting, he also put in the story conference work to ensure that the script was making the points he wanted to make in the way he wanted them made. After one session, he complained of a sequence that it was "like a string of sausages, each one good, but not satisfying. I'm left hungry. I want a big steak!" This drive for improvement extended to the actual filming. Location work was done in Tahiti, as well as more extended shooting near Santa Barbara and on Catalina Island, where Thalberg would periodically fly to referee various disputes, including Gable's complaints that Laughton was stealing scenes by refusing to look directly at him. "This was [Gable's] technical naivete, his innocence of the art of acting, his lack of inner resource," claims Laughton biographer Callow, adding, "As it happens, the conflict was very good for the movie . . . in Gable's case, the most complex piece of work he did until the performances of his last years."

Because of the film's pedigree, plus the novel's large number of readers, MGM at Thalberg's urging put on one of the more wide-ranging publicity pushes of the day. An ad in *Ladies Home Journal* under the headline "Somewhere south of Heaven"

daringly left half the page blank to emphasize the dreamy isola-
tion of Tahiti, while an ad in *Time* took the opposite, hyperfac-
tual approach, headlining "131,000 Feet of Film; 175,000 Hours;
14,000 Miles for Two Hours of Entertainment For you." And
more than one ad emphasized the no-longer taboo name of its
producer, "Irving Thalberg, master-maker of motion pictures."

Given the studio's emphasis on prestige and status, Thalberg and Mayer did not often focus on what was considered the
lesser genre of comedy. But in 1935, despite his intense involvement with *Mutiny*, Thalberg found time, Mayer's qualms
notwithstanding, to salvage the Marx Brothers' careers with the
success of *A Night at the Opera*. But his and Mayer's earlier experience with the films of Buster Keaton was a low point in studio
mismanagement, a nonmeeting of the minds so frustrating that
Keaton titled the chapter in his autobiography, *My Wonderful
World of Slapstick*, on his decision to join MGM "The Worst
Mistake of My Life."

Keaton had been in the business since he was born to traveling vaudevillian parents who involved him in their act "practically from birth." He had a similarly fortuitous introduction
to film in 1917 via his friend Roscoe "Fatty" Arbuckle, who was
making two-reel comedies for independent producer Joseph
Schenck, Nicholas's brother. From 1920 on, still under Schenck's
banner, Keaton began making first his own two-reelers and then
longer features. Though some were distributed by first Metro
and then Metro-Goldwyn-Mayer, they were financed by Schenck,
who was also Keaton's brother-in-law. (Keaton married Nathalie
Talmadge, Schenck wed Norma, and third sister Constance had
been an early Thalberg romantic interest.)

But in 1927 Schenck left independent production and advised Keaton to sign with MGM, with the promise that brother
Nicholas would look after him. Fellow comics like Charlie Chaplin advised him not to do it ("They'll all try to tell you how to

make your comedies. It will simply be one more case of too many cooks"), but Keaton trusted Schenck and he knew and liked Thalberg, with whom he occasionally played bridge. "He had shown that he had the keenest appreciation of story values, both comic and tragic, of any executive in Hollywood," Keaton wrote in his autobiography, adding in a radio interview, "He was not a businessman like Mayer, he was a creator."

Keaton started at the top, with 1928's *The Cameraman*, a harum-scarum story of a novice newsreel cameraman eager to impress a girl. As had become his pattern, the film was less a compelling narrative than a platform for Keaton's engagingly spur-of-the-moment physical gags, with one thing leading to another and another. The film's best gag was Keaton and another actor trying to squeeze into a small beach changing room and, Keaton reports, "Thalberg almost had hysterics when he saw the day's rushes in a projection room."

Unfortunately, *The Cameraman* was the only film on which Keaton was allowed to use the entire team he came in with, the team that understood how he worked. Worse still, sound arrived soon after, and the studio, distrusting Keaton's intuitive method that relied on inspiration and improvisation, felt that the new medium demanded finished scripts that left no room for the kind of inspired happenstance he excelled at. Thalberg undoubtedly appreciated Keaton's humor, with the comic reporting, "No truck driver ever guffawed louder at my better sight gags than did that fragile, intellectual boy genius," but he did not seem to understand its sources. As Keaton himself concluded decades later, Thalberg "lacked the true low-comedy mind. Like any man who must concern himself with mass production, he was seeking a pattern, a format. . . . Though it seems an odd thing to say, I believe that he would have been lost working in my little studio. . . . Our way of operating would have seemed hopelessly mad to him. But, believe me, it was the only way."

Also, though he enjoyed his comedy, Thalberg was not

blessed with the foresight to know that future generations would place Keaton on a par with Garbo as the greatest artists on the MGM payroll. So, instead of overseeing the man himself, he passed that task to Lawrence Weingarten, whose main credential at that point was that he was married to Thalberg's sister, Sylvia. Though Weingarten had later success producing sophisticated Katharine Hepburn/Spencer Tracy vehicles like *Adam's Rib*, he was, in Samuel Marx's words, "lost in the Buster Keaton pictures." Making matters worse, Weingarten did not respect Keaton, saying if he "had still been a big thing for Joe Schenck, he wouldn't have turned him over to Metro-Goldwyn-Mayer." Keaton returned the favor, describing Weingarten as little more than "the fat cop on the corner."

Keaton had in fact been eager to do sound films, saying at one point, "There's nothing wrong with sound that a little silence won't cure." He continually asked for his own unit, and if not that, pleaded with writers, "Don't give me puns, don't give me jokes, no wisecracks." Perhaps afraid to set a precedent and, as he had been with David O. Selznick when he clashed with Hunt Stromberg, predisposed to side with the supervisor, Thalberg refused the special-unit request. He could also point to the fact that every one of Keaton's seven MGM sound films, even the trio of benighted pairings with nonstop talker Jimmy Durante, made money, which was not true of all the silent classics.

Artistically frustrated and experiencing problems in his marriage, Keaton began to drink heavily. He had his own bungalow (nicknamed Keaton's Kennel) just outside the MGM gate, and it was the site of considerable carousing. None of this chaos sat well with Mayer, who had never been the Keaton fan Thalberg was. In February 1933, with Thalberg sidelined after his Christmas heart attack, Mayer sent Keaton a one-sentence note firing him on the spot. This upset Thalberg, who was purported to have said, "I can't make stars as fast as L.B. can fire them."

And, in fact, when Thalberg returned to the lot after his

post–heart attack European trip, he attempted to rehire Keaton to do the comic's idea for a spoof of *Grand Hotel* to be called "Gland Hotel." Keaton always appreciated that "Irving Thalberg, with the chips down, was willing to fight for me," but he had gotten it into his head that he wouldn't return to the lot unless Mayer invited him, and that wasn't going to happen. According to Samuel Marx he told Thalberg, "You studio people warp my character," and it was not until 1937, after the executive's death, that he returned to the lot as simply a gag writer. Rediscovered and celebrated in his later years, he remained until the end the rare artist without artistic pretension. Speaking in 1995, Keaton's widow, Eleanor, said that if the comic could see the way he was currently revered, "he would be in total shock. He wouldn't believe it. In fact, he didn't believe it when his films started coming back. . . . Geniuses were great thinkers to him, he thought calling him that was unreliable information."

While Keaton's relationship with MGM was torturous, the Marx Brothers had a much easier time of it, predictable initial reservations from Mayer notwithstanding. In an odd coincidence, Thalberg's passion for bridge, as it had with Keaton, played a role in making things happen.

If Keaton was a superb silent performer, the brothers (Harpo's perpetual silence notwithstanding) were sound comics to their core. Led by the dazzlingly verbal Groucho (who had been an unlikely boy soprano at St. James Protestant Episcopal Church on New York's tony Upper East Side), the brothers had been hits first in vaudeville and then on Broadway. Paramount signed them when sound came in, and they made five films for the studio, with diminishing financial results. Paramount chose not to renew their contract, and straight man Zeppo left the group and joined with brother Gummo to found a successful talent agency. That left Groucho, Harpo, and Chico unemployed, with *Los Angeles Times* critic Edwin Schallert concluding "every indication points to the Marx Brothers being through with the movies for the time being." Enter that game of bridge.

According to Bob Thomas, Groucho received a cross-country phone call in mid-1934 from Chico, who told him, "I've been playing bridge with Irving Thalberg, and he says he'd like to do some pictures with us. He had to fight with Mayer, who thinks we're all washed up in pictures, but Irving is firm; he wants us to work with him." This interest was in keeping with one of Thalberg's tenets, which he'd previously applied to Marie Dressler and others. As David Lewis summarized it, "If people had real talent, he knew that talent could always be redeemed through careful nurturing, even though it had failed elsewhere."

When the three brothers sat down with Thalberg, the executive had a clear if daunting idea of the direction he wanted to go, telling them, "Your recent pictures haven't been that good. . . . Yes, they laughed, but after they left the theater, they didn't remember what they had seen. I'd rather get half the laughs, and give the audience some story and romance to remember." Particularly because he believed men liked the Marx's brand of anarchic comedy more than their wives, "we'll give the women a romance to become interested in." The brothers were intrigued, and after Samuel Goldwyn advised them, "If Irving wants you, go with him, he knows more in one finger than I know in my whole body," the deal was struck.

Before Thalberg went to work in earnest there were, according to numerous accounts, issues of access to the elusive executive to be worked out. It's not clear whether any of the stories is true, but the most plausible seems to be that the brothers blockaded the door to Thalberg's office with heavy filing cabinets after he had kept them waiting longer than they liked.

In any case, after some false starts the script for what was to become 1935's *A Night at the Opera* took the form of the brothers not only mocking that august cultural institution but also helping a pair of young singing lovers (Kitty Carlisle and Allan

Jones) find happiness. The final writing was done by comedy veterans George S. Kaufman and Morrie Ryskind, and Ryskind left an amusing recollection of giving some pages to Thalberg. "He read through its entire length without the faintest smile crossing his face. When he was finished he handed it back to me and said, 'Morrie, that's the funniest scene that I have ever read.' I've always wondered what his reaction would have been if he hadn't liked it."

Because the brothers had come up through live performance, sharpening their routines by trial and error, Thalberg suggested the idea of touring the finished *Opera* script in a four-shows-a-day, multiweek circuit of West Coast theaters to make sure the timing of the jokes was just as it should be. "From our viewpoint, the gag-testing nature of the tour was particularly great stuff," Chico told a newspaper interviewer. "We have been in pictures for a long time and we had almost forgotten what a wallop, what a buildup for our comedy actual audience reactions had always given us." Even decades later, Billy Wilder talked admiringly of the Thalberg system. "That was the whole secret of the Marx Brothers," he told interviewer Cameron Crowe. "Then they knew what they had. I stole that, the method of timing the laughs. They had it timed, with a clock."

Once filming began, the main glitch had to do not with the comedy but the singing. Kitty Carlisle, who'd gotten her role after Oscar Levant had taken her to dinner at Thalberg's Santa Monica beach house, was a trained soprano who was looking forward to singing the film's arias from *Il Trovatore* and *I Pagliacci*. But Thalberg, ever in search of insurance, had recorded a Metropolitan Opera singer and planned to choose between the two versions. Advised by her agent to coerce Thalberg by refusing to work, she finally got an audience with the producer, "who tried to talk me into his deceitful plan. I cried all over his office; I cried in his wastebasket; I cried on his desk, and I cried all over the top of his head. In the end he gave in." There was a price to be paid, however: Carlisle's agent was barred from the lot for a year.

All Thalberg's plans paid off, and *A Night at the Opera* was the biggest Marx Brothers hit to date. (At one point in a negotiation with Thalberg, agent Zeppo joked that he would rejoin the brothers unless MGM signed his client.) Their next film, *A Day at the Races,* was to surpass it, but there was sadness attached to that box-office accomplishment, as Irving Thalberg died less than two weeks into shooting. "After Thalberg's death, my interest in the movies waned," Groucho said later. "I appeared in them, but my heart was in the Highlands." To the end of his life, Groucho would publicly credit Thalberg with saving the group's career. Privately, he lamented to his niece Maxine, "Why is it the great men always go so early? The schlemiels live to be a hundred."

While its standing as the glossiest, most glamorous of studios was already established by 1936, neither Mayer nor Thalberg was capable of not dreaming bigger and better for MGM and themselves. For Mayer, always restlessly looking for the next new thing, it meant involvement with a new actress from Europe, Luise Rainer, an interest that would both pay off handsomely and cause unforeseen difficulties. Thalberg, on the other hand, was in an increasingly conservative frame of mind, interested not only in furthering the career of the star he'd already established in his wife but in contending with the unforeseen rise in union activism among the writers he was closest to. The only place he allowed himself to dream was in planning the next stage of his Hollywood life. But the quixotic, will-o'-the-wisp Rainer, destined to have a career like no other, would unexpectedly figure in his work as well.

Though she became one of the studio's significant actresses, stage acting, as part of Max Reinhardt's celebrated Vienna theater group, was her first love. "When I went to America I thought they would take one look at me and send me home again," she told Marie Brenner in a 1998 interview. "I never dreamed of becoming a movie actress, never." After costarring with William Powell in *Escapade,* she was to act with him again in 1936's *The Great Ziegfeld.*

Though it plays more stodgy than sensational, *The Great Ziegfeld* was a big deal in its day, clocking in at two hours and fifty-six minutes as it detailed the life of the celebrated Broadway producer who had, the *New York Times* dryly noted, "a princely disregard for the cost accountant." *Thin Man* couple Powell and Myrna Loy played the producer and his second wife, actress Billie Burke, and space was made for cameos by original Ziegfeld performers like Fanny Brice. The film won two Oscars, for best picture and best actress for third-billed Rainer as Ziegfeld's first wife, the singer Anna Held, who had a memorable laughter-through-tears-on-the-telephone scene congratulating her husband on his new marriage. It was a role that Louis B. Mayer did not want her to take.

"They had written the telephone scene, it was nothing," Rainer remembered. "I said, 'Can I write that scene?' . . . And I went to Louis B. and said, 'Look, I very much want to do this film. There is a scene . . . I might be able to make something out of it!' He was very annoyed. He thought I was wrong! He said, 'You're out after the film is halfway over!' I said, 'I don't care how long the part is!'" Inspired by a performance of Jean Cocteau's play *La Voix Humaine* she'd seen in Europe and supported by producer Hunt Stromberg when Mayer wanted to cut the scene from the finished film, Rainer did well enough to win that Oscar for one of the shortest of best-actress performances.

Though Rainer's next major role would be for Thalberg, the executive for the moment had other things on his mind, including politics. This was something of a surprise, for it was Mayer, not Thalberg, who had always been the political animal of the two. Thalberg's trajectory was different. As he liked to tell radical young people he counseled like Maurice Rapf, Harry's son, and Budd Schulberg, he had been something of a boy leftist in his youth. "Every young man is a socialist when he is young," he told the pair. "Even I was full of idealism as a boy and wanted to change the social order." He gave the same message to older colleagues like writer Donald Ogden Stewart, who reported, "Irving disclosed that in his Brooklyn high school days he had been a member of the Young Peoples' Socialist League and had made ardent street corner speeches."

But as he grew older and more established, Thalberg began, not really surprisingly, to become more conservative and to act accordingly. As his friend Samuel Marx noted, "Thalberg thought himself fair-minded and took great pride in that image, but he opposed all who sought to destroy the status quo." As has been noted, he consistently viewed socialism and communism as more of an ongoing threat than Nazi fascism, telling an exiled German prince at a $100-a-plate Los Angeles fundraising dinner that "when a dictator dies his system dies, too, but once communism is allowed to spread it will be hard to root out." The most radical example of this conservatism had come in 1934, when Upton Sinclair, author of the muckraking classic *The Jungle* and a writer with a strong socialist bent (Thalberg called him "that Pasadena Bolshevik"), ran for governor of California. After a surprising win in the Democratic primary, Sinclair and his EPIC ("End Poverty In California") campaign platform were given a good chance of besting bland Republican incumbent Frank Merriam in the general election. One of the reasons that didn't happen was the clandestine MGM creation of a trio of fake newsreels called "California Election News." Given free to theaters, they consisted of bogus man-on-the-street interviews, and, most incendiary, staged scenes of mobs of out-of-state transients forming to invade California and collect benefits once Sinclair was elected.

As journalist Kyle Crichton revealed in his memoir, at the

same dinner where Thalberg displayed sangfroid about the number of Jews who might be killed by Hitler, he also admitted, much to the shock of actor and fellow diner Fredric March, his role in the ads, as well as the reasons behind his actions:

> "I made those shorts," said Thalberg quietly.
>
> "But it was a dirty trick!" shouted Freddy March, leaning forward angrily. "It was the damnedest unfair thing I've ever heard of!"
>
> "Nothing is unfair in politics," said Thalberg, not raising his voice. "We could sit down here and figure dirty things out all night, and every one of them would be all right in a political campaign. . . .
>
> "I used to be a boy orator for the Socialist party on the East Side in New York. Do you think Tammany ever gave me a chance to be heard? They broke up our meetings, and we tried to break up their meetings. . . . Fairness in an election is a contradiction in terms. It just doesn't exist."

Thalberg's increased conservatism cut closer to the bone in 1936, when he strongly and publicly opposed the nascent efforts of Hollywood screenwriters, including his own, to unionize under the umbrella of the Screen Writers Guild (forerunner of today's Writers Guild of America). If his involvement in the fake newsreels was not public knowledge until Crichton's book was published in 1960, his antiunion stance was known at the time and caused serious, even shocking rifts with several of his closest colleagues, some of them irreparable.

The first to get an inkling of Thalberg's stance was one of the writers who had been closest to him longest, Frances Marion. Marion had been key in the formation of the Guild and had been elected vice president unopposed at its initial April 6, 1933, meeting. Thalberg was still in Europe at the time, but in his first meeting with Marion once he returned to the lot in August, he immediately brought up her Guild activity in the starkest terms, calling, she wrote later, "my participation in any opposition against studio policies a betrayal."

> "That's nonsense," I said lightly. "We're not flying a red banner, we're only asking help for a lot of helpless people. You, who are so generous-hearted, should understand this."
>
> He was looking at me coldly. "I thought you were my friend," he said.
>
> "I am your friend, Irving."
>
> "Then promise me that you'll stop all this agitation among ingrates."

Marion made no such promise, and organizing by writers continued to be a persistent frustration to Thalberg, who frequently brought up what he considered its pernicious nature to the pro-union people he talked to, including Salka Viertel ("Writers were not laborers and it was wrong for them to unionize") and David Lewis, who reported, "An anguished Thalberg said to me, 'We live in a paradise. Everyone has a good life, and it's going to be destroyed by organized labor.'" Even more pungently, he once declared, "Those writers are living like kings. Why on earth would they want to join a union, like coal miners or plumbers?"

Things came to a head in an electric meeting Thalberg, no doubt with Mayer's approval, called of all his writers in early May 1936. More than sixty showed up at the same projection room that had been the site of Mayer's plea for a studio-wide pay cut three years earlier. Several participants left recollections, and though some reacted positively ("I was very moved by the speech myself," said John Lee Mahin), the majority were stunned, not only by what Thalberg said but by his affect and his tone. "Thalberg's manner and voice were cold as ice, he spoke briefly and wasted not a single word," wrote Bob Thomas, whose information probably came from Samuel Marx, who avoided the meeting in his own books. Talking about the effect of a work stoppage on everyone on the lot, "in carefully measured tones he added: 'If you wish to put all these people out of work, it is your responsibility. For if you proceed with this strike, I shall close down the entire plant, without a single exception.' His words were received with stunned silence. . . . Thalberg started to leave the room. Then he turned and added his final words: 'Make no mistake. I mean precisely what I say. I shall close this studio, lock the gates and there will be an end to Metro-Goldwyn-Mayer productions. And it will be you—all you writers—who will have done it.'"

"I liked Thalberg very much," said Maurice Rapf, also present. "He was always nice to me. But the idea that he was a sweet, sensitive character was dispelled in five seconds at this meeting. . . . It was a very tough speech. He just spoke and left. People who had known him and worked with him and thought he was a nice guy saw him so tough and so hard that we were absolutely shocked."

Perhaps because of his instinctive fear of socialism, perhaps because practices writers objected to—like the arbitrary assigning of credit and having different individuals unknowingly competing against each other on the same project—were central to his system, Thalberg was immovable in his opposition. Yet, this meeting aside, he did respect the views of people he respected, never more than when a conservative, pro-company Screen Playwrights union was briefly formed to take on the leftist Guild. He said on more than one occasion, "He's entitled to his own opinion" and told one pair of pro-Guild writers, "If anybody tries to threaten you, to tell you your job is in danger, you come and tell me." Maybe, like Ben Hecht ("All those fatheads do is keep voting"), he was frustrated by both sides, or, possibly, as writer George Oppenheimer conjectured, Thalberg was "opposed to the Guild, not so much because of an antilabor bias, but because of his patriarchal attitude toward all who worked for him. He wanted to be the one to dispense favors, and any organization that deprived him of his patronage was his enemy."

With the Guild ultimately prevailing and both sides wanting to avoid a permanent breach, Thalberg and Marion worked out a modus vivendi after he "agreed to disagree" on unionization issues, telling her at a moment of equanimity, "You and I are simple people. We have position in the industry." But things were not that simple with another Thalberg favorite, Donald Ogden Stewart, who had written the Shearer-starring *The Barretts of Wimpole Street* and had a hand in *Dinner at Eight*. For Stewart, the rupture was so significant that it runs as a theme through a section of his elegant autobiography, *By a Stroke of Luck!*. As had happened with actor Charles Bickford, Thalberg's compelling persona proved to be a difficult one to disentangle oneself from.

Stewart arrived on the lot in 1932 and was subjected to a classic Thalbergian trial by fire. Asked to produce a scene for a film already in production, "I got the shock of my life. I had never heard such contempt for anything I had written. . . . On my third attempt he nodded and mumbled, 'not bad.' 'Not bad, you son-of-a-bitch!' I wanted to yell—but I was to learn that 'not bad' from Irving was the equivalent of an Academy Award."

Soon one of the highest-paid writers on the lot, Stewart acknowledges that "Irving became a sort of father, as he did for everyone who worked closely with him," making it easy for Stewart to lose sight of his other writing aims. Those goals reasserted themselves when his contract expired, but that was not the end of the story. "I told Irving that I didn't want to be a screen writer any more. I wanted to write plays, my own plays. Father looked at me sadly, and made me feel that he hadn't heard what I'd said but that he'd forgive me if I signed for just one more year." That and a barrage of other blandishments failed, but at 7 a.m. on the morning Stewart was set to leave town, Thalberg showed up at his house. "If you don't want me to sign that contract, don't let him in," the writer warned his wife, but it was already too late. "I heard Irving's voice as he called, 'Don, are you up-stairs?' I signed the contract—but I got permission to write my play first."

As Stewart got more interested in left-wing politics in general and the Guild specifically, a distance gradually lengthened between the two men. After Stewart crossed a picket line to attend the Academy Awards as Thalberg's guest, he quieted his conscience by making "loud derogatory wisecracks" during the ceremony. "It was my first real assertion of my self against father Irving, but I had to get drunk to do it." When he later chaired an anti-Nazi meeting with leftist connections, "the door of my MGM office opened and there stood Sam Marx, the Story Editor." After conveying Thalberg's compliments about the script Stewart was working on, he also proffered an invitation to dinner at Thalberg's house on Thursday night. When Stewart said he was busy, "Sam looked at me a moment, then said, 'That's the night of that meeting, isn't it?' I nodded, and he came over to my desk. 'Look, Don,' he said, and he seemed a bit uncomfortable; 'Irving's been a very good friend of yours—and he will be very hurt if you make a speech there.'"

Stewart didn't argue, but he did make the speech. He also became a key player in the Guild's battle against the Screen Playwrights, acknowledging, "When I eagerly rushed into this forbidden activity, I knew it meant the final break with Thalberg." When he and Viertel made passionate pro-Guild remarks to their boss, Thalberg said little but "merely regarded us with the sad reproachful eyes of a betrayed parent." The deed was done and soon after Stewart decided "to abandon Hollywood in favor of an Eastern residence." He was to return to the lot, and even won his screenwriting Oscar for *The Philadelphia Story* there, but that was years later, after "the Undoubted Boss" had died.

18

Saying Goodbye

AT ʀᴏᴜɢʜʟʏ the same time that Thalberg was taking on the Guild, he was also weighing options concerning his future. While his name and reputation are forever linked in film lore to MGM, he would have undeniably left the studio for solo production if he'd lived long enough. Well before his planned departure he was moving purposefully in the direction of what David Lewis called "the first real production company financed by a major studio, yet totally independent."

Frustrated with having to run his creative choices past anyone, Thalberg had been angling to have his own company ever since he returned from his long European trip, but Schenck had initially turned him down. Mayer, as quoted by biographer Crowther, was even more adamant about not giving ground at MGM. "I wouldn't yield and Irving wouldn't yield," Mayer recounted. "Thalberg wanted first call on all and every artist on the lot. I told him, 'I will have to throw up my hands! Irving, you ought to be fair. . . . I will give you every darned thing you want as if you were my own son, but I've got to run that plant successfully.'"

One of the options Thalberg explored was getting financing for his company elsewhere and joining Mary Pickford and Samuel Goldwyn at United Artists. But, as a remarkable, carefully reasoned February 7, 1936, "Dear Mary and Sam" letter in the Academy archives demonstrates, Thalberg foresaw problems there. "I cannot," he wrote, "at my stage of the game, so involve my friends that there is financial risk or difficulty. . . . Your gallantry and readiness to move ahead . . . is a magnificent gesture of confidence toward me but one which in the last analysis is very hard for me to accept. . . . We are attempting a little more, through enthusiasm, than, through mature judgement, we should."

Things got so strained between the two adversaries that Goldwyn, Thalberg's friend but a longtime Mayer antagonist, set foot on the MGM lot for the first time since the merger to ask Mayer to "ease up" on his colleague. "Be a little more careful, a little more considerate. He is a very sensitive boy, and he isn't all that strong." Mayer, as he frequently did where his younger colleague was concerned, relented, and Thalberg got a new contract for the future I. G. Thalberg Corporation, set to open for business on January 1, 1939, the day after his old contract expired. Loew's would finance and distribute his films, but Thalberg would have complete creative autonomy. "It was really a fabulous contract for that time and no one else in the industry could have commanded it," said David Lewis. "No one."

Juggling all these difficult situations exacted a toll on Thalberg, and Goldwyn wasn't the only one to notice how exhausted he looked. Adela Rogers St. John, for instance, told biographer Bob Thomas that Thalberg "seemed to be a little figure made of white ashes; he had that certain kind of frailness that you see in young people before death." Yet it was inconceivable that Thalberg would cut back on his workload, involving himself instead in several of the most significant films of his career. "For years Irving had been warned by doctors to slow his pace," Anita Loos observed, "but he felt it better to die of overwork than be bored to death by inactivity."

The film that involved Thalberg most at this point was his *Romeo and Juliet* with Norma Shearer as Shakespeare's ill-starred heroine. Shearer's involvement was not the only reason the film took pride of place on his agenda: it presented multiple difficulties and epitomized Thalberg's lifetime goal of a cinema that was as elevating as it was popular. The public, he told Samuel Marx, will "reach upward to the highest level we can set for them," and he was determined to be up to the task.

Not everyone saw it this way. Reports are mixed as to how pleased Shearer initially was about the role, though, bolstered by two acting coaches, she ended up fully on board. Mayer for his part had never believed Shakespeare could succeed at the box office, especially at MGM prices, and several other executives felt that the actress was too old to take on the title role. Studio story guru Kate Corbaley announced, according to Samuel Marx, "There was no question in [her] mind that he would be wrong to present Norma Shearer as Juliet. . . . 'How can he star a thirtyish wife and mother in the role of a fourteen-year-old virgin?' she demanded of me."

East Coast publicity head Howard Dietz, used to disconcerting nighttime Thalberg calls though he was, was nevertheless nonplussed when his boss insisted on a conversation when he was running late to the first Joe Louis/Max Schmelling heavyweight title fight.

> "Just one consideration before you hang up, Howard, just answer me yes or no. Do you think we should make *Romeo and Juliet*?"
>
> "Offhand, no," I replied, "but we can discuss it after the fight."
>
> "What do you mean 'no'?" said Thalberg. "It's the greatest love story ever told, it's a work of art."

"Who'll play Juliet?" I asked.

"Norma," he replied.

"I doubt if she would be right for it," I said. "She's not that young."

"Juliet can be any age."

"I don't think *Romeo and Juliet* is box office."

"With Norma, it will be a cinch."

As Dietz aptly wrote, referencing both his disappearing chances of getting to the legendary bout on time and his conversation with Thalberg, "The fight was over."

Clearly, Thalberg, in addition to everything else intent on having his wife take on the greatest roles possible, was not to be dissuaded. He even persuaded Nicholas Schenck, on the one hand happy to foment West Coast discord but on the other worried about the cost, to overrule Mayer and okay the film by promising to keep the budget under $1 million, an estimate it's possible he never intended to meet.

With Shearer in place as the star, Thalberg began selecting the other pieces of the puzzle. Contract director George Cukor, known to be a favorite of actresses and a man with theatrical experience, was to direct, his first time for Thalberg. The play itself was adapted by Talbot Jennings (who'd done the same for *Mutiny on the Bounty*), with William Strunk Jr., a Cornell Shakespearean scholar (best known today for coauthoring *The Elements of Style*) signed on as literary consultant and tasked, Thalberg told him, "To protect Shakespeare from us."

In terms of casting, multiple actors were considered for Romeo, including the unlikely possibility of Clark Gable, who told Thalberg, Samuel Marx reported, "I don't look Shakespeare, I don't talk Shakespeare, I don't like Shakespeare and I won't do Shakespeare." The role eventually went to Leslie Howard, whose tony accent was genuine and who at forty-two was age-appropriate for Shearer.

Behind the scenes there was more than enough work to go

around. An enormous replica of Verona's Piazza San Zeno was constructed on a previously vacant studio five acres, and Juliet's garden was made to grow along the entire interior length of Stage 15, the studio's largest. It was all so huge that when novelist Graham Greene reviewed the film for the *Spectator*, he noted the presence of "a balcony so high that Juliet should really have conversed with Romeo in shouts like a sailor from the crow's nest sighting land."

Perhaps sensing this would be his last opportunity to work with Shearer, Thalberg, who rarely went to sets, made frequent appearances on this one, sometimes standing alone in the shadows, just watching. He saw to it that no expense was spared, no potentially useful footage unshot. The famous balcony scene took four full days to shoot, and when Margaret Booth came to edit it, she told Kevin Brownlow, "I had five versions. . . . One with tears, one without tears, one played with close-ups only, another played with long shots only, and then one with long shots and close-ups cut in."

Given Thalberg's expectations, MGM inevitably went all out in the publicity department, with multifocus advertising geared toward the movie fan ("In All the Brilliant Pages of Show History Nothing Can Compare"), the romantic ("William Shakespeare's most beautiful love story"), even the young male market ("THRILLS for Every Red-Blooded Boy!") The reviews were surprisingly strong, with the *New York Times*' Frank Nugent proclaiming, "Never before, in all its centuries, has the play received so handsome a production." Indeed, the notion, which must have gratified Thalberg, that this was a better version of Shakespeare than anyone thought this young art could produce was a frequent theme. As *Time* magazine proclaimed, *Romeo and Juliet* "proved that the cinema has at last grown up."

Despite all this acclaim, the box office was stubbornly less agreeable. *Romeo and Juliet's* budget more than doubled Thalberg's initial cost estimate, and as a result the film's loss was some

$900,000, a record deficit for a producer who prided himself on not having to absorb them. Yet though this rankled Thalberg, there were satisfactions to be had. As he had admitted in an unusual bylined essay in the film's program, "the picturization of Romeo and Juliet is the fulfillment of a long cherished dream," and no one could take that away from him.

An unexpected footnote to Mayer and Thalberg's *Romeo and Juliet* saga has to do with *Fury*, another 1936 release that in terms of subject matter and tone was so far from standard MGM fare that it's a bit of a shock that the studio made it in the first place. Produced by future director Joseph L. Mankiewicz and directed in his first American foray by the German auteur Fritz Lang, with Spencer Tracy in a star-making role, it is, at least until the final upbeat moments, a dark and disturbing look at both the American weakness for lynch-mob justice and the uncomfortable depths an average citizen could sink to as he attempts revenge for being wronged.

It came about because Mayer, always on the lookout for good producers, especially ones he anticipated might have Thalberg's qualities, thought he had found one in screenwriter Mankiewicz, the younger brother of the ill-starred Herman. This Mankiewicz wanted to direct (and did so elsewhere with superb films like *All About Eve* and *The Barefoot Contessa*), but Mayer was of the firm opinion that producing was more important. "No, you have to produce first," he told the young man. "You have to crawl before you can walk." More willing to take chances on people he believed in than he's given credit for, Mayer greenlit *Fury* even though it was hardly his kind of picture. "Mayer said 'I think it stinks,' and we had a big fight about whether it should be made," Mankiewicz remembered. "Mayer then said, 'Look, I'm going to do something right away, at the beginning of your career. I'm going to let you make this film, young man, and I'm going to spend as much money advertising this picture as Irving Thalberg spends on *Romeo and Juliet*. Otherwise, if it fails, you'll always say we didn't get behind it properly. This way, I'm going to prove to you that this picture won't make a nickel.'" Actually, unlike the Thalberg film, *Fury* did earn a profit, but Mayer, ever wily and always unwilling to lose an argument, did his best to hide that fact from his producer.

Though *Romeo and Juliet* turned out to be the last Thalberg film released in his lifetime, the nature of his MGM system meant that he was simultaneously working on several others, including two, *Camille* and *The Good Earth*, that began shooting while he was still alive and turned out to be especially notable. The Garbo-starring *Camille* was released first, premiering in late 1936, and is arguably the pinnacle of both Thalberg's and the actress's careers, a moment in time when everything providentially came together to produce a romantic drama of enviable strengths and few apparent weaknesses.

The film's venerable story of ill-fated courtesan Marguerite Gautier and Armand Duval, the earnest young man who loves her deeply, had had numerous iterations since Alexandre Dumas *fils* wrote the novel *La Dame aux Camelias* in 1848. It was a role Garbo, who knew that both Bernhardt and Duse had played it on stage, was determined to have, though in a letter to Salka Viertel she worried, "It's so like *Anna* [*Karenina*] that I am afraid. . . . It's devastating to do the same story again."

Also worried was young Robert Taylor, not long removed from the Pasadena Playhouse and now picked by Thalberg to costar with the formidable Garbo. "We can't miss with these two," Thalberg enthused to Frances Marion, who was working on the script, eventually rewritten by playwright and poet Zoe Akins. But Taylor had a secret weapon. He was romantically involved with Barbara Stanwyck, and, according to Stanwyck biographer Victoria Wilson, she went over Akins's script line by line "night after night, talking over the scenes, telling Bob how to say each line."

Until Akins was brought in, that script had not quite pleased Thalberg, who also worried that the story's nineteenth-century underpinnings, its origin, explained Cukor, in "a time when a woman's reputation, her virtue, was a terribly important thing," would not resonate with current audiences. "We have a problem," is how Thalberg put it. "The audience must forget within the first five minutes that this is a costume picture. It must be contemporary in its feeling, but one thing mitigates against that effect: the point that a girl's past can ruin her marriage." Thalberg's assistant David Lewis, who got an associate producer credit on the finished film, came up with the solution. "On the way home, I was driving Overland Avenue when an idea hit me," Lewis wrote. "I pulled into a gas station and called Thalberg. 'Instead of the story being based only on the boy's life being ruined, suppose we have a special case of a very jealous boy? It isn't a question of his life being ruined by her past, it's a question of his *jealousy* [of Henry Daniell's icy, unimaginably wealthy romantic rival Baron de Varville] ruining his life.' He embraced it immediately. 'Can you come back to the studio?' he asked. I returned and we talked. He loved the idea; it opened his mind."

Though Clarence Brown had directed six of Garbo's films, including *Anna Karenina*, Thalberg assigned Cukor, who felt as he did that Garbo "was born to play this part." Cukor ended up marveling not only at Garbo's gifts but also at Thalberg's multifaceted understanding of them. "She must never create situations," he told the director. "She must be thrust into them; the drama comes in how she rides them out." Recalling a later script meeting between himself, Thalberg, and screenwriter Akins to discuss the scene where Marguerite and Armand plan a possible marriage, "Thalberg said, 'They should play this scene as though they were plotting a murder!' That was a very interesting idea."

As for Thalberg himself, he seemed to sense even in the early shooting days before his death that the performance was going to be something remarkable even for Garbo. Cukor remembers him enthusing about seemingly ordinary dailies of Marguerite sitting in a theater box with some friends. "He saw a couple of days' rushes and said, 'She's awfully good. She's never been this good.' I said, 'Irving, how can you possibly tell? She's just sitting there.' He said, 'But she's relaxed, she's open.'" In another interview Cukor adds the phrase "I know, but she's *unguarded*" to Thalberg's response. However he expressed it, Thalberg's enthusiasm was clear, so much so that not even a random act of Garbo aloofness could dampen it. "He was always quite shy with her," Cukor remembered. "He came on the set of *Camille* one day and she was preoccupied, so he said, 'Well, I've been turned off better sets than this,' and left with the greatest grace. He looked and behaved like a prince."

Though *Camille* presented problems, they were not out of the ordinary, especially compared to the other key film Thalberg started but did not live to finish, *The Good Earth*. The Pulitzer Prize–winning Pearl Buck novel about the turbulent lives of Chinese farmer Wang Lung and his wife O-Lan had spent two years at the top of the best-seller list, the kind of cultural validation that always attracted Thalberg. As was becoming almost a reflex as their relationship worsened, Mayer did not see it as a film, arguing, "Irving, the public won't buy a picture about American farmers. And you want to give them *Chinese* farmers?" Once again Nicholas Schenck broke the tie in Thalberg's favor, but Mayer's worries were not unjustified: the project took three years to get to the screen, and its journey was especially tortuous.

At first, however, the path seemed clear. Thalberg selected one of his go-to writers, Frances Marion, to do the script and at her suggestion assigned her former husband George Hill, who'd done *The Big House*, to direct. An MGM expedition to China was mounted with the usual studio thoroughness to both film background material and gather props, and Hill returned with a staggering eighteen tons of properties. The director, however, did not live to start principal photography: he took his own life in August 1934. The energetic Victor Fleming was set to take over, but illness sidelined him, and the veteran Sidney Franklin got the call. But not before Fleming had supervised extensive agricultural construction over the five hundred acres near Chatsworth in the San Fernando valley that would be the film's principal location. The effect of the detailed preparations was overpowering, especially for actors like star Paul Muni, who noted during shooting, "I forget the camera and think I am really on a farm on the other side of the world. . . . And just think, WE ARE TEN MILES FROM THE CORNER OF HOLLYWOOD AND VINE!"

It was Thalberg's idea to star Muni, a veteran of Maurice Schwartz's Yiddish Art Theater and so skilled in makeup he'd been called "the new Lon Chaney," as Wang Lung, a role Muni was initially dead set against. "I'm about as Chinese as Herbert Hoover," he told Thalberg. "I won't look Chinse, no matter how much makeup I use, and I won't sound it." But Thalberg, who'd considered and rejected the idea of shooting in China and using local actors, did not concern himself with issues of ethnic identity. "I am in the business," Samuel Marx heard him say, "of creating illusions." He so believed in Muni he engineered a complex loan arrangement with Muni's studio. "They traded us like baseball players," Muni later told biographer Jerome Lawrence. "Warner Brothers got Gable. Thalberg got Leslie Howard [for *Romeo and Juliet*], me, and an outfielder." Yet even Thalberg would be unnerved by the intensity of Muni's determination to get the role right. As director Mervyn LeRoy, a friend of Muni's, remembers it, "One day, Thalberg called me in a panic. . . . 'He's down in Chinatown every night. He even sleeps there. I want him to act Chinese—but he doesn't have to become a real Chinese.' . . . I called Paul [and] mentioned Thalberg's concern, and we laughed together about it. I imagine he continued visiting Chinatown until he felt he had his character down pat."

Thalberg and MGM's attitude toward using Chinese actors was contradictory. On the one hand, each of the film's six top-billed roles was played by a Caucasian, and even James Stewart tested for a part until his 6-foot-4 frame ruled him out. But the studio expressed pride in using some sixty English-speaking Chinese in subsidiary roles. The cause célèbre in this regard was American-born Anna May Wong, who had been a star at least since she held the screen with Marlene Dietrich in Josef von Sternberg's 1932 *Shanghai Express* (and now appears as a face on the U.S. Mint's American Women's quarters program). Once Muni was cast, the Production Code's antimiscegenation clause forbade casting a non-Caucasian opposite him romantically, but Wong claims she was offered and rejected the opportunity to test for the role of conniving second wife Lotus. "If you let me play O-Lan, I'll be very glad," she said she told Thalberg. "But you're asking me—with my Chinese blood—to do the only unsympathetic role in the picture."

After considering Stanwyck and others, Thalberg gave the part to the ethereal Luise Rainer, the Oscar winner the previous year for *The Great Ziegfeld*. In her own way, like Muni, the actress needed to live the role to perform it. "I never acted, I felt everything," she told Marie Brenner on the eve of her eighty-eighth birthday, recounting a story of being so moved by playing her own death scene "that she sat on a curb at Metro, weeping. 'A big limousine comes by and stops—it was Joan Crawford,' Rainer told me. 'She said, "Luise, what happened? Why are you crying?" I did not want to sound like a phony about acting, so I told her that I had received terrible news from Europe about my family.' After Rainer returned to her house in Brentwood that evening, a large bouquet of flowers from Crawford arrived."

Though handling the myriad demands of a project like this was Thalberg's strength, he was not equally adept at every aspect of filmmaking, and music was considered an area of weakness. (As recently as 1999, conductor/composer Andre Previn entitled his memoir of his Hollywood years *No Minor Chords* after a memo that, twenty-five years after it arrived over Thalberg's signature, was still "on the wall in the music department, under glass and heavily bolted. . . . It read as follows: 'From the above date onward, no music in an MGM film is to contain a "minor chord."'") As reported by Sasha Viertel, who witnessed it, a nonmeeting of the minds occurred between Thalberg and the unbendingly modern composer Arnold Schoenberg. Having heard some early Schoenberg music on a radio broadcast from New York, "Thalberg decided that Schoenberg was the man to write the score for *Good Earth.* . . . I explained that long ago Schoenberg had given up the style . . . and had been composing twelve-tone music, which I doubted Irving would like. However, I promised to do my best to arrange a meeting."

Intrigued by the potential for an impressive salary, Schoenberg agreed to the meeting but, Viertel recalled, was quite late because he had been mistaken for a tourist and put on a studio tour.

> We sat down in front of Thalberg's desk, Schoenberg refusing to part with his umbrella in case he forgot it on leaving.
>
> I can still see him before me, leaning forward in his chair, both hands clasped over the handle of the umbrella, his burning genius eyes on Thalberg, standing behind his desk. . . . When he came to "Last Sunday when I heard the lovely music you have written . . ." Schoenberg interrupted sharply: "I don't write 'lovely' music."

Things went from bad to worse from there on, with Schoenberg insisting he would have to direct the actors as well as write the music, as "they would have to speak in the same pitch and key as I compose it in." Though he obviously wasn't going to agree, Thalberg remained, in Viertel's words, "fascinated by Schoenberg" and stayed serenely confident. "He'll write the music on my terms, you'll see." It never happened.

Thalberg was much more in his element in dealing with one of the film's knottier problems, how to create a cinematic version of the catastrophic locust storm that is one of the novel's high points. It is typical, perhaps, of Thalberg's approach to everything that the sequence's ultimate success was the result of the combination of numerous individual elements. To news-reel footage of actual locust swarms were added shots of coffee grinds and small pieces of burned cork exploded out of pressure guns and blown into a large white screen. Providentially, just at this time a genuine locust storm blew up in Utah, and the studio not only had it photographed but also had real insects captured and sent to California. Some were photographed "on what is probably the smallest movie stage ever constructed," and others were released on the set. The result of all this work was, thankfully, more than convincing.

Dealing with all the films on his current schedule, not to mention his long-gestating idea to cap Norma Shearer's career by starring her as the guillotined French queen in historical drama *Marie Antionette*, exhausted even someone of Thalberg's enormous capacity for work. Then, over Labor Day weekend in 1936, he did something uncharacteristic: he decided to take a brief vacation. It turned out to be a devastating choice, an atypical time away that ended up leading directly to his death.

The destination was the Del Monte Lodge up the coast from Los Angeles in Monterey, the place where Thalberg and Shearer had honeymooned almost exactly nine years earlier, so the vacation doubled as an anniversary celebration. A party of friends was gathered, including Samuel Marx, for the incorrigible Thalberg hoped to get a bit of work in as well. Ever the demon bridge player, he joined an outdoor game with some friends on the hotel's veranda late Sunday afternoon. One source says he had a jacket with him that he gave to Chico Marx's wife, Betty, but Thalberg biographer Mark A. Vieira, whose description of these last days is the most detailed, relates that Shearer brought him a sweater that he defensively refused to wear.

Thalberg woke up sick Monday morning, but by Tuesday afternoon, back in Los Angeles, he seemed to be better. Then came the next in a series of choices that undermined his chances of complete recovery. He had agreed to sponsor and offer advice on a Hollywood Bowl performance of the medieval morality play *Everyman* that was to benefit Jewish aid organizations; his role involved sitting outside for hours during rehearsals as well as showing up for the Thursday night opening in the chilly evening air.

"On Friday, September 11," Vieira writes, "something happened. Thalberg's condition changed—suddenly and drastically. The common cold was gone. In its place was a combination of symptoms: a raw throat, fever, dehydration, aches and nausea." Physicians were consulted, including Thalberg's personal doctor and his German heart specialist from Bad Nauheim, now a refugee in New York, who agreed to be flown out to see his patient. By Saturday there was a new diagnosis: lobar pneumonia. There were discussions over several days about the Mayo Clinic and its pioneering use of antibacterial sulfa drugs and whether either the drug could be flown to Los Angeles or Thalberg flown to Minnesota. Though nothing came of it, Shearer had asked David Lewis early on, "Would you fly east with Irving? It's necessary and he wants someone to fly with him."

As for the patient himself, he was sinking, as were his spirits. "I'm not getting the right treatment," he told a visiting Bernard Hyman. "They don't know what they're doing. They're killing me." When Hyman demurred, he replied "No, Bernie. This time I'm not going to make it." By the time the sulfa drugs were agreed on, it was too late in the week to get the experimental treatment out of the Mayo Clinic, and it was considered too risky to put the patient on a plane, so an oxygen tent was called for. Paradoxically, Thalberg's heart doctor arrived and said that the organ, its years of debilitating weakness notwithstanding, was in good shape. Early Monday morning, though the patient was increasingly weak, business was on Thalberg's mind: he asked one of his secretaries what the New York weekend grosses were for *Romeo and Juliet*. There are also poignant reports that he told Shearer "Don't let the children forget me." Thalberg went into a coma and at 10:16 a.m. on Monday, September 14, the end came. Ben Hecht, writing later, summed up with a concision that has unexpected emotional heft: "He caught cold, went to bed, and died." Just like that.

19

◆▸◈◂◆

Mayer Being Mayer

No ONE IN Hollywood had been more likely to die young than Irving Thalberg, confidently projected not to live past thirty due to his congenital heart defect. But Thalberg had so adroitly evaded that inevitability, had been such a fabulous invalid for so long, that the news of his sudden death at age thirty-seven, Albert Lewin remembered, "was kind of an earthquake, not only for Metro, but for the whole industry." It was as if one of the pivotal lines in *Everyman*, the play Thalberg had devoted his last days to—"O death, thou comest when I had thee least in mind"—had leapt off the Hollywood Bowl stage and made its way into the world.

Newspapers and trade publications reacted accordingly. The *Los Angeles Examiner* ran an eight-column front-page banner headline reading "Picture Industry Mourns Thalberg, Star-Maker," while at the *Los Angeles Times* critic Edwin Schallert's appreciation was headlined "Brilliant Career at Absolute Zenith

When Death Came to Film Pace Setter." *Daily Variety* paid tribute to "the miracle man of the pic industry," while noted columnist Irvin S. Cobb wrote, "Big an industry as the moving picture industry is, the death of one slender, shy, frail man has stunned it. . . . Irving Thalberg was an authentic genius of the films. . . . Here, to the limits of his own craft, was not only a Napoleon but a Daniel Boone and a Balzac rolled into one."

This shock at Thalberg's early death was something those who worked with him had special difficulty getting over, both at the time and when they came to write about it. Anita Loos noted "unable to work" in her appointment book every day for a week after Thalberg's death and later said, "When Thalberg died, I looked around and saw that the ship was going to sink and got out." Samuel Marx wrote three books in which Thalberg figured prominently but could never bring himself to write about the death in detail. He did reveal that when his secretary told him, "Mr. Thalberg died," his initial response was to ask, referring to Thalberg's father, "You mean William?" Lenore Coffee speculated, "Had he been less important his life might have been saved by the new sulfa drugs. . . . The doctors would not use them without the consent of the family, and the family was reluctant to make so drastic a decision." And Helen Hayes reported that when her husband Charles MacArthur, perhaps Thalberg's closest male friend, heard the news on their tennis court, he "played furiously for hours, until he was exhausted and spent. Then he came into the house and began to cry."

It was not only Thalberg's intimates who were affected; those who'd not been close and even those who had been antagonists felt a loss. Sasha Viertel, who had clashed with Thalberg over *Queen Christina* and mocked his impasse with Arnold Schoenberg, wrote in her memoir that she "felt terribly sad" at his passing and commented in more detail to fellow screenwriter S. N. Behrman that "he was 'Hollywood' in all its pretentiousness and falseness but he had a certain dignity and talent. I liked him very much." Even F. Scott Fitzgerald, whose screenwriting career had been sidetracked by Thalberg, wrote ambivalently that the man's "final collapse is the death of an enemy for me, though I liked the guy enormously."

Shattered by the ordeal of her husband's illness, Norma Shearer initially tried to exhaust herself even more. David Lewis, who stayed close to Shearer, reported that she was distraught at her part in the decision not to pursue the sulfa drug treatment. "She was thereafter tortured with the thought that, had she made the right decision, Irving might have lived. The night after his death, in fact, she had wandered the cold beach, hoping to make herself incurably ill. She got pneumonia, but Norma was physically strong and recovered."

Though their relationship had deteriorated, there had been a time when Louis B. Mayer had been as close as family to Thalberg, and, initially at least, reports are that those feelings revived. Mayer's statement to the press began, "I have lost . . . the finest friend a man could ever have." Though out of tact he had intentionally stayed away during the younger man's final illness, Mayer had monitored the situation and been the first to show up at the Santa Monica oceanfront house after Thalberg's death. Shearer told him that in his last days her husband had talked of his regret that his once-intimate relationship with Mayer had soured. Mayer, for his part, said he shared that remorse and the two embraced. About what happened later, however, there is disagreement.

Because both of Thalberg's observant parents were still alive, attention was paid to the Jewish precepts that burial should be as close to death as possible and not on the upcoming holiday of Rosh Hashanah, so the funeral service was held on the morning of September 16 at Wilshire Boulevard Temple. Attendance was by invitation only, with an admission card necessary, and filling the impressive rotunda were what the *Los Angeles Times* described without irony as "several hundred of his closest friends

Thalberg's funeral, complete with elaborate flower-covered casket, drew a crowd reminiscent of a movie premiere. (Marc Wanamaker/Bison Archives)

and associates," seated by a dozen ushers who included such stars as Douglas Fairbanks, Clark Gable, and Fredric March. Thalberg's burnished copper casket, impressive in itself, was covered with an enormous blanket of flowers: "A great sheaf of white gardenias was interwoven with hundreds of sweet peas . . . and dozens of fresh white roses, bordered with exquisite white orchids," detailed the *Los Angeles Examiner*. Outside the synagogue was an enormous crowd, estimated at seven thousand to ten thousand people "banked in rows four deep in Wilshire boulevard and on verdant lawns bordering Hobart boulevard." They sometimes forgot they were at a funeral service, not a movie premiere, and their behavior was said to have inspired similarly chaotic scenes in 1937's *A Star Is Born*. Bosley Crowther condescendingly characterized the event as "one of those grotesque affairs, peculiarly marked by the freakishness and mob sentimentality of Hollywood," and Graham Greene waspishly noted that Thalberg "had a funeral success second only to Rudolph Valentino."

Inside, where the service lasted little more than half an hour, everything was decorum itself. Rabbi Edgar Magnin read a message from President Roosevelt and said of Thalberg, "He was as simple as a child, despite his greatness." Speaking of the couple he had married, the show-business-savvy rabbi added, "The love of Norma Shearer and Irving Thalberg was a love greater than that in the greatest motion picture I have ever seen—*Romeo and Juliet*." From the elevated choir loft, opera singer and former MGM star Grace Moore sang from the Twenty-Third Psalm, and the *Examiner,* opting for a rare use of transliterated Hebrew in daily newspapers, relayed Magnin's recitation of "words from the Book of Job: 'Adonoi nosan, Adonoi lokach, y'hi shem Adonoi mi vorach'—The Lord gave and the Lord hath taken away; blessed be the name of the Lord." Jewish law notwithstanding, Thalberg was buried in a marble mausoleum at Forest Lawn, Hollywood's nonsectarian cemetery of choice, behind closed iron doors at the far end of the Sanctuary of Benediction.

Mayer, who the *Examiner* said had "sat for many minutes with his eyes downcast" at the Temple service, left Forest Lawn in a chauffeur-driven limousine along with Eddie Mannix, one of the executives he was closest to. According to Samuel Marx, who starkly ends his book *The Make-Believe Saints* with the anecdote,

> Mayer sat back and looked out the window away from his companion. . . . Mayer suddenly elbowed him in the ribs. He was smiling.
>
> "Isn't God good to me?" he exclaimed.

That quote, which Mayer biographer Scott Eyman traces to Mannix's wife Toni, is the most controversial one in the Mayer/Thalberg canon. It conflicts with the reports of the touching

Mayer/Shearer rapprochement, though it echoes Frank Capra's report. "My wife and I saw Mayer dance publicly all night at a cabaret on the Strip the day Thalberg died." And in truth that ambivalence, the way Mayer could alternate self-interest of the naked "monster from the id" variety (to quote MGM's post-Mayer science fiction classic *Forbidden Planet*) with genuine empathy was characteristic. "He was a very impetuous man," one associate remembered, "given to sudden infatuations, temper outbursts, emotional moments." A man largely without filters, Mayer said what he felt when he felt it, with consistency being the inevitable collateral damage.

Inside the studio (which, at Mayer's command, had closed for an entire day while others simply observed five minutes of silence) this back-and-forth was also in evidence. As David Lewis related, "Everyone wanted to diminish the Thalberg charisma—they wanted to obliterate his distinctive stamp of perfectionism. God, how they tried. The entire M-G-M upper echelon wanted to erase the fact that there had ever been an Irving Thalberg." Though Mayer stood apart at times—he once berated an executive for belittling Thalberg and told Lewis, "Nobody will ever speak badly of Irving in your presence again, never"—he also wouldn't release Thalberg associates to work elsewhere. "Mayer would never agree to it," Lewis wrote. "They wanted to hold onto the Thalberg people in case they went elsewhere and did well, but they also wanted to denigrate the Thalberg image and put their own in its place."

When it came to the Thalberg projects that were just beginning, Lewis says, "Immediately after Irving's death, everyone at M-G-M who was in a position to do so started grabbing." Even those projects closest to being finished, specifically *Camille* and *The Good Earth*, had to fend off ostensible improvements ("Things were tried that almost sank the film" said Lewis, *Camille*'s associate producer), but because they had protectors the films were able to withstand the pressures.

Under the sure hand of George Cukor, *Camille* did most of its filming after Thalberg's death, and the director remembered that Eddie Mannix "called me up and said, 'This will be Irving's last picture, is there anything you can do to improve it in any way?' . . . I was very touched." The protagonist's last moments, marked by graceful lines like "Perhaps it is better if I live in your heart where the world can't see me," retain an extraordinary emotionality. Garbo biographer Barry Paris reports that the death scene had a singular repercussion. Garbo was averse to watching herself on screen, "with one exception—one piece of film she watched the day after shooting and perhaps the only one with which she was ever satisfied: The last ten minutes of *Camille*."

Though it had been filming for more than six months when Thalberg died, the complexity of *The Good Earth*'s production meant it took longer to finish, so it, not *Camille*, became the film that contained Thalberg's lone on-screen credit, the reluctant final valedictory mandated by Mayer. Positioned after Leo's roar and before the main title, it filled the screen with its message: "To The Memory of Irving Grant Thalberg We Dedicate This Picture, His Last Great Achievement." A film distinctly of its time in its casting choices, *The Good Earth* gave the Academy the opportunity to overlook both Garbo's sublime *Camille* performance and Rainer's dissonant Viennese accent and award the latter an unprecedented second straight Best Actress Oscar.

Thalberg's death was not the only one to disconcert Hollywood in general and MGM in particular at that time. Less than nine months later, on June 7, 1937, star Jean Harlow died. If Thalberg had been sadly young, the actress, just past her twenty-sixth birthday, was even more so, with the gossip sources of the time hinting that after the tragedy of Paul Bern she had been close to finding happiness with costar William Powell. *Time* magazine had put her on its cover in 1935, the year after she starred in her sharpest MGM film, the crackling *Bombshell*, an inside-Hollywood satire. When Franchot Tone's beau tells her Lola Burns character, "I'd like to run barefoot through your hair," an entranced Lola deftly skewers her MGM colleagues by exclaiming, "Gee, not even Norma Shearer and Helen Hayes in their nicest pictures were ever spoken to like that!"

Harlow was on set making *Saratoga*, her sixth film with Clark Gable, when she was stricken with intense abdominal pains and went home. She died a week later, and a voice-over actress and a double were eventually used to complete the project. (Mayer told the *Los Angeles Times* that he planned to "rewrite the story to fit some other feminine personality," but public demand to see Harlow one last time changed his mind and the jury-rigged *Saratoga* ended up the actress's biggest success.) As with Thalberg's death, Harlow's had the despair of the unnecessary about it. Initially misdiagnosed by her personal doctors and kept out of hospitals by a domineering Christian Science mother who feared losing control, the actress died of uremia caused by kidney failure. "The day the Baby died," said screenwriter Harry Ruskin, using Harlow's nickname, "there wasn't one sound in the M-G-M commissary for three hours. Not one goddamn sound." Harlow was buried close to Thalberg in Forest Lawn's Sanctuary of Benediction amid a deep air of sadness at her youth and the fact that on a personal level she had never found acceptance for who she was. That *Time* magazine cover story had pointedly closed with an anecdote about Harlow making a witty remark at a party only to be asked, "'Who did you hear say that?' Jean Harlow paused bitterly before making another remark which was both brighter and indubitably her own: 'My God, must I always wear a low-cut dress to be important?'"

Norma Shearer was still among the living, but she was not to appear on theater screens for a full two years after *Romeo and Juliet*. In part she was adjusting to life without Thalberg, the husband who had increasingly guided her decisions, and who had decided that her next film was to be *Marie Antoinette*. But she was also engaging in a bit of financial gamesmanship with MGM about her husband's financial legacy.

Though it was not public knowledge, Thalberg, Mayer, and attorney J. Robert Rubin were participants in an MGM profit-sharing agreement. Since Thalberg was no more, Mayer and Rubin felt the compact was null and void, but Shearer felt entitled to her husband's percentage. Since she couldn't say that publicly, she announced that she was no longer interested in *Marie Antoinette* and was leaving the business unless she got a new contract. Since MGM had already invested hundreds of thousands in preproduction expenses for the film, she had Mayer over a bit of a barrel. A new contract was soon forthcoming, Thalberg's share of the profits through the 1938 end of his contract went to his estate, and work began in earnest on *Marie Antoinette*. Not for nothing had George Cukor said that Shearer was a star who "looks at her work with the mind of a producer."

Even for MGM, a studio that did not rush into things, *Marie Antoinette* had had a long gestation period. It began, as was the norm with Thalberg, with a prestigious book: Stefan Zweig's highly regarded 1932 psychological biography of the French queen, *Marie Antionette: The Portrait of an Average Woman.* Zweig presented the future queen as a young woman who turned to frivolity because her husband the Dauphin suffered from sexually crippling phimosis. Later, after a passionate friendship with Swedish diplomat Count Axel von Fersen, she made peace with her fate during the French Revolution. Thalberg announced the forthcoming movie as part of a shipboard press conference when husband and wife returned from Europe in 1933.

In this they initially reckoned without William Randolph Hearst, who had also read the book and invariably envisioned Marion Davies for any and all costume dramas. "W.R. wanted me to do it, and I was going to try my best," Davies remembered later. "I could visualize myself as Marie Antoinette with a big white wig and an upturned nose." Though they were reluctant to cross Hearst, neither Thalberg nor Mayer felt that Davies was right for the part, and Mayer tried to square the circle by telling the powerful publisher the actress could play the role if he bore the film's costs. After losing out to Shearer on both *The Barretts of Wimpole Street* and *Romeo and Juliet*, Davies as well as Hearst felt the meager offer was, in the actress's apt platitude, "the straw that broke the camel's back." Hearst ended Cosmopolitan Productions' relationship with MGM and promptly signed a new deal for Davies to star at Warner Bros.

More than that, Hearst had Davies's fourteen-room bungalow, "filled with Hearst antiques and run by a full staff of servants," removed from the lot. The location, nicknamed "The Trianon" by Charlie Chaplin after the Versailles pleasure palace, had for years doubled as MGM's unofficial visiting dignitary welcoming center, with George Bernard Shaw, Winston Churchill, and others feted by Mayer, Thalberg, and Hearst with glamorous celebrity luncheons. Hearst had it broken into sections and transported across town to Warners' Burbank lot, a move worthy of a Hollywood king or even a French one.

MGM then faced a difficulty of a different sort, getting a story grounded in sexual dysfunction past the Production Code. Thalberg, always the studio's go-to individual with tough cases because of his singular ability to artfully split hairs, did what perhaps only he could have done, persuade code administrator Joseph Breen to allow a brief, one-time-only allusion to impotence when the future Louis XVI tells Marie Antoinette on their wedding night, "Well there'll never be an heir. Because of me." Breen himself, in a fascinating internal memo, acknowledges that agreement and emphasizes that "Mr. Thalberg is following the formula of making his point . . . and thereafter forgetting all about it." Breen also felt relieved by Thalberg's agreeing to "make a picture dealing with Marie Antoinette and the French Revolution—and not a picture dealing with a charming woman who finds herself married to an impotent man."

Mayer, here circa 1930s with William Randolph Hearst and Winston Churchill, cherished his proximity to the power elite. (Private Collection; J. T. Vintage/Bridgeman Images)

With a story this complex, it's not surprising that several writers, including Thalberg favorite Donald Ogden Stewart, worked on the script for long periods of time. Stewart reported wearily, "Fourteen months later the head of Queen Marie was still firmly on her shoulders and I was still consulting with my colleagues as to the best way of explaining the French Revolution in terms that would not lose audience sympathy for Norma Shearer."

Also taking place was extensive physical preparation for

filming, always a studio hallmark, that reached a kind of obsessive zenith with this production. Permission was granted for the first time to have the Palace of Versailles photographed for motion picture reference, and some twelve thousand photos were taken to assist Cedric Gibbons in designing his massive sets. E. B. Willis of the studio's property department made an epochal buying trip to France, acquiring so many period objects that his shipment "to this day retains the record for the largest number of antiques ever received at the port of Los Angeles at one time."

Thalberg's death inevitably put *Marie Antoinette* on hiatus until Shearer decided whether to proceed. In an August 1938 *Good Housekeeping* cover story headlined "Norma Shearer Returns," she told writer Dixie Willson that thoughts of Thalberg had been with her as she made up her mind. "He was so ambitious for me. He wanted me to do so many things I never quite got done," she said. "And so—I wished to go back to my work, the work we both had loved, the work which had made our lives so exciting and wonderful." Once she was on board, Shearer made her opinions known about casting. Though the studio would have preferred the in-house Robert Taylor, Shearer fancied the young Tyrone Power, who had to be borrowed from Fox. Though Thalberg had wanted Charles Laughton for the Dauphin, the future king, the role went to stage actor Robert Morley in his film debut. He was a natural wit who came to describe the elaborate production as *Marie and Toilette*. "The film was leisurely and deluxe," he remembered. "We were all treated like visiting maharajahs. Huge cars waited all day outside the stages to carry us one hundred yards to our dressing rooms."

Though some of this luxury was built into the nature of the project, Louis B. Mayer (who exclaimed to Morley, "God, how I hate epics!") did not want it encouraged. Budgetary concerns always on his mind, and no doubt still smarting from Shearer's victory in the profit-sharing dispute, Mayer engineered the departure of the director Thalberg had selected, the deliberate

Sidney Franklin, and had him replaced by one of his favorites, the fast and furious Woody Van Dyke, who a friend of Morley's described as someone who "I am pretty sure, thought a Dauphin was a large fish."

Van Dyke was only given a weekend to prepare and even the director's friend and sympathetic biographer Robert C. Cannom allowed that "Miss Shearer did become apprehensive because of Van's reputation as a speed demon." But, as a gimlet-eyed professional of whom Morley said, "her knowledge of lighting was as great as the cameraman's," Shearer knew enough not to complain. And with producer and Thalberg loyalist Hunt Stromberg making sure that egregious speed-induced miscues were corrected, even Morley admitted, "Once they got to know each other, Shearer and [Van Dyke] got along famously."

Though the finished film took in an estimated $3 million, impressive in its day, its extravagant production costs made a financial loss inevitable. That *Marie Antoinette* did as well as it did is partly attributable to an ad campaign that placed heavy emphasis on spectacle, including a trailer that shamelessly proclaimed, "4 Years in Preparation, 152 Speaking Parts, 5500 Extra Players, 98 Massive Sets, 20 Years of Tumultuous Drama Crowded Into 2 Hours of Roaring Screen Thrills." While Shearer liked it enough to make it one of two of her films (the other being *Romeo and Juliet*) she kept prints of, many observers, even the usually sympathetic Hedda Hopper, felt otherwise. Given the dangerous state of the pre–World War II world, "the time for such a picture is out of joint," the gossip columnist wrote. "Had Irving Thalberg lived, I'm certain he never would have made it."

Though projects he initiated like Jeanette MacDonald and Nelson Eddy in *Maytime* and the Marx Brothers' *A Day at the Races* continued to appear sporadically on the studio schedule, Thalberg's lingering influence of course waned as Mayer became MGM's undisputed power source. Though he both enjoyed having even more say in what the studio produced and probably resented the frequent Hollywood assertion (here articulated by Budd Schulberg) that hiring Thalberg had been "undoubtably the single best move Louie ever made," Mayer understood what Thalberg had brought to their equation and wanted to find a replacement. Thalberg's exacting taste may have been difficult to deal with and what he did for pictures hard to immediately put your finger on, but its absence would eventually be felt. If it was true, as screenwriter William Goldman said decades later, that moviemaking was a business where "nobody knows anything," Thalberg stood out as someone who actually knew something. As an anonymous source quoted in the August 1939 issue of *Fortune* had asserted at Thalberg's funeral, "They won't miss him today or tomorrow or six months from now. But two years from now they'll begin to feel the squeeze."

Replacing Thalberg in practice, however, proved more challenging than any theoretical imperative. Mayer considered various individuals for the job, but the searches did not progress to a lasting conclusion. He may have been thinking of the bright young Joseph L. Mankiewicz as an eventual choice when he made him a producer, but Mankiewicz, who wanted to direct in any case, soured on the job when his interactions with F. Scott Fitzgerald on the *Three Comrades* script led to a famous plea, "Oh Joe, can't producers ever be wrong? I'm a good writer—honest. I thought you were going to play fair."

Things got a little further with Mervyn LeRoy, who had directed the highly profitable *Tugboat Annie* for the studio. Mayer lured him away from Warner Bros. in 1937 to take a lead producing role (even though he was married to Harry Warner's daughter) by paying him such a large sum, $6,000 per week, that he had to say it was $3,000 to avoid alienating the other producers. LeRoy, who claimed that a deal for him to work for Thalberg had been on the executive's desk when he died, soon found that he missed directing. "About a year after I got there," he wrote, "I went to Mayer and said I wanted out. I volunteered to take a cut in salary if he would let me direct again. He never stood in my way, although I think he was disappointed." Mayer's search for another Thalberg, which Howard Dietz characterized as "like looking for another Kohinoor [diamond]," still had some years to run.

Until that ever-elusive gem might be found, MGM was run by an executive committee, often called the College of Cardinals, whose shifting members included familiar faces like Eddie Mannix, Harry Rapf, soft-spoken talent whisperer Bennie Thau, and producers Bernard Hyman and Hunt Stromberg. Mayer, understood as first among unequals, was sometimes dubbed the Pope. Dore Schary, who began on the lot as a writer, chose military rather than ecclesiastical imagery to describe the system: "Mayer was commander in chief. The executives . . . were field generals. Producers and directors were colonels, majors, and captains, depending on their credits. Writers were privates. The unit idea was designed to prevent any one executive from developing the threat Thalberg had been to Mayer's seat of power."

Perhaps the most out-of-the-box member of the executive committee was Mannix, who did not fit the usual profile. He was an Irish Catholic who some thought was a model (his religion grafted onto Mayer's persona) for non-Jewish studio head Pat Brady in Fitzgerald's *The Last Tycoon*. The burly Mannix had worked for the Schencks as far back as their days owning New Jersey amusement parks, probably starting as muscle of sorts. Nicholas Schenck's continued distrust of the West Coast led him to send Mannix out to Culver City as essentially a corporate spy, perhaps hoping that his anomalous background would keep him from going native. It didn't work, and Mannix's loyalty to Mayer and Thalberg became unswerving.

No matter who was on the committee, one problem with Mayer's system was that it was both expensive and expansive: director Josef von Sternberg described it as "a hydra-headed aggregation of producers and supervisors which always increased in number, for whenever one head was chopped off two arose in its stead." When Leo Rosten's study *Hollywood: The Movie Colony, the Movie Makers* listed twenty-one producers who made $100,000 or more in 1938, fully ten of them, more than any other studio, came from MGM. Just as damaging, and even worse in the long run, was the tendency of committee decisions to favor safer, middle-of-the-road films. To veteran screenwriter Casey Robinson, it felt as if Mayer had decided "he would never have a strong man again. And it developed into a system where they had committees for everything. . . . Now the thing wrong with a committee is that it can only make a compromise. Bravery is gone, courage is gone, and it's wasteful. But it's worse than that, because all you can develop with that kind of a system are formula stories." Or as Charlie MacArthur put it with more concision, working for MGM after Thalberg was "like going to the Automat."

Mayer himself, however, might well have been flattered at the comparison. Like the high-volume Automat eateries, he was aiming for quality but only if it could be mass-produced and scaled up. As a man in the business of reliably entertaining massive numbers, he rarely was interested in one-offs; without Thalberg as an opposing voice, repetition did not scare him. Though Thalberg had increasing felt taking risks was worth it if the highest quality was at stake, Mayer gradually became less and less willing to experiment. If something was successful, he opted for more of the same, and then more of that. Joseph L. Mankiewicz biographer Kenneth Geist provides a telling anecdote of the young producer going to see Mayer in the wake of Warner Bros.' success with the musical *42nd Street* with an idea of his own:

> After patiently listening to Mankiewicz outline the story, Mayer said, "So you think that's a very clever idea for a musical?" To which Joe replied, "Yes, L.B., I think it's new, dif-

ferent, enchanting." "New, different, enchanting," mocked Mayer, rising from his desk. "Young man, let me tell you what I want from you. I want *43rd Street, 44th Street, 45th Street.*" As Mayer came barreling toward him, Mankiewicz fled the office, only to be pursued down the hall by the agitated studio chief yelling, "Don't come to me with anything new. Give me *46th Street, 47th Street . . . !*"

Mayer was not just being hyperbolic. Even while Thalberg was alive, MGM had become enamored of recurring enterprises like Tarzan and The Thin Man, and that was only the start of a trend essential for a studio that aimed at producing fifty films a year. The Maisie series was a case in point. Though the initial 1939 film was originally intended for Jean Harlow ("The Explosive Blonde" was the advertising tag line), these stories of strong-willed, good-hearted Maisie instead made a B-picture star out of Ann Sothern. Lasting for ten films over eight years, with self-explanatory titles like *Gold Rush Maisie* and *Congo Maisie*, the films did so well that Mayer told Sothern, "Your pictures pay for our mistakes."

Another classic MGM series, and one so successful it spawned its own popular spin-off, was the run of Dr. Kildare films. They starred Lew Ayers as idealistic young Dr. James Kildare and Lionel Barrymore (acting out of a wheelchair because of crippling health problems) as his crusty big-city mentor Dr. Leonard Gillespie. Starting with *Young Dr. Kildare* in 1938 and ending in 1941, the studio produced nine Dr. Kildare films, and a further six Dr. Gillespie films were added for good measure.

Among the examples of MGM's undeniable passion for these kinds of films, however, there is, to paraphrase J. R. R. Tolkien, one series to rule them all: the Andy Hardy films, starring Mickey Rooney and featuring promising young actresses including (of course) Judy Garland, Ann Rutherford, and even Lana Turner. Much beloved by Mayer, fifteen of these films were made between 1937 and 1946 (with one more added in 1958), and the omnipresence of those pictures has solidified the series' place in American cultural history.

The Hardys first appeared in the modest (it ran only sixty-nine minutes) *A Family Affair*, but when theater owners reported unexpected audience satisfaction, a series was launched with Rooney as ultimate teenage scamp Andy, MGM veteran (and frequent Garbo costar) Lewis Stone as stern but fair Judge Hardy, and Fay Holden as nurturing mother Emily. The films became money machines (1938's *Love Finds Andy Hardy* cost $212,000 and grossed $2.2 million worldwide) and made young Rooney the country's top box-office draw from 1939 through 1941, besting the likes of Spencer Tracy and Clark Gable. In show business for much of his young life, Rooney had a reputation for an active social life, which the moralist Mayer tried in vain to curtail. As the actor later remembered it, Mayer told him "You're Andy Hardy. You're the United States. You're the Stars and Stripes. Behave yourself. You're a symbol."

Mayer's determination to put on film, in the Hardy series and elsewhere, his belief in the power of family and the eternal importance of mothers was legendary. It was no accident that one MGM film, 1938's *Of Human Hearts*, concludes with John Carradine's irate Abraham Lincoln summoning Union Army surgeon James Stewart directly from the battlefield to the White House to chide him for failing to write to his mother. "Oh, you ungrateful fool," the chief executive thunders. "Write her every week, you understand me. If you fail, I'll have you court-martialed." Mayer's passion for the Hardy family was his most successful attempt to deify both his own beloved mother and the American way of life that had been so good to him, and he was shrewdly protective of it. According to Bosley Crowther's biography, Mayer told the Hardy team, "Don't try to make these films any better. Just keep them the way they are." Should anyone question the worth of journeyman George Seitz, Mayer would claim, "If you had a stronger director the films wouldn't be as good." Mayer was proud of his ability to be his own best audience, and as late as 1950, in an interview with the *New Yorker's* Lillian Ross long after the Hardy films' prime, he was still gratified at their success and his part in it.

"'They make an Andy Hardy picture.' He turned his powerful shoulders toward me. 'Andy's mother is dying, and they make the picture showing Andy standing outside the door. *Standing.* I told them, 'Don't you know that an American boy like that will get down on his hands and knees and *pray*? They listened. They brought Mickey Rooney down on his hands and knees.' Mayer leaped from his chair and crouched on the peach-colored carpet and showed how Andy Hardy had prayed. 'The biggest thing in the picture!' He got up and returned to his chair."

In 1939, three years after Thalberg's death and seven after the *Fortune* piece that was a factor in the divide that bedeviled the two men, the upscale business magazine returned to again take the measure of the studio. This time the focus was on parent company Loew's and the financial problems it and MGM might be jointly facing, but in other respects, this new piece ended up curiously echoing the earlier one. "Thalberg," the unnamed writer wrote, "is almost as pervasive an influence at Culver City today as he was in his lifetime. Recent errors of executive judgement are ridiculed in his name and compared with the master's performance in similar situations." As for Mayer, he was still being dismissed as "essentially a businessman. . . . His job remains what it was, to oversee the entire studio." If Mayer took offense at this, if he felt his creative contributions to things like the Hardy films had been slighted, there's no record of it. He was probably too busy dealing with the studio's current output, which was considerable.

For 1939 was also a year often referred to as Hollywood's greatest, a golden span that saw the release of some of the studio system's most celebrated products. MGM under Mayer pro-

duced its share of memorable films, including the Ernst Lubitsch–
directed *Ninotchka*, one of the best and most lighthearted of Greta
Garbo's career. Advertised as "Garbo Laughs," it starred the actress as a dour Soviet commissar who learns to love capitalism
and crack a smile by hanging out with Melvyn Douglas's Pari-
sian playboy. Reminiscing about the film's success, Frances Marion pointed out "several of us at the Metro studio recalled
Irving Thalberg's insistence that Greta would give a surprising
performance if ever the studio put her in a comedy."

MGM was also central to the year's biggest film, *Gone With
the Wind*, which the studio did not make but—thanks to some
cutthroat dealmaking on Mayer's part—did make a fortune on.
It was based on Margaret Mitchell's massive best-seller, just the
kind of book MGM usually snapped up, and accounts differ as
to why Thalberg, who was still alive when the book was published, passed on it. The most persuasive version, told to biographer Bob Thomas by Thalberg associate Albert Lewin, is that
Lewin had procured an early synopsis and showed it to Thalberg what turned out to be scant months before his death. He
told Lewin, "You're absolutely right. It's sensational. The role is
great for Gable and it will make a terrific picture. Now get out
of here with it." Thalberg's reason? "I have just made *Mutiny on
the Bounty* and *The Good Earth*. And now you're asking me to
burn Atlanta? No! Absolutely not! No more epics for me now.
Just give me a little drawing room drama. I'm tired. I'm just too
tired." Though rival bidder David O. Selznick worried, "Thalberg is liable to take a gamble without even reading it," that did
not happen, and Mayer's son-in-law and the head of Selznick
International Pictures ended up paying $50,000 for the rights.

Because the book had such a powerful impact on readers,
there was nationwide interest as to who would be cast as southern belle Scarlett O'Hara and her brash and bold antagonist
Rhett Butler. Opinions varied widely about Scarlett, but America was of one mind in considering Clark Gable ideal for the

part of Rhett. There was only one problem: Gable (who was "scared stiff" at the prospect of the role) was under contract to MGM, which in effect meant that Mayer decided whether he would be made available and at what cost to his son-in-law's production company. Mayer did not do the actual negotiating himself, but he and Nicholas Schenck got what they wanted: in addition to Gable, Selznick was given $1.25 million to cover half of the production costs and MGM was given distribution rights (which meant 15 percent of the gross) plus a whopping 50 percent of the profits. Given that the film became the most successful in Hollywood history, this was an exceptionally good deal.

Gable had also been an inadvertent factor in the rise of Judy Garland, the star of another of MGM's 1939 successes, *The Wizard of Oz*. A vaudevillian from an early age like frequent co-star Mickey Rooney, Garland was signed by the studio in 1935 at age thirteen. Accounts differ as to how involved Mayer was in that, but two things characterized her years at the studio, especially the early ones: wonder at the warmth of her expressive voice and a determination to remake the way she looked. This was a process all MGM stars were subjected to, but, as *Oz* authority Aljean Harmetz reported, it was especially so for Garland: "In the next seven years, the voice would be trained, the teeth capped, the nose restructured, the thick waist held in by corsets and the body reshaped as well as possible by diet and massage."

All this made an uncertain actress feel increasingly vulnerable, something the studio capitalized on by casting her as an insecure teen in *Love Finds Andy Hardy*. Mayer, always dogged about talent, made Garland a kind of special project, with dire results. "From the time I was thirteen," she later remembered, "there was a constant struggle between M-G-M and me—whether or not to eat, how much to eat, what to eat. I remember this more vividly than anything else about my childhood." This led to a studio recommendation of diet pills, in addition to the sleeping pills and others she already took.

Worse was yet to come. Mayer mocked Garland to her face, calling her "my little hunchback," and, according to an unpublished autobiographical fragment uncovered by biographer Gerald Clark, he molested her as well. As Clark recounted, "Whenever he complimented her on her voice—she sang from the heart he said—Mayer would invariably place his hand on her left breast to show just where her heart was. 'I often thought I was lucky,' observed Judy, 'that I didn't sing with another part of my anatomy.'" Ida Koverman tried to protect the girl from the studio as much as she could, but it was a losing battle. "'In our house, the word of Louis B. Mayer, who ran the studio, became the law,'" Garland remembered. "When Mother wanted to discipline me, all she had to say was, 'I'll tell Mr. Mayer.'" And then Garland got a big in-studio break.

As part of his determination to fashion the studio into his idealized version of an American family, Mayer was big on throwing ostentatious birthday parties for his stars. In early 1937 an elaborate event was planned for Clark Gable, and Garland, with the help of musical arranger and friend Roger Edens, delivered a celebrated number. Called "Dear Mr. Gable" and consisting of a spoken prelude to the classic "You Made Me Love You," it captivated the studio hierarchy and led directly to her starring role in *The Wizard of Oz*. (According to Garland's second husband, director Vincente Minnelli, a truculent Gable told Garland years later, "You've ruined every one of my birthdays. They bring you out from behind the wallpaper to sing that song, and it's a pain in the ass.")

Actually, the Yellow Brick Road to Oz was not direct, for Mayer initially went after Shirley Temple (under Fox contract and unavailable) for the role of Dorothy, the little girl from Kansas who helps new friends Scarecrow, the Tin Man, and the Cowardly Lion and gains wisdom of her own after a tornado deposits her in the mythical land of Oz. Though a money loser on its initial release, *Oz* gained so many viewers via repeated television airings that its promoters took to calling it the most-seen film in history. Given its progression to classic status, disputes as to who gets credit for what have multiplied. Though the film was a tribute to what historian Thomas Schatz characterized as "the genius of the system" rather than the work of any auteur, Mayer did make some crucial early groundwork decisions.

Probably motivated by the success of the Disney fantasy *Snow White and the Seven Dwarfs*, Mayer approved the purchase of the rights to the L. Frank Baum novels from Samuel Goldwyn. (In an interesting twist, Goldwyn had initially purchased them at the suggestion of future MGM screenwriter George Oppenheimer.) Mayer also assigned Mervyn LeRoy to produce but not direct, and had prolific songwriter Arthur Freed, who wanted to produce, made assistant producer. After that, the MGM system went to work, churning through numerous writers (estimates go as high as more than a dozen) and four directors. Richard Thorp had his footage discarded and George Cukor, who called the source material "a minor book full of fourth-rate imagery," lasted scant days, but long enough to create Dorothy's on-screen look. Victor Fleming, nominally a he-man type but, according to LeRoy, "a kid at heart," shot most of the film, with King Vidor finishing up when Fleming replaced Cukor on *Gone With the Wind*. Freed was the key player in the film's style of musical drama that he would take with him when he started the studio's Freed Unit after *Oz* wrapped. And it was Mayer once again, probably at Freed's suggestion, who overruled doubters and decided that "Over the Rainbow" would stay in the picture. Yes, some folks wanted to cut that exquisite Garland number, they really did.

Always insatiable in his hunger for talent, Mayer, probably thinking of his success with Garbo, looked for newcomers in Europe as well as this country, invariably tacking search excursions onto whatever took him overseas. In fact, a single visit to

England in 1937 to inspect the newly opened MGM British studio led to the signing of two of the biggest of MGM's future female stars, Greer Garson and Hedy Lamarr.

Garson was hardly a nobody in August of that year when Mayer by purest chance saw her in a London stage production. The *London Express* had dubbed her "The Most Sought After Young Actress in London," and James Agate of the *Times* called her "this new, young meteor," adding confidently that she would avoid Hollywood and "remain with us because, heaven be praised, she is not extraordinarily beautiful." In this bit of benighted prophecy he reckoned without Mayer's highly developed gift for spotting potential film talent. The executive admired Garson's demure charisma and poise from the moment he saw her, and having sent a backstage message that convinced her that he was indeed "Mr. Metro-Goldwyn-Mayer" ("Hyphens and all?" is said to have been her reaction), he dined with her, met her mother (Mayer was always at his best with mothers), and eventually signed her to a seven-year contract at twice what he had initially offered.

It took a year to find the right vehicle for Garson's debut. That turned out to be the smallish but crucial role of the vibrant wife in yet another 1939 hit, *Goodbye, Mr. Chips*, a woman who enlarges the life of an old-fashioned schoolmaster (Oscar winner Robert Donat) before herself dying young. That was also Garson's first step in the gradual process of becoming Mayer's favorite and replacing Norma Shearer as the first lady of the MGM lot. The irony here was that it was Thalberg who had bought the property when it was in galleys in 1934; the finished film had a gracious title card featuring the signatures of six key personnel reading, "We wish to acknowledge here our gratitude to the late Irving Thalberg, whose inspiration illuminates the picture." It was the last of Thalberg's projects to reach the screen.

All this was in the future, however, when Mayer boarded the *Normandie* for his ocean voyage back to America after signing Garson. On board was young Viennese actress named Hedwig Kiesler, sometimes called "the most beautiful woman in Europe" and already infamous for starring in the racy Czech film *Ecstasy*. Mayer had had an inconclusive meeting with her in London, but an agreement was both completed and signed on the boat. Newly renamed Hedy Lamarr, the actress played exotic roles in numerous films, and despite the lack of a defining hit remained so popular that an MGM World War II fundraising drive offered a kiss from her for the purchase of a $25,000 government bond. Though it is often accurately said that Mayer seemed to gradually lose interest in her, as with Garson his acumen in seeing her potential for the studio remains impressive.

MGM needed these new talents because the old ones were fading. Appropriately enough for a studio that prided itself on its female stars, one of its 1939 hits was *The Women*, which proved to be, as far as MGM was concerned, the last triumph for both Norma Shearer and Joan Crawford. Based on a successful Clare Boothe Luce play and having an unprecedented all-female cast, it featured snappy patter (Rosalind Russell says of her womanizing husband, "I wouldn't trust him on Alcatraz") in a story of supposed high-society friends cattily fighting one another over men.

Shearer was easily cast as the woman whose husband is stolen, but Crawford had to actively campaign with Mayer and director George Cukor for the unsympathetic role of the thief of hearts, Crystal Allen, whom Crawford later described as "the hard-boiled perfume clerk who uses every wile to catch another man's husband." Mayer was against it ("I don't know that you should play a heavy, Joan. It might hurt your career"), but Cukor agreed. This led to some tense moments on the set between the two actresses. "Norma and Joan Crawford never were what you'd call bosom pals," deadpanned Hedda Hopper, also in the film. "During Norma's close-ups, Joan would sit out of camera range and knit." Loudly. All of which added tension and emotion to the characters' mano-a-mano confrontation in a store dressing room, when Crawford's Allen snaps at Shearer's haughty and refined Mary Haines, "You noble wives and mothers bore the brains out of me."

Both actresses starred in a few more films at MGM after *The Women,* but the thrill was gone. Without Thalberg to advise her, Shearer made some questionable role choices before leaving acting in order to focus her professional energies on burnishing the Thalberg name. As for Crawford, perennially feeling under-appreciated by studio middle management and eager to push herself into more dramatic roles, she persuaded a reluctant Mayer to have MGM release her from her contract in 1943. "We were so totally owned by the studio," Crawford reminisced later, "we could have had 'Property of MGM' tattooed on our backsides without raising the slightest objection." Crawford signed with Warner Bros. almost immediately and soon after, in a remarkable career turnaround, won 1945's best-actress Oscar for *Mildred Pierce,* leading to other successes, a new contract, and the *Variety* headline "Crawford's Back and Metro Hasn't Got Her." Crawford relates with relish that Mayer made his disbelieving producers look at each of her hits three times. "'She's through is she?' he said. 'Why couldn't we have done this here? Every one of them is Academy timber!' He was right."

Two other major stars were to leave MGM, one after a dramatic confrontation with Mayer, the other more or less drifting away. Luise Rainer was the first, and her departure was indisputably stormy. Possessed of the kind of *artiste* personality Mayer never felt at ease with, her back-to-back Oscars notwithstanding, Rainer, as she wrote her playwright husband Clifford Odets, did not enjoy feeling like "a bolt in their machinery." "It is more important to me," she told *Modern Screen,* "to be a human being than to be an actress." Rainer had benefited from Thalberg's protection, but after he died a clash with Mayer was inevitable. After what was to be her final film for MGM she met with the studio chief and told him, "Mr. Mayer, I cannot work anymore. It simply is that my source has dried out. I have to go away, I have to rest." Rainer recalled his impervious response: "'What do you need a source for? Don't you have a director?' . . . 'If you can't release me from my contract, at least give me a leave of absence,' she said. 'Luise, we've made you and we're going to kill you,' he told her." Rainer's response: "Mr. Mayer, you did not buy a cat in a sack. . . . In twenty years you will be dead. That is when I am starting to live!"

A more consequential if more gradual departure was Garbo's. In 1941 she followed up *Ninotchka* with the unpopular George Cukor–directed *Two-Faced Woman*, painfully playing a woman pretending to be her own more carefree (albeit imaginary) twin sister. This remarkably tone-deaf performance by one of the greatest of film artists plays like a get-me-out-of-here cry for help. Long ambivalent about the demands of stardom, Garbo at age thirty-six took a break that never ended, even though Mayer only reluctantly gave up hope.

Two-Faced Woman became so notorious that the people who made it took perverse pride in their participation. "I claim the dubious distinction of having written the picture that drove Greta Garbo off the screen," George Oppenheimer wrote, and as late as 1958, when Cukor autographed a magazine article on *Two-Faced Woman* to a friend, he added a tart postscript: "It was this picture that caused Miss G's retirement from the Silver Screen."

As Adrian revealed to Irene Mayer Selznick, Garbo was hardly a sentimentalist when it came to studio leave-takings. When the designer said goodbye after creating all the actress's costumes for more than a dozen years, Garbo was characteristically blunt. "I'm very sorry you are leaving," she told him. "But, you know, I never really liked most of the clothes you made me wear."

20

Old and in the Way

In 1938 a new, gleaming white, fully air-conditioned MGM administration building, named in honor of Thalberg but soon saddled with the nickname the Iron Lung (where "paralytic minds were at work," quipped Joseph L. Mankiewicz), opened roughly on the spot where Buster Keaton had had his infamous bungalow. To Elia Kazan, it was "the great white hornet's nest of overpaid executives," but to Mayer it was his new home. As befitted the man in sole charge of the studio, he moved into a new luxurious office on the third floor, an office that was talked about. A lot.

The main topic of conversation inevitably was size, with movie stars being especially impressed by how big it was. Esther Williams called it "a masterpiece of Hollywood ingenuity. It was designed to intimidate, from the grandeur of the ante-rooms, where his secretaries sat, to the mammoth walnut doors that opened to his office." Once inside, said Debbie Reynolds, "you entered this enormous room, all in white, for what some people called 'the quarter-mile walk' to a desk the size of a small helicopter pad, all highly polished and shining." Even Samuel Goldwyn, who presumably had an imposing office of his own, reportedly told Mayer, "It's like Mussolini's! You need an automobile to reach your desk." Perhaps because Maurice Rapf reports that for a time an autographed photo of Il Duce hung on the wall behind Mayer, references to the Italian dictator became something of a leitmotif in Mayer lore. Marion Davies reported that Hearst told her after meeting Mussolini that his office was "this huge room—almost as big as Louis B. Mayer's office." Taking the other side was actor James Mason, who insisted, "No, not Mussolini. . . . One did not have to walk very far in the office of L. B. Mayer, which was more like a small courtroom."

As Williams observed, Mayer's lair, as befits what Adela Rogers St. John characterized as his "consulting room, safety zone and, I must admit, torture chamber for stars," was laid out with psychological impact in mind. The most detailed description comes from two journalists who report that Mayer sat "on a chair constructed to make him seem taller than he actually was, behind an enormous horseshoe-shaped desk, his back to a window equipped with drapery and venetian blinds that could be adjusted so that his own face remained in shadow while those of his visitors were fully lit." Around him were photographs of the people he admired, a virtual *goyishe* Hall of Fame including Francis Cardinal Spellman and the two Hoovers, Herbert and J. Edgar. But in the place of prominence, actor Joel McCrea reported, was "a picture of his mother on his desk. 'Only God was more important to me than her,' he said."

Mayer's treasured mother was central to the one feature of his reign that met with universal approval: the quality of the chicken soup—the traditional food for the Jewish soul—served in the studio commissary, soup that was, Samuel Marx claimed, "almost as famous as some of its film stars." Costing a bargain thirty-five cents per bowl, it graced the menu because Mayer "had vowed to his mother that when he became rich he would always have chicken soup with real chicken in it." Taught to studio chefs by the Mayer family cook, the recipe was, complete with matzoh balls, acclaimed as everything from "excellent" (Edward G. Robinson) to "exquisite" (Eleanor Powell) by all who tried it. Even as epicurean a palate as that of British producer Alexander Korda, his nephew Michael reported, approved, though he characterized the dish as "chicken soup with dumplings a la Louis B. Mayer."

If chicken soup was an aspect of Jewish life that Mayer connected to, in other ways his relationship to the religion and culture of Judaism was complex, a situation that became more apparent as World War II approached. On the one hand, he believed. Not only did he have his strictly religious father live with him for many years, according to friend and frequent houseguest Fanny Holtzmann, the attorney and *Rasputin* antagonist, he avoided Reform High Holy Days services at the Wilshire Boulevard Temple but instead went with his father to an old-school Orthodox synagogue. "There," he told her, "I put on a *tallis*. I stand with other Jews as my people have done for thousands of years—and I feel closer to God."

And his grandson Jeffrey Selznick, in a powerful anecdote recounted to biographer Gary Carey, witnessed another Mayer moment of deep immersion in traditional Judaism. Asked by his grandfather in the late 1940s to accompany him while he said Kaddish on the anniversary of Mayer's mother's death, Selznick reported going in a limo to "the heart of [New York's] Garment District, where Mayer stopped the car in front of a modest, somewhat dilapidated synagogue that was Middle European in appearance and ambiance. Once inside, Mayer put on a yarmulke and prayer shawl, and for over an hour, 'with tears streaming down his cheeks,' he sobbed and recited Kaddish and other prayers. Afterwards, he had to walk several blocks to compose himself."

On the other hand, though Mayer said, "I am a Jew and try to be a good one," those photographs on his wall, even his friendship with the notorious antisemite Henry Ford, testify that Mayer had an equally strong yearning to be accepted by America's Christian hierarchy. Even more than that, however, Mayer's religion had in some ways become the studio with his name on it. In this he would be making common cause with author Bruce Barton, a founder of advertising powerhouse BBD&O, who in 1925 wrote the best-selling *The Man Nobody Knows*, which recast Christ as a powerful corporate executive who pointedly said, "I must be about my Father's *business.*" As a result, Mayer saw all issues, even ones involving Jews, through a commercial, what's-good-for-MGM, lens. So when it came to deciding how to deal with the lucrative German market in the run-up to the European war, for instance, what made business sense was the dominating factor. (This proved to be true, if only at first, even with the postwar anticommunist blacklist, with Mayer initially protecting his writers by saying, "I wouldn't fire anyone because someone said someone was a Communist, as long as there was no communism in our pictures—and it couldn't get in.")

Growing up as he had, Mayer of course understood that antisemitism was real. He even gave a speech on St. Patrick's Day in 1937, emphasizing that "in some lands, an increasing number, you are persecuted if you are a Jew, you cannot earn anything, may not vote; you can be driven from your home, torn from the arms of your loved ones." Like Thalberg, he was concerned about the rise of Adolf Hitler but did not know exactly how concerned to be. He suggested William Randolph Hearst meet with Hitler on the publisher's 1934 trip to Europe but was happy to accept at face value Hearst's bland assurances about the German leader's intentions.

While Warner Bros. released anti-Nazi films as early as May

1939's *Confessions of a Nazi Spy*, MGM, the studio which "had the biggest financial stake in Germany," was slower to respond. Mayer, worried about that profitable German market, had the Clark Gable/Norma Shearer *Idiot's Delight*, released the same year, "remove any incendiary political references" and use inoffensive Esperanto "whenever a foreign dialect was needed." Moreover, when some studios withdrew from Germany because of the Nazi demand that they no longer employ Jews, MGM was one of only three to remain. The reason, *Variety* explained, was that they "have too much coin tied up there. . . . They are loath to forget it and mark the sum down as a net loss."

Given how passionately Mayer felt about America, once the United States entered the war one would have thought he would be all in. He was, eventually, but once again what was good for the studio (which meant keeping those under MGM contract out of harm's way) initially trumped all other considerations. Mayer was angry when James Stewart and Robert Montgomery enlisted before Pearl Harbor (Stewart paid for his own flying lessons so he could join the Army Air Force), and for a time he managed to keep his top male stars out. When Mickey Rooney made a morale-boosting movie called *Thousands Cheer*, Mayer told him, "This show will do more for America than ten Mickey Rooney's in uniform." But when Clark Gable's wife, actress Carole Lombard, died in a plane crash coming home after a successful war bond fundraising tour, Gable could not be held back. He enlisted as an aerial gunner, telling a friend, "I'm going in, and I don't expect to come back, and I don't really give a hoot whether I do or not." Mayer continued to fight for exemptions for his stars, and in 1942 Selective Service head General Louis Hershey agreed with him, ruling that moviemaking was "an activity essential . . . to the national health, safety, and interest." Despite this, to Mayer's chagrin, Rooney chose to enlist, as did Gene Kelly and Robert Taylor.

Mayer eventually turned his efforts to help the war effort

to his area of expertise, the making of motion pictures, and there he had greater success. As always, sentiment was his default position, especially in MGM's biggest wartime success, *Mrs. Miniver*, which hit theaters in June 1942, six months after Pearl Harbor. Under William Wyler's sure direction, its seamless portrait of a happy, carefree England suddenly forced to confront the deadly agonies of the Blitz was very much what the American public wanted to see at this early, uncertain stage of the war, a model example of a film that confidently rose to meet its moment in history. "I was a warmonger," Wyler admitted later. "I was concerned about Americans being isolationists. *Mrs. Miniver* obviously was a propaganda film."

Norma Shearer had been offered the starring role, but she felt too young to play the wife and mother of the title, especially one old enough to have a son attending Oxford. Second choice Greer Garson had resisted as well, though Mayer, as noted, eventually wore her down. Her portrayal of a woman who started as, in her own words, "foolish and extravagant" but ends up being able to face down Helmut Dantine's chilling downed German pilot in her own kitchen, was strong enough to win her the best-actress Oscar, one of seven the film won, including best picture and best director for Wyler. More impressive were the political plaudits, with Hitler's propaganda minister Joseph Goebbels, of all people, calling it an "exemplary propaganda film for German industry to copy" and Winston Churchill chiming in that the film was worth, depending on which source you believe, either six military divisions or a hundred battleships to the Allied war effort.

But though *Mrs. Miniver* is considered the definitive World War II home front movie, it was not Mayer's personal favorite. That distinction belongs to 1943's Mickey Rooney–starring *The Human Comedy*, based on a work by a writer Mayer had a particularly fractious relationship with, William Saroyan. Saroyan, who'd written the Pulitzer Prize–winning play *The Time of Your*

Life, did not particularly want to write for the movies, but he was swayed by the money Mayer offered. "No Jew can ever cheat an Armenian," he reportedly said. "The Armenians have been cheating the Jews for centuries." The episodic *Human Comedy* script Saroyan turned in detailed the impact the war had on the members of one family in the fictional Ithaca, California. Saroyan wanted to direct himself, but the task fell to Clarence Brown, who coaxed a remarkably subdued, Oscar-nominated perfor- mance out of Rooney as the teenage bicycle messenger who, in a scene Mayer particularly prized, delivered messages of war- time death to about-to-be-grieving mothers. Though Saroyan won an Oscar for best original story, he never lost his frustration with Mayer. He attacked his former employer in a bylined piece in *Variety* and later wrote a play lampooning the executive called *Get Away Old Man*, which closed on Broadway after thirteen performances. He even reversed his earlier position about who cheated whom, writing in the *Saturday Evening Post* in 1963, "Old L.B. gypped me, but as he *had* to, as he had no choice in the matter, as it would have killed him had he so much as *tried* not to gyp me, I don't see how I can hold it against him."

The war years were strong ones for MGM, with audiences not only embracing *Mrs. Miniver* and *The Human Comedy* but also seeking the familiar comfort of the series films Mayer so believed in, and his income rode that wave. Starting in 1937, when the combination of salary and bonuses earned Mayer $1.3 mil- lion, he was almost fetishistically proclaimed by the media as the highest-paid individual in America, making even more money than President Roosevelt. Quite an achievement for a tough Jew- ish kid who survived a hard-scrabble immigrant childhood, and, especially after the war ended, Mayer began to live more and more like the uncrowned king of Hollywood he felt himself, with justification, to be. Up to and including indulging himself in the expensive, ultra-Gentile sport of kings, horseracing. As his daughter Irene Mayer Selznick put it, "he lost his head, not over women, but over horses."

Indulging himself, however, is perhaps the wrong image here, because Mayer went about the business of buying, breeding, and racing thoroughbreds with the kind of methodical resolve he'd devoted to building his studio. He'd first gotten involved in the late 1930s on the advice of a doctor who told him he needed a diverting hobby, but Mayer, attracted by the recognition as well as money that winning promised, didn't know how to do things by half measures. Advised as he was by a small circle of experts, his shrewd purchases included future horse of the year Busher, which he once compared to Greer Garson, calling the actress "a classy filly who runs the track according to orders and comes home with blue ribbons."

Mayer's success was such that he purchased five hundred acres south of Los Angeles near Perris and turned it into the up-to-the-minute Mayer Stock Farm, winning the New York Turf Writers Association 1945 accolade as the country's top breeder in the process. "He was the country's leading money winner" that year, Irene Mayer Selznick remembered, "and, beginning in 1945, for three years running, the country's leading breeder of stakes winners." Though he'd started out, in director and friend Clarence Brown's words, knowing "about as much about horses as a hog knows about Sundays," by the time sportswriter Vincent X. Flaherty visited the farm in 1946, Mayer was sought out for his wisdom. "In the movies," he told Flaherty, "a man likes to develop stars. In racing it is very much the same way. You take a horse and train him and bring him along and watch him develop. You get a lot of satisfaction watching them blossom out."

An area where Mayer was not getting the kind of gratification he felt he was due was his relationship with his wife Margaret. The marriage had initially been a love match and while Margaret Mayer had never become the kind of sophisticated partner Norma Shearer had been for Irving Thalberg, that did

Mayer turned himself into one of America's top horse breeders,
but that didn't mean every visit to the track was a happy one.
(Bettmann/Getty Images)

not present a problem until a series of medical crises occurred.
"Toward the end of 1933, when Mother was forty-eight, con-
trol of her health had been taken out of her hands; she required
a hysterectomy," daughter Irene Mayer Selznick remembered.
"The operation was routine, but nothing was ever again the same.
Overall, it was the worst calamity that ever hit our family."

Afflicted with melancholia after the surgery, Margaret Mayer
became an on-and-off patient at a sanatorium in Massachusetts.
"My father was lost," Mayer Selznick wrote. "He wandered
around brooding, homeless and bereft. We didn't know what

to do about him, nor was anyone else able to console him. . . . Even approaching fifty, he was probably the most unsophisticated, straitlaced man in town. Only gradually did he turn to diversion." Samuel Marx agrees that up to this point in his MGM career, "there were rumors that he slept with stars, but they were spread by people who didn't know him, because it was precisely what he would not do. He was the most circumspect man in his studio; he knew that revelations of an affair between him and a leading lady could lead to a devastating scandal that would probably ruin both of them."

Still, Mayer had never been above what Frances Marion, speaking from experience, called "a neat little pinch on the bottom," and it was common knowledge that, ever his own version of a father figure, he enjoyed having his female stars sit on his lap. As Margaret Mayer's condition persisted, however, he took to marathon bouts of dancing at night spots like Ciro's, with Mickey Rooney cattily reporting, "Mr. Mayer liked to rhumba himself with a variety of young ladies, now that he'd sent his wife to a sanitarium in the East." And writer Budd Schulberg confirms that during this period his mother, the talent and literary agent Ad Schulberg, had an affair with Mayer. But what Mayer also did, resembling nothing so much as an antediluvian Andy Hardy, was launch into a series of chaste, hands-off courtships of younger women he had become infatuated with and hoped to marry.

The most celebrated of these nonaffair affairs was with a young woman named Jean Howard, half Mayer's age, who was one of MGM's numerous aspiring actresses when she became the focus of the mogul's attention. "Mayer was a Puritan," producer Walter Wanger told Samuel Marx. "He was like a bashful boy around Jean. He didn't tell her about his feelings and I'm sure she didn't realize what had happened." Howard herself candidly told Marx, "He didn't even hold my hand. I liked him very much but he seemed a mental adolescent in perpetuity. . . . I'm sure I would have gone to bed with him if he had asked me." Instead, Mayer asked her to meet him in Paris with a chaperone, where he planned for a marriage proposal. In the interim, however, Howard fell in love with agent Charles Feldman, and when a private investigator informed Mayer in Paris, Howard reports, "he roared around the room and then, suddenly, made a move to throw himself out the window." Mayer was restrained, but in retaliation he barred Feldman (who soon married Howard, with Wanger as the best man) from the MGM lot for years.

Finally, in 1944, Mayer officially separated from his wife, abruptly moving out of their oceanfront Santa Monica home after forty years of marriage. In the same year he met another young actress, this one with more stardom ahead of her. Tap dancer Ann Miller left a detailed record of her recollections of their relationship in her memoir, *Miller's High Life*. Miller was introduced to Mayer as a potential dancing partner when she was only twenty and, she admits, "I probably had the emotional maturity of a fourteen-year-old." Given her age, Miller's mother "always went along on my dates with Louis B. Mayer because he always invited her." The trio also had at-home evenings "and many times at all hours the telephone would ring and it would be one of those big Hollywood star-ladies wanting to come over and hold L.B.'s hand—meaning spend the night—in return for a certain part in a certain film." Mayer's response: "You see, Ann, this is why I like you. You would never do anything like that. This is the ugly side of Hollywood." What Miller also wouldn't do was marry Mayer. "When he proposed marriage to me, all hell broke loose," she remembers. "Absolutely no way, said my mother," and that was that.

The divorce between Louis B. and Margaret Mayer on grounds of desertion (his) was finalized on April 28, 1947, with the *Hollywood Citizen-News* excitedly headlining "MAYER MUST PAY WIFE $3,240,000." "He knew deep down it was the wrong thing to do," publicist Howard Strickling told Bosley Crowther.

"He really hated himself for it." A year and a half later, on December 4, 1948, another newspaper, the *Los Angeles Examiner*, ran a very different banner: "L.B. MAYER WEDS TODAY; ELOPES WITH LORENA DANKER." Though she was some twenty years younger than her husband, the former actress and dancer was a more decorous choice for Mayer: Danker was a widow with a twelve-year-old daughter. The couple eloped to Yuma, Arizona, to escape publicity, but reporters caught on, leading to a situation the *Los Angeles Mirror* headlined as "Mayer-Danker Wedding Held in Yuma Jailhouse." The new wife wanted a new house, and Mayer obligingly moved to St. Cloud Road in tony Bel Air. And, as grandson Daniel Selznick told biographer Scott Eyman, there was another big change as well: "There was no photo of his mother on St. Cloud Road."

Mayer could have been forgiven for thinking MGM's success would continue in the postwar world, but it was not to be. Initially the momentum created by doing more of the same seemed to be working. The Freed Unit kept making prestige musicals, following celebrated Judy Garland wartime hits like *Meet Me in St. Louis* with the postwar *The Harvey Girls, Ziegfeld Follies*, and *Easter Parade*. Mayer signed another star, swimming champion Esther Williams, aka "The Million Dollar Mermaid," and her aquatic musicals were major money makers as well. When a fawning June 1947 *Reader's Digest* profile was headlined "The Unchallenged King of Hollywood," Mayer probably felt it would always be thus, but the decline was already upon him.

The 1947 Oscar race was the first time since the awards' first year that MGM did not have even one best-picture nominee. And in the 1947–48 fiscal year the studio lost money, an unthinkable circumstance. Some had complained that Mayer was focusing his attention elsewhere (Hedda Hopper sniped that he "became more interested in horses than in actors"), and in February 1947, for a variety of reasons, including what his daughter characterized as "time and concentration diverted from his job," he held what one newspaper called "the greatest single stable sale in American history" and got out of the horse business. Even this was not enough, and the long-dormant search for "a new Thalberg" was resurrected. But sometimes, as the saying goes, when God wants to punish you, he gives you what you want.

The search soon focused on Dore Schary, the recently departed head of production at RKO, but also someone Mayer had considerable previous experience with. Schary had come to MGM as a writer in 1933 and had shared the best-story Oscar for his work on 1938's *Boys Town*, but his determination to go his own way had also caused friction. As he tells it in his *Heyday* autobiography, Schary's passion for *Joe Smith, American*, a B-picture he was working on, led in 1941 to his first-ever meeting with the top man: "Mayer radiated power—physical and psychological . . . while always well groomed, [he] was surrounded by a faint glimmer of crudeness." At one point Schary made an off-the-cuff remark about the untapped potential he felt B's had: "I believe that low cost pictures should dare—should challenge—that they also should be used as a testing ground for new talent." Mayer's response the next day was characteristically unexpected: "He held me with an intense look, then half smiled. 'All right, you're in charge of all the B pictures.'" The job involved working with the veteran executive Harry Rapf, and when Rapf and Schary disagreed, Mayer took Schary's side in a particularly explosive meeting. "Mayer opened with a barrage of abuse. "Goddamit, Harry . . . you stupid kike bastard—you ought to kiss this man's [pointing to me] shoes—get on your knees.' . . . When I got out of Mayer's office, I dashed to the men's toilet and threw up my breakfast." Within a few years Schary had left MGM to work first for David O. Selznick and then for R.K.O.

Differences in temperament and politics (Schary was a pro-

Roosevelt New Deal Democrat who eventually wrote the Tony-winning *Sunrise at Campobello*) were brushed aside as Mayer began to see the much younger man as the Thalberg replacement he both needed and thought he wanted, an American-born Jew who had the requisite devotion to his mother. Mayer invited Schary to his home and "with no preface offered me the job as vice-president in charge of production," the first time all MGM's producers would be reporting to one man since Thalberg's heyday. Mayer would be happy, the executive said, "to have you come home to MGM where you belong." Schary, of course, had his doubts: "MGM was ridden with conflict, envy and rivalry. It was peopled with employees who had been there for years—spoiled and wasteful, and yet many of them talented but hobbled by the old College of Cardinals system inaugurated by Mayer." Schary sought assurances that he would be in charge in fact as well as in name, and these both Mayer and Nicholas Schenck in New York gave him. In June 1948, with a holding of breath all around, the deal was made official.

Initially, all went well. Schary implemented some needed economies, and the studio showed a small profit for the 1948–49 season, but not everyone was happy. After Schary talked about budget cuts to costume designer Irene, she fumed to her sketch artist Virginia Fisher, "This didn't even happen during the Depression! How in the hell does he expect us to do our work? He may understand money but not what it takes to make an MGM movie." An attempt to enhance good feelings came in 1949, MGM's twenty-fifth anniversary, which the studio decided to celebrate in style with a gala February 10 luncheon capped by a soundstage photo of fifty-eight of its stars, arranged alphabetically in tiered rows from June Allyson to Esther Williams and Keenan Wynn. (Lionel Barrymore and Lassie were given special dispensation to sit on their respective aisles.) Vincente Minnelli did not go, but he heard from screenwriter Adolph Green that Mayer gave "this very involved talk . . . trying to rationalize why

Dore was now there." Green also noted the presence of choco-
late ice creams molded in the shape of the MGM lion. "We sat
through the long speeches," he said, "looking at all these lions
melting."

For agreement or no agreement, it was never quite clear
where the lines of responsibility between the two men had been
drawn. Schary (though he wrote of Mayer, "Many times I found
his judgments of great value") was eager to claim what he considered to be his rights, and the older man was reluctant to sur-
render his. James Mason maintained, "I would never have been
able to answer a test paper concerning the precise limits of each
man's authority," and Esther Williams, who knew and worked
for both, explained that "as VP of production, Schary had control over stories, stars, and directors, but Mayer was still VP in
charge of the studio as a whole; and Schary was theoretically
answerable to him. It was literally The Clash of the Titans. Unless Schenck intervened, there was always a question of whose
word was final." Making this confusion worse, the two men had
"diametrically opposite approaches to moviemaking, so the an-
imosity between them became personal."

Mayer liked Big Picture spectacle, while Schary, tending to
what were called message pictures, had a more high-tone approach that ran the risk of failing badly with audiences. "Dore
Schary was sort of like a rabbinical student who feels badly about
having become a mountebank," observed costume designer Lucinda Ballard. "He was so moralistic and always wanting to do
something about God or the pilgrims, which people didn't want
to see, and it really was one of the things that wrecked him in
the end." To the people on the ground, like Vincente Minnelli,
Mayer, for all his faults, was often the preferred devil they knew:
"For if he lacked innate taste, he had the ability to entrust a picture to his underlings and keep his nose out of it," while Schary
was in the habit of "assuming prerogatives Mayer had never
presumed to take."

The first major dustup between these titans came with the 1949 World War II drama *Battleground*. The muted script about the relentless adversity facing the Army's 101st Airborne division as it attempts to hold off a German drive during the Battle of the Bulge had been a favorite project of Schary's while he was at RKO, and in fact the only thing he asked of new owner Howard Hughes when he left that studio was that he be allowed to take it with him. Schary decided to produce the film himself, and Mayer, who had disliked this kind of nonheroic war movie since *The Big Parade*, agreed to let him do it because "It will teach you a lesson." Unfortunately for Mayer, the lessons to be learned were for him (not that he took them): the William Wellman–directed film turned out a critical and box office success and ended up winning Oscars for screenwriter Robert Pirosh and Paul C. Vogel's luminous black-and-white cinematography.

Also causing difficulty for Mayer was one of his biggest stars, Judy Garland, whose psychological and drug-related problems, which the studio had had a hand in creating, were coming to a crisis. Garland was suspended twice in less than a year for causing time-consuming production delays and had to be replaced both times, first by Ginger Rogers in 1949's *The Barkleys of Broadway* and then by Betty Hutton in 1950's *Annie Get Your Gun*. When reports of problems on 1950's *Summer Stock* were added to the mix, Garland took the unusual step of publishing "an open letter" in the pages of *Modern Screen* to reassure the writers of "more than 18,000 letters" she'd received from fans worried about her.

Yet James Mason, who was to costar with Garland in one of her best films, 1954's *A Star Is Born*, wrote that "Judy was by no means a temperamental star. . . . Judy was essentially a witty, lively, talented, funny, adorable woman." The problem, as Mason saw it, was that because she had "developed as a child star at MGM the unfortunate habit of taking uppers and downers . . . Judy had made a sort of bad name for herself because in a commercial town like Hollywood reliability is the big thing." The tolerant Mason felt that "to get something as unique as Judy's talents, some patience and certain sacrifices were needed," but this MGM and its leader were willing to make allowances only up to a point. Mayer, who had insisted that the studio pay for hospitalization for Garland after the *Annie* episode, seemed to both genuinely care for his former child star, still only twenty-eight in 1950, and be frustrated that this case of an actress who yearned for MGM to "treat me like they do Greer Garson" resisted tidy solutions.

As if to underline that, Garland made an attempt at suicide in June of 1950, after which, according to biographer Gerald Clarke, "Mayer had paid her a visit. What they said to each other has not been recorded, but their meeting, which lasted an hour and fifteen minutes, was emotional." Three months later, to relief all around, MGM canceled her contract, though as late as 1955, two years before his death, Mayer was still distraught at what had come to pass. "Like my own daughter she was to me, but then she got sick," he said in a newspaper interview. "It became too much to ask my producers and directors to work with her. She had to go. It broke my heart. She had to go." Metro songwriter Harry Warren maintained, "If she had been at Warners, they would have dropped her three years earlier," and Garland's daughter Lorna Luft wrote, "She always spoke lovingly of him to us children and to my father. . . . She loved L. B. Mayer to the end of her life."

Perhaps most troubling to the core of the man at this juncture was the likely terrifying suspicion that he was slowly drifting out of fashion and into cultural irrelevance. No longer was he his own best audience, no longer could he say with confidence, as he had in that 1947 *Reader's Digest* article, "If 75 percent of the American people didn't feel as I do about the American family, we wouldn't be here." Not even getting a 1950 honorary Oscar for "distinguished service to the motion picture industry" (biographer Scott Eyman calls it "The Kiss of Death Award") was likely to ease the pain. Nothing illustrates Mayer's doomed predicament more acutely than the drama behind the filming of 1951's *The Red Badge of Courage*, as well as Lillian Ross's *New Yorker* reporting about it that became *Picture*, arguably the original nonfiction novel and still one of the irreplaceable books on Hollywood.

Based on the Stephen Crane novel of the Civil War and starring World War II hero and B Western star Audie Murphy as a young man who must face up to his conflicts about combat, the well-meaning but uninspired *Courage* became, in the words of director John Huston, "a cause célèbre before it was ever made. It was a film over which the old and new orders at MGM fought. . . . Whoever prevailed would control the studio, and the loser would be relegated to limbo." Given the stakes, there was considerable back-and-forth on both sides about the film, with Mayer at one point proclaiming, "I wouldn't make that picture with Sam Goldwyn's money," but then insisting Huston proceed anyway, telling the director, "John Huston, I'm ashamed of you! Do you believe in this picture? . . . Then stick by your guns! Never let me hear you talk like this again!" Schary for his part both wrote a memo to Mayer saying the film "has a chance of becoming a highly important motion picture that will bring honor to the studio" and confessed to Lillian Ross its commercial flaws: "The story—well there's no story in this picture. It's just the story of a boy. It's the story of a coward." The make-or-break decision went to Nicholas Schenck, who, after the success of *Battleground*, had no trouble siding with Schary.

That we know as much as we do about *Courage* and the workings of MGM is due to Lillian Ross. She had become friends with Huston in New York and his invitation for her to observe the making of *Courage* for a *New Yorker* series led to a year and a half of unprecedented access for this sharp and fearless woman into the film's inner turmoil. Because it had not been the habit of film journalists to do her kind of realistic fly-on-the-wall reportage, nobody she talked to expected her to make public what she heard and saw. Her unblinking eye spared no one, not Schary ("A man who seems to be favorably disposed toward the entire world . . . but there is in [him] a definite hint of a firm-minded and paternalistic Sunday-school teacher"), and certainly not Mayer. As Ross related to her editor William Shawn, Mayer had told her "that he has always refused interviews, but for some reason he didn't explain he was more than willing to talk to me for the story." The centerpiece of her interview, and perhaps the most memorable scene in the book, was a patented Mayer outburst about the dire state of motherhood in contemporary American film.

> "Don't show the good, wholesome, American mother in her home. Kind. Sweet. Sacrifices. Love." Mayer paused, and by his expression demonstrated, in turn, maternal kindness, sweetness, sacrifice, and love, and then glared at [Arthur] Freed and me.
>
> "No!" he cried. "Knock the mother on the jaw!" He gave himself an uppercut to the chin. "Throw the old lady down the stairs!" He threw himself in the direction of the American flag. "Throw the mother's good, home-made chicken soup in the mother's face." He threw an imaginary plate of soup in Freed's face. "*Step* on the mother! *Kick* her! That is *art*, they say. Art!"

That unhinged scene is easily read as amusing, and Mayer was no stranger to acting foolish at this stage of his career. But if viewed in another light, there is real poignance here, the how-the-mighty-have-fallen bewilderment of a man who's stayed on the job too long, who cannot comprehend that time has noticeably passed him by. This reality, much to his dismay, was soon to be impressed on him in no uncertain terms. As beleaguered *Courage* producer Gottfried Reinhardt put it, "We unleased a civil war of our own at MGM. Louis B. Mayer was the first casualty."

Given how momentous, even epoch-ending the concluding incident was, there is an unexpected lack of unanimity over its specifics. Tired of things not going his way, of films he had no patience with getting made ("I wouldn't walk across the room to see a thing like that," he said of the 1950 noir classic *The Asphalt Jungle*), Mayer lashed out in Schenck and Schary's direction. The specific tipping point might have been Mayer's dissatisfaction with the way a stock option plan was handled, or Schenck's overruling him over whether *Courage*, which had been cut to sixty-nine minutes after disastrous screenings, should be shelved ("He refused to release it, but I changed *that*," Schenck told Lillian Ross), or maybe just general malaise, but at one point Mayer insisted, by letter and/or phone, "It's either me or Schary." Message received, the ever-correct Schenck (Mayer liked to say his longtime antagonist had "two faces—the smiler and the killer") responded with a letter opting for Schary. Mayer for his part quashed any possible reconciliation by fiercely insisting to an intermediary that his opponents "can take the studio and choke on it." On June 22, 1951, the announcement came: after twenty-seven years, twelve with Irving Thalberg, fifteen without, Mayer and Metro-Goldwyn-Mayer were going their separate ways. As screenwriter George Oppenheimer summarized, "Mayer had brought Dore to Metro and, in so doing, signed his own death warrant. For a while Dore was his son. Then he became a stepson, and finally a bastard. It was inevitable that these two should clash."

MGM insiders, the people who knew Mayer personally, had seen this coming. Frances Marion reports running into him in the hall outside his office and hearing him say, "I'm tired of being Atlas. My shoulders ache from carrying this ungrateful world that I built up. What I need is a long rest. Peace! I'll never find it here with these bloodhounds at my throat." And Esther Williams remembered encountering Mayer at celebrity hangout Chasen's a few months before the split, when he told her, "They're kicking me out, Esther. If I start up another studio, would you come with me?" She tactfully turned him down by saying, "'Thanks, Mr. Mayer, but where are you going to find a pool like the one on Stage 30? How can I go with you if you don't have a pool?' . . . He looked at me, crestfallen, and it was painful to see him like that. Mayer had always been short; now he looked small, which was very different indeed. He seemed quite vulnerable as he wished me well and returned to his table."

The statement Mayer issued when his departure was announced was upbeat, with the bullish mogul insisting, "I am going to remain in motion picture production, God willing. I am going to be more active than at any time during the last 15 years," but this proved to be a difficult agenda to put into practice. Without the structure of the studio to bolster and support him, Mayer found it difficult to proceed.

Nothing came of rumors that he would buy control of RKO, of Republic, even Warner Bros, and though he evinced enough interest in a new super-widescreen product called Cinerama to become chairman of the board, nothing came of that either. Films he thought he wanted to make, like the musical *Paint Your Wagon* and a biblical epic about Joseph and his brothers, did not go anywhere. He tried to buy the rights to Agatha Christie's hit play *Witness for the Prosecution* but was outbid. As someone whose idea of golf was playing three to five balls simultaneously, he was not likely to take up the game more seriously, but he did believe in exercise: Lillian Ross reports seeing him on Wilshire Boulevard in Beverly Hills, "walking, with great energy, along the street; he was taking his nightly constitutional." Dore Schary, for one, was not sympathetic: "He had no inner life to sustain him. All he had was bitterness and a burning yen for revenge."

Mayer in 1956 did have one last opportunity to take that revenge on those he felt had wronged him. By this time, his old antagonists Schenck and Schary had both fallen in corporate combat, but Mayer's zeal for battle remained undiminished. He joined with Canadian financier Joseph Tomlinson, Loew's largest single shareholder, in what has been called "an attempted studio coup" or, according to Louis Nizer, best-selling author of *My Life in Court* and chief attorney for the anti-Mayer faction, "one of the bitterest fought contests in the history of American industry." The resulting fight with new Loew's president Joseph Vogel, a struggle aptly characterized by one Mayer biographer as "long, complicated, ugly and finally tedious to anyone not fascinated by the machinations of corporate power play," was not finally resolved, in Vogel's favor, until October 15, 1957. By that time, Mayer, who had announced, "I have come back because I am lonely for Leo the Lion," had other things on his mind. Within two weeks, he would be dead.

Mayer had been initially hospitalized in the summer of 1957 at the Stanford Hospital in San Francisco, had gone home and then was admitted once again to the UCLA Medical Center. The diagnosis was leukemia, and though Mayer was apparently never told, there was the sense that he knew. His nephew and MGM producer Jack Cummings told Bosley Crowther that he was in the hospital room when Mayer's intravenous feeding tube came loose. It was reattached but Mayer responded, "It's not going to work. I can't go on." At one point near the end he cried, "Has she come yet? Is she outside?" Neither of his daughters was present at the moment, and Irene and Edith, who had an ongoing feud, disagreed over which daughter he was asking for. On October 29, 1957, Louis B. Mayer died. Perhaps his last recorded words were to publicity chief and friend Howard Strickling: "Don't let them worry you. Nothing matters, nothing matters."

21

Afterlife

ON ONE LEVEL, Louis B. Mayer's funeral echoed Irving Thalberg's. Each was held before a cast of thousands at the Wilshire Boulevard Temple, each was presided over by Rabbi Edgar Magnin, and each featured a vocal solo by an MGM star, with Jeanette MacDonald rather than Grace Moore doing the honors this time with a rendition of "Ah, Sweet Mystery of Life." But twenty years had passed, Hollywood was different, and the death of a disenfranchised senior citizen did not register the same way as the loss of an individual taken before his time. There was an inevitable era-closing feeling about the Hollywood reaction to Mayer's death, with even Rabbi Magnin noting, "This is the end of a volume, not a chapter." Spencer Tracy, enough of a Thalberg man to have reportedly gone on an alcoholic binge when he died, nevertheless read the eulogy, largely written by David O. Selznick, which called Mayer "a man of contrasts—part sentiment and idealism, part pure practicality."

In an editorial that still echoes today, the *Los Angeles Examiner* noted that with Mayer's death, "absolute personal rule has given way to executive caution and deftness. The old spirit of guess and venture largely has been replaced by the decisions of surveys and computers."

Unlike Thalberg, Mayer was buried in a Jewish cemetery, the Home of Peace in East Los Angeles, where he joined fellow movie business grandees like Carl Laemmle, three of the Warner brothers, and his MGM colleague Harry Rapf, all of whom were in turn eventually joined by Rabbi Magnin himself. Mayer had not been long interred before carping witticisms began to make the rounds, with Rapf's son Maurice quoting Samuel Goldwyn saying of Mayer's large funeral, "The reason so many people showed up was to make sure he was dead." In a similar vein, screenwriter I. A. L. Diamond told biographer Maurice Zolotow he was next to Billy Wilder at the funeral and heard him say, "It shows that if you give the public what they want, they will come out for it." As Irene Mayer Selznick perceptively noted, "If my father had died, like [Adolph] Zukor, at over a hundred, things might have been different. Zukor managed to outlive all his enemies, so when he died, there was barely anyone around to remember how rough and ruthless he could be."

Within a few days, the Mayer naysayers were given a boost when the contents of his will became known. It wasn't that he gave the lion's share of his wealth to establishing the Louis B. Mayer Foundation for charitable works; that was above reproach. It was that this steadfast champion of family and family values had stiffed his daughter Edie, her producer husband William Goetz, and their children. Mayer's reason, as stated in the will, was true as far as it went: "I have given them extremely substantial assistance during my lifetime through gifts and financial assistance to my daughter's husband, and through advancement of his career." Mayer was in part referring to the $375,000 he had contributed to Darryl F. Zanuck's Twentieth Century Pictures, a predecessor to 20th Century–Fox, on condition that Goetz be named a partner. What finalized the rift was politics. Goetz, like Dore Schary, was a staunchly liberal Democrat, and Mayer was furious when his son-in-law and his studio rival joined forces to hold a fundraiser at Schary's home in support of presidential candidate Adlai Stevenson, the Democrat running against Republican Dwight D. Eisenhower. Mayer took his grudge with him to the grave, an action that caused Goetz to write to Schary that his was "the biggest contribution anyone made to the Stevenson campaign."

For the studio both Mayer and Thalberg gave their working lives to, worse was yet to come, far worse. Successive executives took over, none particularly memorable, and though MGM continued to make notable musicals like *An American in Paris* and *Singin' in the Rain* (which featured a cameo by that trailer on wheels that Irving Thalberg had gifted Norma Shearer), the nonmusicals lacked the studio's characteristic style and sheen. Even the good ones, like *Cat on a Hot Tin Roof, Bad Day at Black Rock*, and the 1959 remake of *Ben-Hur*, were indistinguishable from what everyone else was doing.

Not only were the stars leaving the lot—even Clark Gable, who left in 1954 after more than fifty films in twenty-three years— the lot itself was being sold off bit by bit by bit. The authors of *MGM: Hollywood's Greatest Backlot* report that "the contents of innumerable studio filing cabinets [went] into a pit as fill for the construction of the intersection of the San Diego and Golden State Freeways," and storied Lot Two, the site of the Andy Hardy street and Tarzan Lake, was leveled for a Studio Estates development that put single-family houses on roads with names like Garland Drive, Hepburn Circle, and Lamarr Avenue. The nadir of management's misguided belief that consuming itself was the way to stay alive was the disheartening way the painstakingly assembled physical objects, the huge number of irreplaceable pieces that made MGM MGM, were summarily auctioned off.

Billed by the David Weis Co. as "AN UNPRECEDENTED IN-
VENTORY OF THE LARGEST COLLECTION OF MOTION PICTURE MEM-
ORABILIA EVER ASSEMBLED," the May 1970 auction disposed of
some thirty thousand items for an estimated $8 million to $10
million in what the *Hollywood Reporter* characterized as "the
greatest rummage sale in history." Biggest ticket items turned out
to be the *Cotton Blossom*, the 172-foot, Mississippi stern-wheel
paddleboat from *Showboat* and a pair of "red sequined 'ruby'
shoes" from Dorothy's wardrobe in *The Wizard of Oz*, each item
going for $15,000. Even dreams, it turned out, have a price tag.

While the Louis B. Mayer Foundation looked for namable
brick-and-mortar projects to fund, including a library on the
AFI campus in Los Angeles and a movie theater in the Motion
Picture and Television Fund's retirement community in Wood-
land Hills, Norma Shearer, the keeper of the Irving Thalberg
flame, became involved in something quite different. Though
she remarried outside the business, to ski instructor Marti Ar-
rouge, and though the two children she'd had with Thalberg
distanced themselves from their parents' world as much as they
could (daughter Katharine became the founder/owner of an independent bookstore in Aspen and son Irving Jr. a professor of
philosophy at the University of Illinois, Chicago), Shearer always
kept up her connection to the business. She was even plugged
in enough to help a young woman named Jeanette Morrison,
whose photograph she chanced upon at the Sugar Bowl ski lodge
in Truckee, California. She brought the photograph to Hollywood, showed it to the right people, and after a screen test smiled
on by Mayer, actress Janet Leigh's career began.

The main posthumous commemoration of Shearer's first
husband, something that has kept his name prominent for decades, was the Academy's decision to present an Irving G. Thalberg Memorial Award, which initially was given annually for "the
most consistent high quality of production achievement by an

individual producer." The idea for this came not from Shearer but, as he emphasized in a letter to a fellow producer, from Thalberg's friend David O. Selznick. "As no doubt has been forgotten," he wrote, "it was I who originally suggested that there be an Irving Thalberg Memorial Award, and gave it its name; it was I who suggested, and even wrote, the phrasing of the award and its purposes." Selznick was so attached to this award that when he became its third recipient in 1939, his wife Irene Mayer Selznick characterized it as "a prize he had dreamed of. He had hit the jackpot." Though Shearer didn't originate the idea and at times expressed mixed feelings about it ("Irving wouldn't have liked that award. He hated that kind of publicity. I told them so at the time"), she soon came to embrace it. So much so that she oversaw not one but two new versions of the sculpted head of Thalberg that stood atop the trophy. She liked her first revision, initially presented in 1943, so much that she sent unsolicited copies to all those who'd received the award in earlier years. The second version of her husband's head commissioned by the actress was first presented in 1966 and, though the award is no longer an annual affair, is still in use today.

But as a movie star herself, Shearer was looking for something cinematic, something that would burnish her husband's name as brightly as possible in the community he'd devoted so much of himself to, and she found it in her substantial involvement in *Man of a Thousand Faces*. This 1957 biopic dealt with the life and times of Lon Chaney, a star in whose career Thalberg had been much involved. Because Ralph Wheelwright's original story had specifically positioned Thalberg as Chaney's key studio connection, permission was needed from Shearer to use his name, and for granting that permission Shearer had been given the right of approval over who played her husband.

Which brings us to November 5, 1956, when Shearer spotted a twenty-six-year-old New York–based women's clothing executive named Robert Evans poolside at the Beverly Hills Hotel and immediately wanted him for the Thalberg role. According to Evans' raffish autobiography, *The Kid Stays in the Picture*, Shearer said of him, "Young actors don't have his presence, authority. He's perfect. He's Irving." All obstacles to Evans getting the role dissolved, and Shearer began intensively coaching him "so I would sound and look as much like Irving as possible. She was obsessive about every detail, every inflection of his voice, every pause, every movement of his head and hands. It wasn't a performance she was after, it was a resurrection." There was a brief kerfuffle over whether Evans was to wear makeup or not ("You must not allow them to put makeup on you, Bob. I don't want you to look like another pretty-boy actor"), but otherwise the filming went smoothly. Evans, however, decided his movie talents lay elsewhere, and as head of production for Paramount starting in 1966, he oversaw hits like *Love Story*, *The Godfather*, and *Chinatown*. But successful as he became, he always retained a fondness for the time he played "the beau ideal of Hollywood producers. No career has ever approached his."

This would not be the last time Thalberg, or Mayer for that matter, would figure as characters in motion pictures. Though studio executives, even world beaters like William Fox and Adolph Zukor, are usually faceless figures unlikely to appear as movie protagonists, these two men were exceptions. Perhaps because of their divergent yet complementary personalities, perhaps because their joint efforts enabled the classic studio system to function at its peak, both together and separately, Mayer's and Thalberg's grip on the imaginations of filmmakers has never lessened. The two men's most substantial recent appearance was a joint one, played as devious MGM coconspirators by Arliss Howard and Ferdinand Kingsley in David Fincher's 2020 *Mank*.

Thalberg is by himself as a character less often than Mayer is, with one of the most charming being in *Young Indiana Jones: Hollywood Follies*, a 1994 Family Channel film for which Bill Cusack plays a youthful Thalberg of whom it is sadly said, "Poor

Irving, he can't stop thinking about movies." By contrast, Mayer has been portrayed by himself more than a dozen times, and a fascinating clip reel could be put together of performances by such top actors as Martin Balsam (*Rainbow*), Howard Da Silva (*Mommie Dearest*), Richard Dysart (*Malice in Wonderland*), and Allen Garfield (*Gable and Lombard*). And this doesn't include the way a fictional character based on Mayer dominates the screen as Michael Lerner's Jack Lipnick does in the Coen brothers' Hollywood spoof *Barton Fink*. Lipnick, who Lerner acknowledged in interviews was inspired by Mayer, can go from joy to fury in a heartbeat. He has an eagerness that extends to kissing an understandably confused writer's feet, an avidity that gives us as good a sense of Mayer's profane energy as any performance has.

In a class by themselves, not because of their qualities but because of their lineage, are the two filmed versions of *The Last Tycoon*, the 1976 Elia Kazan–directed feature starring Robert De Niro and Robert Mitchum, and Billy Ray's 2016–17 Amazon series starring Matt Bomer and Kelsey Grammer. Both are engrossing versions of F. Scott Fitzgerald's unfinished novel of the same title, the roman à clef that did so much to enshrine Thalberg and Mayer in popular consciousness that Bob Thomas began his first-ever biography of Thalberg with a substantial chapter on the Fitzgerald book.

As we have seen, Fitzgerald, initially hired to work on *Red-Headed Woman*, put in his time at MGM, and *The Last Tycoon* was not his first fictionalization of its inner workings but his third. Even though the author had notorious difficulty mastering the mechanics of screenwriting, his fluid writing style and supple insights, employed in fiction, are strikingly effective. First to see publication was 1932's half confessional, half observational short story "Crazy Sunday." It tells the story of screenwriter Joel Coles, invited with a friend to an exclusive Sunday tea at the home of celebrated director Miles Calman and his movie star wife Stella

Walker. As he fears, Coles drinks too much and insists on singing a noticeably unfunny song that angers the entire group. The
story then veers into romantic melodrama, but though the characters are invented, the truth of the underlying situation, and
then some, is vouched for by writer Dwight Taylor, the friend
who accompanied Fitzgerald, in his memoir *Joy Ride*.

Invited to Sunday tea at the oceanfront Santa Monica home
of Thalberg and Shearer and quickly inebriated despite everyone's best intentions, Fitzgerald starts on a sour note when he's
introduced to the actor Robert Montgomery, "who was standing in all the grandeur of his polo outfit. 'Why didn't you bring
your horse in?' he said slowly, and there was not a vestige of
humor in his face when he said it." Then began the impromptu
singing, "the kind of song which might have seemed amusing if
one were very drunk and still in one's freshman year at college."
Stars John Gilbert and Lupe Vélez begin hissing their displeasure, and Taylor says, "I will never completely forget the horror
of that precise moment."

Taylor also includes a memorable snapshot of their host at
that instant: "I could see the little figure of Thalberg standing
in a doorway at the far end of the room, with his hands plunged
deep into his trouser pockets, his shoulders hunched slightly
in that characteristic posture of his which seemed to be both a
withdrawal and a rejection at the same time. There was a slight,
not unkind smile on his lips as he looked down toward the group
at the piano. But he did not move." Taylor manages to get Fitzgerald home, and though Shearer sent a gracious telegram the next
day that made its way into the story ("I thought you were one of
the most agreeable persons at our tea"), the event did not help
Fitzgerald's standing at the studio. Coincidentally or not, he was
let go within a week.

Published eight years later, Fitzgerald's Pat Hobby stories
had a quite different tone. Initially appearing in *Esquire* from January 1940 through mid-1941 and first gathered in book form

two decades after Fitzgerald's death, these seventeen tales remain some of the most amusing and insightful fictions about Hollywood. The Pat Hobby in question is a broken-down screenwriter still scrambling to secure a toehold in the business despite having "more screen credits than a dog has fleas." Pat Hobby was not based on Fitzgerald but rather informed by his observations and experience in the business, someone he perhaps feared on his darkest days he might eventually become.

Though Fitzgerald was proud of the stories and fussed over them continually, he wrote them mainly to pay the bills, to earn money to support himself while he toiled on what was to be his final major opus, *The Last Tycoon*. Often considered the preeminent Hollywood novel, even though incomplete, it features the Thalberg-modeled Monroe Stahr as protagonist. Edmund Wilson, an old friend of Fitzgerald's, put together the version that was published less than a year after the author's death, calling it an "unfinished draft," but Fitzgerald scholar Matthew J. Bruccoli insists that "the surviving text is not just an unfinished novel: it is work in progress toward an unfinished novel—a novel in the process of development and refinement."

The story is narrated by Bennington junior Celia Brady, whose crush on Stahr, a work-obsessed widower who claims "pictures are my girl," is complicated by the fact that her father, Pat Brady (a blend of Louis B. Mayer and the Irish Eddie Mannix), is the head of the unnamed studio where Stahr is the "production genius." Even in its unfinished state *The Last Tycoon* is that rare novel where the work environment that envelopes its people (like Stahr watching dailies and commenting, "And there's a hair in the picture—there on the right, see it? Find out if it's in the projector or the film") is more involving than the private lives of the characters. As Raymond Chandler, someone who knew a thing or two about plot, acerbically observed, Stahr was "magnificent when he sticks to the business of dealing with pictures and the people he has to use to make them;

the instant his personal life as a love-hungry and exhausted man enters the picture, he becomes just another guy with too much money and nowhere to go."

So how can it be that this unformed, unfinished, flawed book not only has a potent reputation of its own but has done so much for Thalberg's visibility and increased interest as well in what Fitzgerald characterized as "the deadly dislike . . . between Thalberg and Louis B. Mayer"? As Edmund Wilson admitted, "It is remarkable that, under these circumstances . . . the character of Stahr [should] emerge with so much intensity and reality." The best answer is the most obvious one: though Fitzgerald's access to Thalberg and Mayer was a limited one, his subtle antennae were always fully engaged, noticing everything, and he perceived almost at once that these two men could support the weight of a novel. It is in general, Bruccoli says, "always risky to read Fitzgerald's fiction as straight biography," and Thalberg's personal life is nowhere on view here. But the man's professional life is another matter, with many pages of the novel containing anecdote after anecdote that ring irresistibly true as to how things worked behind the scenes.

Even when Fitzgerald first casually met Thalberg in 1927, the executive made a vivid impression, witness a key story the writer wrote a detailed impression of for himself just before beginning *The Last Tycoon*. In the novel the monologue appears as follows: "Suppose you were a railroad man. You have to send a train through there somewhere. Well, you get your surveyors' reports, and you find there's three or four or half a dozen gaps, and not one is better than the other. You've got to decide—on what basis? You can't test the best way—except by doing it. So you just do it." In his notes, though not in the novel, Fitzgerald expands on how he remembered Thalberg's thinking: "You know in your secret heart and no one else knows, that you have no reason for putting the road there rather than in several other different courses, but you're the only person that knows that you don't know why you're doing it and you've got to stick to that and you've got to pretend that you know and that you did it for specific reasons. . . . When you're planning a new enterprise on a grand scale, the people under you mustn't ever know or guess that you're in any doubt because they've all got to have something to look up to."

The MGM studio for which Mayer and Thalberg provided "something to look up to," masterminding new enterprises on a grand scale, is no longer an independent entity. Amazon acquired MGM for $8.5 billion in 2022, and many of the classic films it produced are now owned by Warner Bros, but it matters not. The complementary ambitions of these two men, the way Mayer, for all his bluster, both shared and empowered Thalberg's zeal for quality, had a transformative effect. In the end, their drive to create something of value from the flickering shadows that obsessed them succeeded more than they dared imagine. They had dreamed big, bigger even than the stars they created, and they likely felt something like astonishment when their dreams came true. Their accomplishment didn't smooth out differences between them or eliminate trouble and woe from their lives, but it has added something of value to our own.

SOURCES

WRITING A BOOK on Louis B. Mayer and Irving Thalberg means owing a great debt to the numerous biographies that came before me. The most helpful were *Mayer and Thalberg: The Make-Believe Saints* by Samuel Marx (New York: Random House, 1987), *Lion of Hollywood: The Life and Legend of Louis B. Mayer* by Scott Eyman (New York: Simon and Schuster, 2005), and *Irving Thalberg: Boy Wonder to Producer Prince* by Mark A. Vieira (Berkeley: University of California Press, 2010).

Other Mayer/Thalberg biographies consulted include Gary Carey's *All the Stars in Heaven: Louis B. Mayer's MGM* (New York: E. P. Dutton, 1981), Roland Flamini's *Thalberg: The Last Tycoon and the World of MGM* (New York: Crown, 1994), Charles Higham's *Merchant of Dreams: Louis B. Mayer, MGM, and the Secret Hollywood* (New York: Donald I. Fine, 1993), Samuel Marx's *The Gaudy Spree: Literary Hollywood When the West Was Fun* (New York: Franklin Watts, 1987), Bob Thomas's *Thalberg: Life and Legend* (Garden City, NY: Doubleday, 1969), and two pioneering books by *New York Times* film critic Bosley Crowther: *The Lion's Share: The Story of an Entertainment Empire* (New York: E. P. Dutton, 1957) and *Hollywood Rajah: The Life and Times of Louis B. Mayer* (New York: Henry Holt, 1960). I also made use of books on Norma Shearer, principally Gavin Lambert's *Norma Shearer* (New York: Alfred A. Knopf, 1990) and Lawrence J. Quirk's *Norma: The Story of Norma Shearer* (New York: St. Martin's, 1988).

Books on MGM were numerous as well. The ones I found most useful were, in alphabetical order by author: Tino Balio's *MGM* (London: Routledge, 2018); Steven Bingen, Stephen X. Sylvester, and Michael Troyan's *MGM: Hollywood's Greatest Backlot* (Solana Beach, CA: Santa Monica Press, 2011); John Douglas Eames's *The MGM Story: The Complete History of over Fifty Roaring Years* (New York: Crown, 1975); Howard Gutner's *MGM Style: Cedric Gibbons and the Art of the Golden Age of Hollywood* (Guilford, CT: Lyons, 2019); Peter Hay's *MGM: When the Lion Roars* (Atlanta: Turner, 1991); and James Robert Parish and Gregory W. Mank's *The Best of M-G-M: The Golden Years, 1928–1959* (Westport, CT: Arlington House, 1959).

Though neither Mayer nor Thalberg attempted an autobiography, a surprising number of people who knew them left literate and compelling memoirs behind. Some are well known, like Salka Viertel's *The Kindness of Strangers* (New York: Holt, Rinehart and Winston, 1969) and Irene Mayer Selznick's beautifully written *A Private View* (New York: Alfred A. Knopf, 1983), but many were new to me and the best of these were pungent as well as informative. Though almost all were memorable in one way or another and will be referenced in specific chapters, I wanted to single out for individual thanks a dozen that I found especially engaging and informative. In alphabetical order by author:

Bickford, Charles. *Bulls, Balls, Bicycles, and Actors*. New York: Paul S. Ericksson, 1965.
Coffee, Lenore. *Storyline: Recollections of a Hollywood Screenwriter*. London: Cassell, 1973.

Dietz, Howard. *Dancing in the Dark: Words by Howard Dietz*. New York: Quadrangle/New York Times Books, 1974.

Lewis, David. *The Creative Producer*. Ed. James Curtis. Metuchen, NJ: Scarecrow, 1993.

Love, Bessie. *From Hollywood with Love*. London: Elm Tree, 1977.

Rapf, Maurice. *Back Lot: Growing Up with the Movies*. Metuchen, NJ: Scarecrow, 1999.

Schary, Dore. *Heyday: An Autobiography*. Boston: Little, Brown, 1979.

Schulberg, Budd. *Moving Pictures: Memoirs of a Hollywood Prince*. New York: Stein and Day, 1981.

Stewart, Donald Ogden. *By a Stroke of Luck! An Autobiography*. New York: Paddington/Two Continents, 1975.

Veiller, Bayard. *The Fun I've Had*. New York: Reynal and Hitchcock, 1941.

Williams, Esther, with Digby Diehl. *The Million Dollar Mermaid*. New York: Simon and Schuster, 1999.

Williamson, Alice M. *Alice in Movieland*. New York: Appleton, 1928.

I am also grateful to have had access to Peter N. Mayer's privately bound Yale dissertation *M-G-M and the Studio System in the Age of Mass Production*, as well as Norma Shearer's untitled and unpublished memoir, which offers a perspective of singular intimacy on both Thalberg and Mayer.

Introduction

The issues of the *New York Times* containing Thalberg's and Mayer's obituaries are in the author's collection. Except for David O. Selznick's comment about his father-in-law, which comes from Crowther, *Hollywood Rajah*, the quotes given when each man died came from the extensive and invaluable biography clip files maintained by the Margaret Herrick Library of the Academy of Motion Picture Arts and Sciences. Irene Mayer Selznick's thoughts about her father and Thalberg come not from her autobiography, as might be expected, but from Carey, *All the Stars in Heaven*.

1. Mayer Before Thalberg

Schulberg's comment comes from his excellent autobiography, *Moving Pictures*, while LeRoy's is from Mervyn LeRoy as told to Dick Kleiner, *Mervyn LeRoy: Take One* (New York: Hawthorn, 1974). Mayer's studio bio is in the Academy's biography file. Mary Astor's thoughts on MGM mothers are in *A Life on Film* (New York: Dell, 1972). Mayer's gratitude about *The Birth of a Nation* comes from Lillian Gish with Ann Pichot, *The Movies, Mr. Griffith, and Me* (Englewood Cliffs, NJ: Prentice-Hall, 1969). Before she was a celebrated columnist, Hedda Hopper was an actress, and her memories are in Hedda Hopper, *From Under My Hat* (Garden City, NY: Doubleday, 1952). The fistfight with Chaplin was reported in the contemporary trade press. The potent fish market observation is in Anzia Yezierska, *Red Ribbon on a White Horse* (New York: Scribner, 1950). Mayer's early lack of social grace is reported in Madge Bellamy, *A Darling of the Twenties* (Vestal, NY: Vestal Press, 1989), and Miriam Cooper with Bonnie Herndon, *Dark Lady of the Silents* (Indianapolis: Bobbs-Merrill, 1973). B. P. Schulberg's request is detailed in Norman Zierold, *The Moguls* (New York: Coward-McCann, 1959). Published only in Britain is screenwriter Lenore Coffee's fine memoir, *Storyline* (London: Cassell, 1973). The "geniuses we have all we need" quote appears in Neal Gabler, *An Empire of Their Own: How the Jews Invented Hollywood* (New York: Crown Publishers, 1988).

2. Thalberg Before Mayer

In addition to Thalberg, Talmey's *Doug and Mary and Others* (New York: Macy-Masius, 1927) offers excellent profiles of Lillian Gish, Samuel Goldwyn, Carl Laemmle, and others. Also wide-ranging is Lewis's *Creative Producer*. Edna Ferber's unexpected quotes about Laemmle and Thalberg come from her autobiography, *A Peculiar Treasure* (New York: Doubleday, Doran, 1939). The Louella-Parsons-meets-Thalberg anecdote is from Gabler, *An Empire of Their Own*. Herman Mankiewicz's mock birthday greeting appears in Richard Meryman, *Mank: The Wit, World and Life of Herman Mankiewicz*

(New York: William Morrow, 1978). Erich von Stroheim's career is the subject of three useful biographies: Thomas Quinn Curtis, *Von Stroheim* (New York: Farrar, Straus and Giroux, 1971), Richard Koszarski, *The Man You Loved to Hate* (Oxford: Oxford University Press, 1983), and Arthur Lenning, *Stroheim* (Lexington: University Press of Kentucky, 2000). Curtis knew both Stroheim and Mayer, and quotes the latter talking about the former: "Von Stroheim was the greatest director in the world. . . . But he was impossible, a crazy artist." Cinematographer William Daniels is interviewed in Charles Higham's informative *Hollywood Cameramen: Sources of Light* (Bloomington: Indiana University Press, 1970). Thalberg's letter is reproduced in *Letters from Hollywood: Inside the Private World of Classic American Moviemaking*, compiled and edited by Rocky Lang and Barbara Hall (New York: Abrams, 2019). Orson Welles's jibe is from *My Lunches with Orson: Conversations Between Henry Jaglom and Orson Welles*, edited by Peter Biskind (New York: Henry Holt, 2013). Michael F. Blake is the key source for Lon Chaney information; books consulted include *A Thousand Faces: Lon Chaney's Unique Artistry in Motion Pictures* (Vestal, NY: Vestal Press, 1995), *The Films of Lon Chaney* (Lanham, MD: Vestal Press, 1998), and *Lon Chaney: The Man Behind the Thousand Faces* (Vestal, NY: Vestal Press, 1993). Tay Garnett's autobiography, with Fredda Dudley Balling, is *Light Up Your Torches and Pull Up Your Tights* (New Rochelle, NY: Arlington House, 1973), while Bessie Love's is, inevitably perhaps, *From Hollywood with Love*.

3. Early Days and Norma

Frances Marion's "brothers under the skin" quote is found in Mark A. Vieira, *Hollywood Dreams Made Real: Irving Thalberg and the Rise of M-G-M* (New York: Abrams, 2008). Irene Mayer Selznick's recollections are from her *A Private View*. The memory of a childhood friend appears in Lambert, *Norma Shearer*. Shearer's difficulties with director Reginald Barker are detailed in both Thomas, *Thalberg*, and Crowther, *Hollywood Rajah*. The "in the mood for dalliance" episode is related in Coffee, *Storyline*.

4. One Out of Many

Mayer's warning to an unwary switchboard operator is from Ron Haver's imposing *David O. Selznick's Hollywood* (New York: Alfred A. Knopf, 1980). Examples of Paramount advertising are from the author's collection. Marcus Loew's candid remarks to Harvard students are in *The Story of the Films as Told by Leaders of the Industry*, edited by Joseph P. Kennedy (Chicago: A. W. Shaw, 1927). Loew's statistics are in Eyman, *Lion of Hollywood*.

5. Unfinished Business

The poignant Thomas Hardy quote appears in Crowther, *Lion of Hollywood*. Erich von Stroheim's dismissal of his editor is from Jay Leyda, *Voices of Film Experience 1894 to the Present* (New York: Macmillan, 1977), while his worry about starvation is in Koszarski, *The Man You Loved to Hate*. *The Merry Widow* souvenir book is in the author's collection. The fight between Mayer and the director is vouched for by both men in Curtis, *Von Stroheim*. The same book offers visual proof of the *Los Angeles Record* front-page banner headline. Information on all things *Ben-Hur*, including the Thalberg and Niblo quotes, is from the massive and authoritative Jon Solomon, *Ben-Hur: The Original Blockbuster* (Edinburgh: Edinburgh University Press, 2016). Mayer's complaint to the film's costar is from Lon and Debra Davis, *King of the Movies: Francis X. Bushman* (Albany, GA: BearManor Media, 2016). Cedric Gibbons's contribution to the set is from Gutner, *MGM Style*, while a detailed explanation of the film's revolutionary hanging miniature technique is in Andre Soares, *Beyond Paradise: The Life of Ramon Novarro* (New York: St. Martin's, 2002). *Ben-Hur* trade ads are in bound volume 30 of *Exhibitors Herald* in the author's collection. The byline magazine piece is Irving Thalberg and Hugh Weir, "Why Motion Pictures Cost So Much," *Saturday Evening Post*, November 4, 1933. The report of Thalberg viewing *Ben-Hur* rushes on his sick-room ceiling is in Vieira, *Irving Thalberg*.

6. The Right Stuff

Frank Whitbeck's recollection is in Beth Day, *This Was Hollywood* (Garden City, NY: Doubleday, 1960). Thalberg's encouragement of John Gilbert is in Eve Golden, *John Gilbert: The Last of the Silent Film Stars* (Lexington: University Press of Kentucky, 2013). Gilbert returns the praise in the unbylined "Silent Director of 'Big Parade' Got Results with Mental Telepathy," *New York Times*, December 6, 1925, and Vidor on the amount of film he watched is in the similarly unbylined "King Vidor Tells of Work in Filming 'Big Parade,'" *New York Times*, February 21, 1926. Multiple sources deal with the making of *The Big Parade*, primarily King Vidor, *A Tree Is a Tree* (New York: Harcourt, Brace, 1952). Gish's original note is in the MGM Collection at the University of Southern California. Vidor's quote about how *The Crowd* "came out of my guts" and Mayer's description of it as "that goddamn toilet picture" are both from Jordan R. Young, *King Vidor's THE CROWD: The Making of a Silent Classic* (Las Vegas: Past Times, 2014). Vittorio De Sica's enthusiasm and Sid Grauman's description of the Oscar vote are both from Nancy Dowd and David Shepard, *King Vidor: A DGA Oral History* (Metuchen, NJ: Scarecrow, 1988). Contemporary MGM toilet flyer from the author's collection.

7. The Women

The sociological study is Leo Rosten, *Hollywood: The Movie Colony, the Movie Makers* (New York: Harcourt, Brace, 1941). Thalberg's belief that women determine movie attendance is from Robert Dance and Bruce Robertson, *Ruth Harriet Louise and Hollywood Glamour Photography* (Berkeley: University of California Press, 2002). Gish's remark on kissing John Gilbert is in Gish, *The Movies, Mr. Griffith, and Me*. Mayer's disbelief when Gish suggested *The Scarlet Letter* is detailed in Stewart Oderman, *Lillian Gish: A Life on Stage and Screen* (Jefferson, NC: McFarland, 2000). Gish's remarks at the AFI Life Achievement dinner are from personal memory, and the comments of Gish's secretary are in Albert Bigelow Paine, *Life and Lillian Gish* (New York: Macmillan, 1932). Joan Crawford's kind words are in Joan Crawford with Jane Kesner Ardmore, *A Portrait of Joan: The Autobiography of Joan Crawford* (Los Angeles: Graymalkin Media, 2017). The eyewitness account of Mayer confronting a restive sales conference is from Dietz, *Dancing in the Dark*, and Hearst's admiration for Thalberg can be found in Marion Davies, *The Times We Had: Life with William Randolph Hearst*, ed. Pamela Pfau and Kenneth S. Marx (Indianapolis: Bobbs-Merrill Company, 1975). Details of the climactic scene in *Show People* are from Dowd and Shepard, *King Vidor: A DGA Oral History*.

8. Rivals

Bob Thomas's notes on his interview with Joan Crawford are in papers housed in the UCLA Library Special Collections. Both Crawford's lookalike comment and the St. John quote are from Crawford, *A Portrait of Joan*. The Crawford/Shearer comparison is from Frederica Sagor Maas, *The Shocking Miss Pilgrim: A Writer in Early Hollywood* (Lexington: University Press of Kentucky, 1999). Crawford's dismissive note on her childhood is from Alexander Walker, *Joan Crawford: The Ultimate Star* (New York: Harper and Row, 1983). Constance Rosenblum, *Gold Digger: The Outrageous Life and Times of Peggy Hopkins Joyce* (New York: Metropolitan Books, 2000), is the authority on the celebrated figure. Thalberg's parsing of sex and love is from Thomas, *Thalberg*. An underappreciated figure in Thalberg's life, attorney Fanny Holzmann, is the subject of a biography by her nephew, Ted Berkman, *The Lady and the Law: The Remarkable Life of Fanny Holzmann* (Boston: Little, Brown, 1976). Crawford's crack about Shearer's in-laws is in Quirk, *Norma*. Louise Brooks's barbed tale is from John Kobal, *People Will Talk* (New York: Alfred A. Knopf, 1985). The Thalberg/Shearer interchange about his first name is one of the most endearing in her book.

9. The Two and Only

Noel Langley's vivid characterizations of Mayer is from the exemplary Aljean Harmetz, *The Making of the Wizard of Oz* (New York: Alfred A. Knopf, 1977). The Herman Mankiewicz remark is in

Schulberg, *Moving Pictures*, while his brother Joseph L. is quoted in Allen Rivkin and Laura Kerr, *Hello Hollywood: The Story of the Movies by the People Who Make Them* (Garden City, NY: Doubleday, 1962). George Cukor's characterization is from a candid book-length interview: Gavin Lambert, *On Cukor*, ed. Robert Trachtenberg (New York: Rizzoli, 2000). Edie Mayer on her father's temper is in Gabler, *An Empire of Their Own*. The same classic Mayer fit is described in both James Kotsilibas-Davis and Myrna Loy, *Myrna Loy: Being and Becoming* (New York: Alfred A. Knopf, 1987), and Kenneth L. Geist, *Pictures Will Talk: The Life and Films of Joseph L. Mankiewicz* (New York: Da Capo, 1978). The needling implicit in Mayer calling his nephew a *macher*, from Sylvia Shorris and Marion Abbott Bundy, *Talking Pictures: With the People Who Made Them* (New York: New Press, 1994), is inescapable to those familiar with Yiddish. *The Grove Book of Hollywood*, ed. Christopher Silvester (New York: Grove, 1998), contains the unexpected Mayer memory of surrealist director Luis Buñuel. There are many versions of Robert Taylor's interactions with Mayer; Victoria Wilson, *A Life of Barbara Stanwyck: Steel True, 1907–1940* (New York: Simon and Schuster, 2013), is one of the most convincing. Graham Greene described hearing Mayer in the essay "Film Lunch," collected in his *The Lost Childhood and Other Essays* (New York: Viking, 1952). Ida Koverman is described in detail in Jacqueline R. Braitman, *She Damned Near Ran the Studio: The Extraordinary Lives of Ida R. Koverman* (Jackson: University Press of Mississippi, 2020). Everything related to Thalberg's 1929 USC talk is found in *Introduction to the Photoplay*, ed. John C. Tibbets (New York: National Film Society, 1977). The text of S. J. Perelman's "And Did You Once See Irving Plain" can be found in Kenneth W. Leish, *Cinema* (New York: Newsweek Books, 1974). Hecht's understanding that Thalberg "knew what shadows could do" is from Gabler, *An Empire of Their Own*. Clarence Brown's description of working with Thalberg is from Philip French, *The Movie Moguls: An Informal History of the Hollywood Tycoons* (London: Weidenfeld and Nicholson, 1969). Fritz Lang talks about Thalberg's pragmatic reaction to *M* in Bernard Rosenberg and Harry Silverstein, *The Real Tinsel* (New York: Macmillan, 1970). The anecdote about Thalberg, Cedric Gibbon, and Paris first appears in Marx, *Mayer and Thalberg*. The Lunts' thoughts on Thalberg are from Maurice Zolotow, *Stagestruck: The Romance of Alfred Lunt and Lynn Fontanne* (New York: Harcourt, Brace and World, 1965). Negative actor reactions can be found in both Edward G. Robinson with Leonard Spiegelgass, *All My Yesterdays: An Autobiography* (New York: Hawthorn, 1973) and Bickford, *Bulls, Balls, Bicycles, and Actors*. Examples of antisemitism appear in Frank Walsh, *Sin and Censorship: The Catholic Church on the Motion Picture Industry* (New Haven: Yale University Press, 1996), and Thomas Doherty, *Hollywood's Censor: Joseph I. Breen and the Production Code Administration* (New York: Columbia University Press, 2007). Thalberg's opposition to film being derided is from Vieira, *Irving Thalberg*.

10. Garbo

The definitive work on Garbo remains Barry Paris, *Garbo: A Biography* (New York: Alfred A. Knopf, 1995), though books written by those who knew her are also of interest. These include Fritiof Billquist, *Garbo: A Biography* (New York: Putnam, 1960), Sven Broman, *Conversations with Garbo* (New York: Viking, 1991) (he recounts the Norma Shearer anecdote), and Scott Reisfield and Robert Dance, *Garbo: Portraits from Her Private Collection* (New York: Rizzoli, 2005). Louise Brooks's observation is from Robert Gottlieb, *Garbo* (New York: Farrar, Straus and Giroux, 2021), and Lillian Gish's is from *The Movies, Mr. Griffith, and Me*. Garbo's personal reflections are from her "The Story of Greta Garbo," originally found in *Photoplay* magazine in 1928 and republished in the Fall 2015 issue of *Silent Film Quarterly*. Clarence Brown's memories of Garbo and Gilbert are from Leatrice Gilbert Fountain with John R. Maxim, *Dark Star: The Meteoric Rise and Eclipse of John Gilbert* (London: Sidgwick and Jackson, 1985), the director's views of Garbo as one of a kind from the essential Kevin Brownlow, *The Parade's Gone By . . .* (New York: Alfred A. Knopf, 1968). Exhibitor fear of Garbo being "too hot for the elder people" can be found in *Exhibitors Herald* in author's collection. The possibility of "Garbo in Heat" is from

Cari Beauchamp, *Without Lying Down: Frances Marion and the Powerful Women of Early Hollywood* (New York: Lisa Drew/Scribner, 1997). Garbo's estimation of her own toughness is related by her grand-nephew Reisfield in *Garbo*.

11. Sound Makes Some Noise

The amusing origin of the MGM abbreviation is from Alice M. Williamson, *Alice in Movieland* (New York: D. Appleton, 1928). Mayer's antics on horseback are referenced in Vanda Krefft, *The Man Who Made the Movies: The Meteoric Rise and Tragic Fall of William Fox* (New York: HarperCollins, 2017). Information on Marcus Loew's funeral is from Crowther, *The Lion's Share*. Dore Schary's "battlefield" quote can be heard on the August 19, 1959, *Turning Point* oral history episode housed at the Wisconsin Historical Society. The "hyperborean temperature" of Nicholas Schenck's blood is described by John Huston, *An Open Book* (New York: Alfred A. Knopf, 1980). The comparison of Mayer and Schenck personal styles is in Schary, *Heyday*. An excellent history of the changeover from silents is Donald Crafton, *The Talkies: American Cinema's Transition to Sound, 1926–1931* (Berkeley: University of California Press, 1999). Mayer's meeting with MGM's editors is related in *My First Time in Hollywood*, ed. Cari Beauchamp (Los Angeles: Asahina and Wallace, 2015). David O. Selznick on his dispute with Thalberg comes from *Memo from David O. Selznick*, selected and ed. Rudy Behlmer (New York: Viking, 1972). Thalberg's fascinating worries on audience acceptance of music in sound films is part of Tibbetts, *Introduction to the Photoplay*. Marion Davies deals with her stuttering in both Davies, *The Times We Had*, and Lara Gabrielle, *The Captain of Her Soul: The Life of Marion Davies* (Berkeley: University of California Press, 2022). Bayard Veiller, *The Fun I've Had* (New York: Reynal and Hitchcock, 1941), contains his blow-by-blow account of working with Norma Shearer. John Gilbert's *Kansas City Star* interview is in a 1932 issue of *Cinema Digest*. Frank Whitbeck's creation of the "Garbo Talks" ad campaign is detailed in Day, *This Was Hollywood*. Garbo teasing Adrian is related in Jay Jorgenson and Donald L. Scoggins, *Creating the Illusion: A Fashionable His-*

tory of Hollywood Costume Designers (Philadelphia: Running Press, 2015).

12. Threats and Opportunities

Mayer's central role in the Oscars is in Nancy Lynn Schwartz, *The Hollywood Writers' Wars* (New York: Knopf Doubleday, 1982). Mayer's bitter interview, perhaps his last, is Gitta Parker and William Woodfield. "What Makes a Star?" *American Weekly*, June 8, 1958. Details of the proposed Fox/MGM takeover are from Crowther, *The Lion's Share*. Fox's fatalistic response is in Upton Sinclair, *Upton Sinclair Presents William Fox* (Los Angeles: Upton Sinclair, 1933). Eddie Mannix's key quote on Thalberg's temperament is from Marx, *The Make-Believe Saints.* Mayer's plaint about Thalberg and money is in Schary, *Heyday.* Quotes from Jason Joy as well as anonymous internal PCA memos are contained in the Motion Picture Association of America/Production Code Administration files in the Academy's Margaret Herrick Library digital collections. Lamar Trotti's irritation about a dinner delayed is in Leonard J. Leff and Jerold L. Simmons, *The Dame in the Kimono: Hollywood, Censorship, and the Production Code from the 1920s to the 1960s* (New York: Grove Weidenfeld, 1960). Cukor's perceptive view of Harlow comes from Lambert, *On Cukor.* Anita Loos's comment on writing with Thalberg is in Kobal, *People Will Talk*, and her memories of *Red-Headed Woman* are in Anita Loos, *Kiss Hollywood Goodbye* (New York: Viking, 1974). The Atlanta board of censors' outrage can be found in Dawn V. Sova, *Forbidden Films: Case Histories of 125 Motion Pictures* (New York: Checkmark, 2001).

13. New Beginnings

Best source on Frances Marion and *The Big House* is Beauchamp, *Without Lying Down.* Thalberg's advice on delaying production is from the screenwriter's autobiography, Frances Marion, *Off with Their Heads! A Serio-Comic Tale of Hollywood* (New York: Macmillan, 1972). J. J. Cohn on Thalberg and physical production is from Peter Meyer, "MGM and the Studio System in the Age of Mass

Production," thesis for the 1978 Scholars of the House project at Yale. The New Orleans Marie Dressler quote is from *Cinema Digest*, December 12, 1932, while the actress's thoughts on Garbo's ability and Mayer gifting her a cottage can be found in Marie Dressler, *My Own Life* (Boston: Little, Brown, 1934.) The Clark Gable lumberjack quote is in Warren G. Harris, *Clark Gable: A Biography* (New York: Crown, 2005). Gable's strong memory of Thalberg's dismissive comments on his ears is in *The Saturday Evening Post Movie Book*, ed. Starkey Flythe Jr. (Indianapolis: Curtis, 1977). Ida Koverman quote is from Day, *This Was Hollywood*. Crawford on the chemistry between her and Gable is in Crawford, *Portrait of Joan*; her thoughts on losing *A Free Soul* to Shearer are from Vieira, *Irving Thalberg*. Further comments on the relationship with Gable are from Hopper, *From Under My Hat*, and Adela Rogers St. John, *Love, Laughter, and Tears: My Hollywood Story* (Garden City, NY: Doubleday, 1975). The early history of *Grand Hotel* is in Samuel Marx's "Looking for a Story" chapter in *We Make the Movies*, ed. Nancy Naumberg (New York: W. W. Norton, 1937). Transcriptions of Thalberg's story conferences are found in the MGM collection at the USC Cinema Library; major thanks to Ned Comstock for making them available. Garbo's tribute to Barrymore is detailed in Gene Fowler, *Good Night Sweet Prince: The Life and Times of John Barrymore* (New York: Viking, 1944). The "opulent zoo" review is also from *Cinema Digest*, September 19, 1932.

14. To Each His Own

Adela Rogers St. John's memory of the charming "Irvie" interchange is from Jeanine Basinger and Sam Wasson, *Hollywood: The Oral History* (New York: Harper, 2022). The less charming Rowland V. Lee story is from his unpublished memoir, "Adventures of a Film Director," from the American Film Institute's Oral History Department, special thanks to Kevin Brownlow for alerting me to it. Donald Ogden Stewart on Thalberg getting his own way is in Flamini, *Thalberg*. Nagle on Thalberg calming Mayer is from Vieira, *Irving Thalberg*, while Mayer returning the favor is from Lillian Ross, *Picture: A Story About Hollywood* (New York: Rinehart, 1952).

The text of the Mayer cable is in Alexander Walker, *Garbo: A Portrait* (New York: Macmillan, 1965). Actor Rod La Rocque's perceptive comments are from Rosenberg and Silverstein, *The Real Tinsel*. Charles Laughton's thoughts on Thalberg are in Simon Callow, *Charles Laughton: A Difficult Actor* (New York: Grove, 1987). Many people commented on Mayer's acting ability, starting with S. N. Behrman, *People in a Diary: A Memoir* (Boston: Little, Brown, 1972). Casey Robinson is quoted in Patrick McGilligan, *Backstory: Interviews with Screenwriters of Hollywood's Golden Age* (Berkeley: University of California Press, 1986), as are John Lee Mahin and James M. Cain later in the book. Greer Garson on *Goodbye, Mr. Chips* comes from Doug McClelland, *Forties Film Talk: Oral Histories of Hollywood* (Jefferson, NC: McFarland, 1992). Jeanette MacDonald on Mayer on his knees is in Crowther, *The Lion's Share*, and its echo is in Huston, *An Open Book*. Katharine Hepburn's unexpected Mayer partisanship is explored in Carey, *All the Stars in Heaven*, and A. Scott Berg, *Kate Remembered* (New York: Putnam, 2003). Ingrid Bergman, Mickey Rooney, and Ann Rutherford's parallel references to God come from Kobal, *People Will Talk*; Mickey Rooney, *Life Is Too Short* (New York: Ballentine, 1991); and Gabler, *An Empire of Their Own*. The Mabel Normand funeral story conference is described in Vidor, *A Tree Is a Tree*. Mankiewicz's reference to Nathan Leopold is in Meryman, *Mank*. The Welles biography is Frank Brady, *Citizen Welles: A Biography of Orson Welles* (New York: Scribner, 1989). P. G. Wodehouse's MGM experience is detailed in Vieira, *Irving Thalberg*. The studio's episodic style is described in Tom Stempel, *Framework: A History of Screenwriting in the American Film* (Syracuse, NY: Syracuse University Press, 2000). Thalberg's rare public admission of self-doubt is in Gilbert Seldes, *The Great Audience* (Westport, CT: Greenwood, 1970). The summation of Thalberg's production method is from Thomas Schatz, *The Genius of the System: Hollywood Filmmaking in the Studio Era* (New York: Pantheon, 1988). Fitzgerald's thoughts on Hunt Stromberg are in Tom Dardis, *Some Time in the Sun* (New York: Scribner, 1976). Albert Lewin, Douglas Shearer, and Conrad Nagle's comments come from Rosenberg and Silverstein, *The Real Tinsel*. Lloyd as the first scientific screener is from Kevin Goetz, *Audience-ology: How Moviegoers Shape the Films We Love* (New York: Simon and Schuster/Simon Element, 2021). Lumet's nostalgia for the Thalberg method comes from Silvester, *The Grove Book of Hollywood*. Howard Hawks on Thalberg style is found in Joseph McBride, *Hawks on Hawks* (Berkeley: University of California Press, 1982). "The Norma Shearer Irving Thalberg Loves," *New Movie Magazine*, May 1934. Letter from W. R. Wilkinson to Thalberg quoted from Eric Hoyt, *Ink-Stained Hollywood: The Triumph of America's Trade Press* (Berkeley: University of California Press, 2022). Capra's disdain is found in *Frank Capra, the Name Above the Title: An Autobiography* (New York: Macmillan, 1971). Opinions on and from Woody Van Dyke are found in Tim McCoy with Ronald McCoy, *Tim McCoy Remembers the West: An Autobiography* (Garden City, NY: Doubleday, 1977); Andrew Sarris, *The American Cinema: Directors and Directions, 1929–1968* (New York: E. P. Dutton, 1968); and *W. S. Van Dyke's Journal*, ed. Rudy Behlmer (Lanham, MD: Scarecrow, 1996). "The Metro troubadours" are described in *George Oppenheimer, The View from the Sixties: Memories of a Spent Life* (New York: David McKay, 1966).

15. Fissures

Details of the December 1932 *Fortune* story are from a copy in the author's collection. Hyperbolic description of Tarzan comes from the MGM trailer. William Wellman's dream of directing Tarzan is in Richard Schickel, *The Men Who Made the Movies: Interviews with Frank Capra, George Cukor, Howard Hawks, Alfred Hitchcock, Vincente Minnelli, King Vidor, Raoul Walsh, and William A. Wellman* (New York: Atheneum, 1975). Details of Paul Bern's death are in several sources, including Samuel Marx and Joyce Vanderveen, *Deadly Illusions: Jean Harlow and the Murder of Paul Bern* (New York: Random House, 1990). Mayer's vivid description of the Schenck/Thalberg confrontation is found in Crowther, *The Lion's Share*. Frances Marion on Mayer turning into an injured lion is in Beauchamp, *Without Lying Down*. The detailed "Dear Dad" letter is in Behlmer, *Memo from David O. Selznick*. Lewis Selznick's last words are relayed by his daughter-in-law, Irene Mayer Selznick, *A Private View*. Mayer's letter to Thalberg and Thalberg's reply are quoted in Crowther, *Hollywood Rajah*. Thalberg's detailed drafts of a letter to Schenck are in Special Collections, Irving G. Thalberg and Norma Shearer Papers, Margaret Herrick Library, Academy of Motion Picture Arts & Sciences.

16. Alone Together

The exhibitor telegram to Thalberg is quoted in the excellent Ana Salzberg, *Produced by Irving Thalberg: Theory of Studio-Era Filmmaking* (Edinburgh: Edinburgh University Press, 2020). Albert Hackett's deft quip is in Schwartz, *The Hollywood Writers' Wars*. Norma Shearer's disturbing German memory is from Flamini, *Thalberg*, while her husband's thoughts on Hitler come from Kyle Crichton, *Total Recall* (Garden City, NY: Doubleday, 1960). *Saturday Evening Post* short stories by George Randolph Chester referenced include "Named by Izzy Iskovitch," April 21, 1923, and "Isidor Iskovitch Presents," September 8, 1923. Also quoted is Carroll and Garrett Graham, *Queer People* (Carbondale: Southern Illinois University Press, 1976). Schenck's offer to Thalberg is related in Crowther, *Hollywood Rajah*. Thalberg's comments to the press are in the comprehensive T. Lawrence Larkin, *In Search of Marie-Antoinette in the 1930s: Stefan Zweig, Irving Thalberg, and Norma Shearer* (London: Palgrave Macmillan, 2019). David O. Selznick on obsession is in Harmetz, *The Making of the Wizard of Oz*; his letter to Mayer, his quote to Buchwald, and Thalberg as his first investor are all in Behlmer, *Memo from David O. Selznick*. Cukor's thoughts on Dressler are in Betty Lee, *Marie Dressler: The Unlikeliest Star* (Lexington: University Press of Kentucky, 1997). Garbo's salary negotiation and Colleen Moore on the star confronting Mayer about hiring John Gilbert for *Queen Christina* are from Paris, *Garbo*, while the "Tomorrow's Tabloids" quote is from the MGM trailer. Garbo's poignant analysis of the John Gilbert affair is found in Behrman, *People in a Diary*. March on costarring with Garbo is in Gwenda Young, *Clarence Brown: Hollywood's Forgotten Master* (Lexington: University Press of Kentucky, 1969). Magazine article is Thalberg and Weir, "Why Motion Pictures Cost So Much." J. J. Cohn and Howard Strickling's thoughts on Mayer and Thalberg are in Carey, *All the Stars in Heaven*. Details of Shearer making fried bread sandwiches for her husband are in Lewis, *The Creative Producer.* George Hurrell talks of his Shearer photographs in Lambert, *Norma Shearer,* and Kobal, *People Will Talk.* Fitzgerald on Thalberg's beach house comes from his "Crazy Sunday," anthologized in *The Short Stories of F. Scott Fitzgerald,* ed. Matthew J. Bruccoli (New York: Scribner, 1989). The unlikely comparison of Marion Davies to Jimmy Durante is from the May 15, 1933, issue of *Cinema Digest.* Correspondence on *The Barretts of Wimpole Street* is from the Production Code Administration files in the Academy's Margaret Herrick Library digital collections. Charles Laughton on the gleam in his eye is in Thomas, *Thalberg.* Capra quote is from Schickel, *The Men Who Made the Movies.* Clark Gable's Academy Award surprise is in Mason Wiley and Damien Bona, *Inside Oscar: The Unofficial History of the Academy Awards* (New York: Ballentine, 1988). John Barrymore's "three white whales" quote is from Vieira, *Irving Thalberg.* A detailed history of the *Rasputin* affair, including photographs of sensation-hungry newspaper headlines, is contained in Sir David Napley, *Rasputin in Hollywood* (London: Weidenfeld and Nicholson, 1990). The place of royalist sentiment in the verdict is from Rapf, *Back Lot,* and Fanny Holzmann's key role is detailed in Berkman, *The Lady and the Law.*

17. Endgame

The key source on Jeanette MacDonald is Edward Baron Turk, *Hollywood Diva: A Biography of Jeanette MacDonald* (Berkeley: University of California Press, 1998). Maurice Chevalier's idiosyncratic response to Thalberg is found in Maurice Chevalier, *With Love* (Boston: Little, Brown, 1960). Calling *San Francisco* "the first disaster musical" is Balio, *MGM.* Anita Loos reminisces about a key scene in Anita Loos, *San Francisco: A Screenplay* (Carbondale: Southern Illinois University Press, 1979), and Rosenberg and Silverstein, *The Real Tinsel.* Thalberg's quote to Louella Parsons is in James Curtis, *Spencer Tracy: A Biography* (New York: Alfred A. Knopf, 2011). Geraldine Farrar's quote is from Callow, *Charles Laughton*. The "do this for me" request is found in Marx, *The Make-Believe Saints*. *Mutiny on the Bounty* ads are in the author's collection. Buster Keaton quotes are from Buster Keaton with Charles W. Samuels, *My Wonderful World of Slapstick* (Garden City, NY: Doubleday, 1960). Keaton's seeing Thalberg as a creator and his comment on Lawrence Weingarten are in James Curtis, *Buster Keaton: A Filmmaker's Life* (New York: Alfred A. Knopf, 2022). His idea that silence would help sound is in Robert Knopf, *The Theater and Cinema of Buster Keaton* (Princeton, NJ: Princeton University Press, 1999), his aversion to wisecracks in Tom Dardis, *Keaton: The Man Who Wouldn't Lie Down* (New York: Scribner, 1979). Eleanor Keaton's thoughts are in Kenneth Turan, "His Silents Are Golden," *Los Angeles Times*, October 29, 1995. Edwin Schallert's quote and much else are in Robert S. Bader, *Four of the Three Musketeers: The Marx Brothers on Stage* (Evanston, IL: Northwestern University Press, 2016). Samuel Goldwyn's opinion and Morrie Riskind's reminiscence are from Stefan Kanfer, *Groucho: The Life and Times of Julius Henry Marx* (New York: Alfred A. Knopf, 2000). Billy Wilder's thoughts on Thalberg are in Cameron Crowe, *Conversations with Wilder* (New York: Alfred A. Knopf, 1999). Kitty Carlisle describes her crying fit in Kitty Carlisle Hart, *Kitty: An Autobiography* (New York: Doubleday, 1988). Luise Rainer's extended interview is found in Marie Brenner, *Great Dames: What I Learned from Older Women* (New York: Crown, 2000). Thalberg calling Upton Sinclair "that Pasadena Bolshevik" is from Samuel Marx, *A Gaudy Spree: Literary Hollywood When the West Was Fun* (New York: Franklin Watts, 1987). Crichton's memory is in Crichton, *Total Recall*. The quotes from John Lee Mahin and Maurice Rapf on Thalberg's writers meeting are in Schwartz, *The Hollywood Writers' Wars*. Stewart relates his disenchantment in *By a Stroke of Luck!*

18. Saying Goodbye

Thalberg's letter to Pickford and Goldwyn is in Special Collections, Irving G. Thalberg and Norma Shearer Papers, Margaret Herrick Library, Academy of Motion Picture Arts and Sciences.

His comment about reaching to the highest levels is in Salzberg, *Produced by Irving Thalberg*. The conversation with Howard Dietz about *Romeo and Juliet* is from Dietz, *Dancing in the Dark*. The idea of hiring William Strunk Jr. is in Thomas, *Thalberg*. Graham Greene's *Spectator* review is found in *Authors on Film*, ed. Harry M. Geduld (Bloomington: Indiana University Press, 1972). Margaret Booth is quoted in Brownlow, *The Parade's Gone By* . . . The review in *Time* magazine is quoted in Parish and Mank, *The Best of M-G-M*. Mayer's belief in producing first is from Hay, *MGM*. Robert Taylor's *Camille* preparation is in Wilson, *A Life of Barbara Stanwyck*. Thalberg quote about Garbo's performance in *Camille* is found in the George Cukor interview in *Conversations with The Great Moviemakers of Hollywood's Golden Age at the American Film Institute*, ed. George Stevens (New York: Alfred A. Knopf, 2006), and Lambert, *On Cukor*. Paul Muni's exuberance about *The Good Earth* location is from Jerome Lawrence, *Actor: The Life and Times of Paul Muni* (Putnam, 1974). Anna May Wong on testing for *The Good Earth* is in Wollstein, *Vixens, Floozies, and Molls*. Thalberg's memo on music is from Andre Previn, *No Minor Chords: My Days in Hollywood* (New York: Doubleday, 1991). The tiny *Good Earth* set is mentioned in the film's program in *Souvenir Programs of 12 Classic Movies, 1927–1941*, ed. Miles Kreuger (New York: Dover, 1977). The source of the Betty Marx anecdote is Kanfer, *Groucho*.

19. Mayer Being Mayer

Albert Lewin's earthquake quote on Thalberg's death is from Rosenberg and Silverstein, *The Real Tinsel*. Newspaper reports are found in the biography files of the Academy's Margaret Herrick Library. Anita Loos is quoted in Beauchamp, *Without Lying Down*, as well as *The Real Tinsel*, while F. Scott Fitzgerald's thoughts are from Salzberg, *Produced by Irving Thalberg*. Mayer's abortive plans for *Saratoga* are reported in James L. Neibaur, *Clark Gable in the 1930s* (Jefferson, NC: McFarland, 2021), while MGM's commissary silence is detailed in David Stenn, *Bombshell: The Life and Death of Jean Harlow* (New York: Doubleday, 1993). Joseph Breen's thoughts on *Marie Antoinette* are in the Academy's Production Code Administration files, while the film's record number of antiques is in Howard Gutner, *MGM Style: Cedric Gibbons and the Art of the Golden Age of Hollywood* (Guilford, CT: Lyons, 2019). Robert Morley's amusing observations come from Robert Morley and Sewell Stokes, *Robert Morley: A Reluctant Autobiography* (New York: Simon and Schuster, 1966), while his equally droll unnamed friend Peter Bull is quoted in Silvester, *The Grove Book of Hollywood*. Information on Woody Van Dyke is from Robert C. Cannom, *Van Dyke and the Mythical City, Hollywood* (Culver City, CA: Murray and Gee, 1948). Hedda Hopper's caustic comment is in Catherine Jurca, *Hollywood 1938: Motion Pictures' Greatest Year* (Berkeley: University of California Press, 2012). Fitzgerald's plea for fair play is from Sydney Ladensohn Stern, *The Brothers Mankiewicz* (Jackson: University Press of Mississippi, 2019). Casey Robinson on the MGM system is in McGilligan, *Backstory*. The *Love Finds Andy Hardy* grosses are in Eyman, *Lion of Hollywood*. Gable is "scared stiff" in Haver, *David O. Selznick's Hollywood*. Quotes from Judy Garland are found in Gerald Clark, *Get Happy: The Life of Judy Garland* (New York: Delta, 2001). Clark Gable's Garland complaint is recorded by Vincente Minnelli with Hector Arce, *I Remember It Well* (London: Angus and Robertson, 1975). The authority on Greer Garson is Michael Troyan, *A Rose for Mrs. Miniver: The Life of Greer Garson* (Lexington: University Press of Kentucky, 1999). The autographed copy of *The Lion's Roar* is in the author's collection. Irene Mayer Selznick's relating Adrian's memory is from Paris, *Garbo*.

20. Old and in the Way

The "hornet's nest" description is from Elia Kazan, *A Life* (New York: Alfred A. Knopf, 1988). Reactions to Mayer's office are found in Williams, *The Million Dollar Mermaid*, and James Mason, *Before I Forget* (London: Hamish Hamilton, 1981). The detailed description is in Christopher Finch and Linda Rosenkrantz, *Gone Hollywood: The Movie Colony in the Golden Age* (Garden City, NY: Doubleday, 1979). Eleanor Powell's chicken soup thoughts are in Kobal, *People Will Talk*, while Alexander Korda's are in Michael Korda,

Charmed Lives: A Family Romance (New York: Random House, 1979). Mayer's "I am a Jew" comment is in Higham, *Merchant of Dreams*. Mayer's early thoughts on firing writers are in Seldes, *The Great Audience*. Mayer's St. Patrick's Day speech is from Eyman, *Lion of Hollywood*. The use of Esperanto in *Idiot's Delight* is detailed in Howard Gutner, *Gowns by Adrian: The MGM Years, 1928–1941* (New York: Harry N. Abrams, 2001). Clark Gable's despair is from Lyn Tornabene, *Long Live the King: A Biography of Clark Gable* (New York: Putnam, 1976). Selective service ruling is in Tracy Campbell, *The Year of Peril: America in 1942* (New Haven: Yale University Press, 2020). Wyler as a warmonger is from Jan Herman, *A Talent for Trouble: The Life of Hollywood's Most Acclaimed Director, William Wyler* (New York: Putnam, 1995). William Saroyan's quote about Armenians cheating Jews is found in Crowther, *Hollywood Rajah*, and Saroyan's change of heart is in his "The Best Angel God Ever Saw," *Saturday Evening Post*, November 16, 1963. Vincent X. Flaherty's column on Mayer's horse farm is in the Academy's Herrick Library biography clip files. Ann Miller's recounting of Mayer's courtship is in Ann Miller with Norma Lee Browning, *Miller's High Life* (Garden City, NY: Doubleday, 1972). Dore Schary's memories of MGM are in Schary, *Heyday*. Irene's reaction to Schary's cuts is in Frank Billecci and Lauranne B. Fischer, *Irene: A Designer from the Golden Age of Hollywood, The MGM Years, 1942–1949* (Atglen, PA: Schiffer, 2014). Lucinda Ballard's tart observation is in Curtis, *Spencer Tracy*. Judy Garland's open letter is from Mark Bego, *The Best of Modern Screen* (New York: St. Martin's, 1986). Mayer's late interview on Garland is quoted in Leyda, *Voices of Film Experience*. Mayer's taunt about not making a film with Sam Goldwyn's money is from Ross, *Picture*. Letter from Ross to William Shawn is in the author's collection. Gottfried Reinhardt is quoted in Lawrence Grobel, *The Hustons* (New York: Scribner, 1989). Mayer's "take the studio and choke on it" anger is found in Eyman, *Lion of Hollywood*. Louis Nizer's view is detailed in Louis Nizer, *My Life in Court* (Garden City, NY: Doubleday, 1961). The "long, complicated, ugly" quote is from Carey, *All the Stars in Heaven*.

21. Afterlife

Details of Mayer's funeral are in the Academy's Herrick Library biography clip files. Billy Wilder's quote is from Maurice Zolotow, *Billy Wilder in Hollywood* (New York: Putnam, 1977). Irene Mayer Selznick on Adolph Zukor is in Carey, *All the Stars in Heaven*. Information on MGM files used as freeway fill and the "greatest rummage sale" quote are from Bingen, *MGM*. Shearer on her husband's thoughts comes from Flamini, *Thalberg*. Robert Evans deals with the details of playing Thalberg on film in both Robert Evans, *The Kid Stays in the Picture* (New York: Hachette, 1994), and Robert Evans, *The Fat Lady Sang* (New York: It Books, 2013). The incidents that inspired "Crazy Sunday" are recounted in Dwight Taylor, *Joy Ride* (New York: Putnam, 1959). The wording of Shearer's telegram is in Matthew J. Bruccoli, *"The Last of the Novelists": F. Scott Fitzgerald and* The Last Tycoon (Carbondale: Southern Illinois University Press, 1977). Also quoted are F. Scott Fitzgerald, *The Pat Hobby Stories* (New York: Scribner, 1962), and F. Scott Fitzgerald, *The Last Tycoon* (London: Grey Walls, 1949). Qualms about the novel's climax are in Rapf, *Back Lot*. Raymond Chandler's ambivalence and the expanded version of Fitzgerald's Thalberg anecdote are both in Bruccoli, *"The Last of the Novelists."*

ACKNOWLEDGMENTS

WHEN I FIRST came across the opening of L. P. Hartley's *The Go-Between*, its celebrated words ("The past is a foreign country: they do things differently there") did not particularly resonate with the college student who read them. But researching and writing a book about the past has meant both understanding that aphorism and living it continually.

So, treating Louis B. Mayer and Irving Thalberg as a distant land I was going to spend extended time in, the first thing I did was consult the best guidebooks I could find, all listed in Sources. But as with all travel, guidebooks take you only so far, and it is essential to talk to people who've been there before. After decades of writing about film, I was fortunate to have friends who'd done exceptional work in classic Hollywood, individuals I could both consult with and lean on for moral support during the years of research and writing. These include:

A. Scott Berg, the superb biographer whose books on Hollywood include *Goldwyn* and *Kate Remembered*. Scott was the first person I talked to when I was considering this book, and the incisive memo he wrote was invaluable during the entire writing process.

Kevin Brownlow, whose *The Parade's Gone By . . .* pioneered serious scholarship about silent film. Celebrated in the field for his knowledge and his generosity, Kevin was a tireless correspondent, writing me frequent notes including information he'd come across about both Mayer and Thalberg, most compellingly an excerpt from an unpublished memoir by director Rowland V. Lee.

The late Ned Comstock, librarian and archivist at USC's Cinematic Arts Library, was mere days from retirement when another friend, Leonard Maltin, suggested I call him. Despite that extremely tight timeline, Comstock was able to send me copies of the most varied and invaluable material, from a handwritten Lillian Gish note to a moving photograph from Thalberg's funeral and transcriptions of the potent story conferences of the executive's MGM hits. It is no wonder that prominent thanks to him can be found in many Hollywood histories and biographies.

Cari Beauchamp. The late author of one of the best Golden Age biographies, *Without Lying Down*, about powerful screenwriter and close Thalberg collaborator Frances Marion, Cari steered me in numerous right directions and kept in touch to make sure I was staying sane.

I'm also grateful for having been able to talk to people with family connections to my subjects. These include Thalberg's granddaughter Deborah Thalberg and her mother Suzanne McCormick, who married Thalberg's philosopher son Irving Jr. and shared memories of her mother-in-law Norma Shearer. Speaking of Shearer, major thanks also go to Darin Barnes, the ultimate authority on the actress, for sharing his personal photo collection (including a winsome shot of Thalberg as a boy) and taking the time to patiently bring me up to speed.

Making the research for this book different from what I anticipated was that it had to be done during the height of the Covid pandemic, when most libraries and research centers were closed to in-person investigation. But even though it was difficult, people made sustained efforts to lend a hand.

This was especially true at the unparalleled Academy of Motion Picture Arts and Sciences' Margaret Herrick Library. Rachel Bernstein, at the time associate director, reference and public services, calmed me down, showed me what was available online, and placed me in the skilled hands of Kristine Krueger, among other things the library's National Film Information Service coordinator. Willing to answer all my questions, no matter how foolish, she was able to email me key documents and help me understand what was possible and what was not. With her in my corner, I felt my task was doable, pandemic or no pandemic. After she retired, senior reference librarian Genevieve Maxwell expertly picked up the slack.

I also want to give a shout-out to the selfless individuals past and present at the Wisconsin Center for Film and Theater Research, who created and maintain the Media History Digital Library and its Lantern search engine. An astonishing resource, the MHDL has scanned more than 2.8 million pages of vintage magazines and books, making it possible to turn the virtual pages of long-gone movie fan magazines and the most obscure trade publications.

Because so many brick-and-mortar archives were closed, I relied on material I already had or was able to acquire, so my thanks go to book dealers who went beyond the call of duty to help me out, including but not limited to Eric Chaim Kline, Bookseller; Marc Selvaggio, Books and Ephemera; and Kevin Smith of Royal Books.

I also relied heavily on a popular resource new to me, the nationwide web of dealers known as eBay. Largely located in small towns where movie passion knew no limits during Hollywood's heyday, these sellers offered an endless supply of old movie paper, including programs, flyers, fan magazines, full-page newspaper ads, even a glossy MGM in-house publication called *The Lion's Roar* I hadn't heard of. Judicious buying enabled me to immerse myself in the Mayer-Thalberg era to an extent I had not thought possible.

Not new to me were the numerous pertinent books in my personal library that I had purchased from Andy Dowdy. His long-gone Other Times bookstore on Pico Boulevard in Los Angeles was the source of many of my key Hollywood books, identifiable by Andy's distinctive price notation in the lightest of pencil. Shopping and hanging out there, which I did on a regular basis, along with Richard Schickel and other critics, was an education in itself.

Other people materialized at key moments, providing essential assistance. In no particular order:

Delia Ephron, who made a connection for me when I needed it most.

Robin Swicord and Nick Kazan, in whose vacation house I wrote the book's proposal.

James Pepper, who ferreted out and sent me numerous YouTube links to both Mayer and Thalberg speaking in public.

Mary Sweeney, who told me that Dore Schary's papers were housed at the University of Wisconsin and put me in touch with Jennifer Barth, project archivist at the Wisconsin Sound Archive, who was able to pinpoint the material I needed.

Christopher Nolan, who alerted me to a particularly savage Orson Welles analysis of Thalberg that had somehow eluded me.

Bayard Veiller, who granted me permission to quote a marvelous anecdote about Thalberg, Shearer, and early sound from *The Fun I've Had*, the memoir written by the grandfather whose name he shares.

Ron Shelton, whose book on the making of *Bull Durham* introduced me to an E. L. Doctorow aphorism about long-form writing being like driving at night in the fog ("You can only see as far as your headlights, but you can make the whole trip that way") that became my mantra for this project.

Two people were involved in this endeavor from beginning to end. My agent Kathy Robbins steered the project from an idea on the phone to the finished book with unerring skill, while Steven J. Zipperstein, Jewish Lives series editor, both assigned the book and astutely edited it. Also essential were Yale editors Ileene Smith and Heather Gold, publicist Elizabeth Pelton, and editorial assistant Elizabeth Sylvia, who did a chunk of the heavy lifting. And special thanks go to copy editor Dan Heaton, who unobtrusively improved every sentence he put pen to, and production editor Jeffrey Schier, who made short work of last minute problems.

The finding of images suitable for publication, an invariably complex process, was made simpler by the hands that pitched in, starting with Marc Wanamaker, whose exceptional Bison Archives was the source of photos I despaired of finding. Key as well were Sherri Jackson and Casey Schweiger of Bridgeman Images, Derek Davidson and Todd Ifft of Photofest, and the staff of Getty Images. And Susan Landesmann spent time coming up with leads on locating an especially difficult photo.

Finally, I want to thank an old friend, the late writer Ross Thomas. Several accidents of fate meant that I ended up writing this book seated between his desk lamp and his venerable Remington manual typewriter, and once I realized this was happening, I began to think of him as the book's guardian spirit. Ross was an impeccable craftsman whose dazzling thrillers are without peer, and if only a fraction of his writing gift rubbed off on me, I will count myself very fortunate indeed.